SHABTAI TZVI, LABOR ZIONISM AND THE HOLOCAUST

by Barry Chamish

SHABTAI TZVI, LABOR ZIONISM AND THE HOLOCAUST

by Barry Chamish

www.LuLu.comPrinted by
) http://www.lulu.com/content/336970(

ISBN:5 800030 505361

Modiin House
Nakhal Zohar St. 40/2
Modiin 71700 Israel

chamish@netvision.net.il

Table of Contents:

EPILOG
THE MURDER OF OFRA HAZA

PREFACE

I worked for nine years gathering the truth about the Rabin assassination and not one of my articles received the kind of recognition accorded my September '04 piece about the radiation experiments on Israeli Sephardi children during the 1950s. It began when the gutsy site www.israelinsider.com published the article. It was then picked up and featured on the news sections of both Google and Yahoo. From there the article spread everywhere. To my dismay, blatantly anti-Israel sites abused the information and its real message.

The message is that the early Labor Zionists were monsters and their descendants, the Oslo "peacemakers," are no less monstrous. According to Rabbi Antelman, Zionism began as an honest national liberation movement that was too quickly infiltrated and corrupted by the secret followers of the false messiahs Shabtai Tzvi and Jacob Frank. Anyone who looks at events from that starting point realizes that had there never existed Labor Zionism, there would not have been a Holocaust.

Now this same demonic force is wrapping its pincers around the Jews of Yesha. These Jews refuse to realize that their enemy is terrified by the revival of Torah Judaism taking place in these territories and will do whatever needs to be done to wipe the revival out and return the country to the Sabbataian values envisioned by the founders of Israel.

Opposing the Sabbataian Zionists during the period of the Holocaust were, what were then known as, the Revisionist Zionists. Today, the wounded and weakened descendants of this good Zionism, are known broadly as the Right. They tried and failed to save the Jews of Europe. The Labor Zionists had far too many powerful allies among the bloodthirsty occultists who run this planet from behind the scenes.

5

The Sabbataian Zionists made a terrible pact with the Nazis, simplified after the best known component, called The Transfer Agreement. They let the Germans have their way with Europe's Jews, and later continued the torture and medical experiments on the Sephardi children who immigrated to their new Sabbataian state.

The purpose of my exposing these sadistic experiments is to strengthen Judaism by removing these anti-Jews from our midst. Over the past 120 years the Sabbataians have infiltrated the Jewish leadership worldwide and oversaw the destruction of over 80% of the people by promoting wars, pogroms, assimilation and the Holocaust.

They have to go! If Judaism is to survive, we must expunge the devils. If that means exposing their worst crimes, so be it. Every moment they sit in power over the Jews is a mortal threat to the survival of the remaining 20%. My exposes may have the power to shake the demons out of our hair. Judaism and Israel will survive the shocking truth, but they will not outlive the continuing existence of Labor Zionism.

CHAPTER ONE –
DESTROYING YESHA

ALM 1 - NAMING THE YESHA SPIES

Poor deluded Israelis believe that the current moment of justice, when the government actually has freed the army to arrest their murderers, is a lasting trend. They will soon learn that the Oslo game is just on brief hold and the real goal of intimidating the Jewish residents of Yesha from their homes is merely on the backburner.

Admittedly, the more perceptive see the signs. Two more Yesha rabbis have been murdered in the past month, Shapira and Dickstein, upping the total to about an even dozen in the past four years. And there is no denying that the murder of Rabbi Eliahu Shapira of Peduel wasn't random terrorism. He was ambushed by a highly trained hit squad which possessed exact intelligence about his whereabouts.

And another Arab girls' school was bombed without deaths and again Jewish settler "extremists" were blamed. These same "extremists" blamed for similar school bombs in East Jerusalem and Tzur Bahr don't exist. They are the creation of a group of Shabak officers, working hand in hand with the CIA and PLO, to remove Israel and its citizens from Yesha. And guess who the Israeli behind the plot is? Read on:

CIA begins training Palestinian officers
By Amira Hass, Ha'aretz 17 September 2002
"A training course for Palestinian Authority security officers got underway yesterday in Jericho. The course is being run by a team of security experts from the Central Intelligence Agency, Jordan and Egypt, and is taking place at the Intercontinental Hotel in Jericho.

"'The session will be part of a training program with the goal of developing the capabilities of the security services as part of the reforms launched by the Palestinian Authority," head of West Bank preventive security, Zuheir Manasra, said on Sunday. The current course will last 20 days, after which, different groups will be trained.

"Palestinian Authority Chairman Yasser Arafat gave his approval to the training, despite the fact that, according to Palestinian sources, Israel prevented 100 Palestinian officers from taking part.

"According to Israeli sources, this is a very 'preliminary' stage of a U.S. plan to implement reforms in the Palestinian Authority. The program was developed by a CIA team that spent several weeks in the region and met with senior Palestinian officials. Also involved in the plan were Egypt, Lebanon and Saudi Arabia.

"As part of the reforms within the Palestinian Authority, the foreign security experts are helping train Palestinian security services, which both Israel and the United States accuse of not doing enough to prevent terror attacks against Israel.

*Officers from the West Bank preventive security service, headed by Zuheir Manasra, were present at yesterday's course, in addition to those of the Gaza Strip General Intelligence, headed by Amin al-Hindi. Palestinian policemen and firemen also took part.

"According to Rashid Abu Shabak, head of preventive security in the Gaza Strip, the U.S. guaranteed the training program would be carried out as planned, but did not impose upon Israel to let everyone participate. The ban on letting officers take part in the course is not a personal one, but rather aimed at certain organizations, such as the West Bank General Intelligence, headed by Tawfik Tirawi.

"While the Palestinian Authority position remains that Palestinians should be able to kill non-civilians for the time being, FM Peres praised the current training program run by the CIA, Egypt and others security services to improve the skills of PA security forces."

8

There you have it. Shimon Peres and CIA director George Tenet are once again buttressing the PLO and the victims of the training will be Yesha Jews.

The plot of the scenario is to once again prove to Israelis and the world that the Jews of Judea and Samaria are violent, irresponsible criminals whose biblical and historical claims to their homeland is forfeited by their murderous behavior. This, the plotters believe, can be achieved by fabricating violent acts and blaming them on selected "settlers." That requires agents planted in the Yesha Council and local councils providing exact intelligence on potential patsies.

So, let's short-circuit the devious operation by naming these agents, from excellent sources.

The first is a near legendary figure in the drama leading up to the Rabin assassination. His name is Nathan and he asked that I not publish his last name. It's a weak firewall since many readers will recognize him, but it's now up. Less than a month before his murder, Rabin addressed a highly hostile group of a thousand English speakers at the Wingate Institute near Netanya. Before he made it to the podium, he was supposedly attacked by a religious settler with murderous intentions. The film of the attack was broadcast worldwide for days. The attack was a fake forged by the Shabak, Israel's secret service. The attacker was either chosen at random or by mistake. That was Nathan, as he explains:

"I was standing with my seven year old son waiting to hear Rabin's speech when I was attacked and beaten senseless. Then I was dragged away."

Unfortunately for the Shabak, they chose the wrong sucker to blame for attacking Rabin. Nathan had been the chief Rabbi of the Hebrew University of Jerusalem for seventeen years. When his hearing was held, even radical leftists like Nomi Chazan testified that he was neither violent, nor extremist in his views. All charges against him were quickly dismissed. Not that Israelis know that. What they remember is that a radical settler tried to harm Rabin at the Wingate Institute, just before he was murdered.

"The Shabak officer who tackled and beat me was Yuval Schwartz. He dragged me away and his beatings continued until I was taken to jail. I was told by people who know him that it was lucky I survived. I admitted nothing to him because there was nothing to admit. I was just standing in the crowd with no malevolent intentions towards anyone, including Rabin. Even then I had the feeling that he was practising on me, seeing if he could get away with blaming an innocent person for attacking Rabin when he didn't. Now, I believe he was conducting a dry run for the Rabin murder."

Which has to be the right conclusion. Yuval Schwartz was the officer in charge of security for the November 4, 1995 rally where Rabin was murdered.Two photos in my possession show Schwartz guarding Peres' rear. And that's where he stays until Rabin's murder; behind or beside Peres. And that's exactly where he was at the moment Rabin was shot. Moments before, the "amateur" film of the murder shows Schwartz conversing with Peres in front of Rabin's limousine. He had far more interest in the movements of Peres than the safety of the Prime Minister. That is mighty selective treatment by the Shabak's Head of Rally Security.

"When I was incarcerated, they placed three Shabak agents in my cell. Two have continued their work in Yesha since then. Everyone seems to think that Avishai Raviv was the only Shabak provocateur around. He's just the one who got caught because he wasn't very bright. The ones in my cell were a lot smarter and have escaped indictment so far. It's a matter of time.

"The less clever one was Sammy Ovadia. The Shabak recruited him because of embarassing family activity. Later, after the Rabin murder, they planted him and his wife in Har Bracha. Today he lives in Netanya.

"The bright one was Ronen Bar Shira. He had been at the top of the settlement bureaucracy; he was the registrar of the Gush Emunim youth movement. Now that must have been really handy for the Shabak. I learned he was recruited over financial irregularities. The two of them tried to trick me into incriminating myself over Rabin, like asking me if I knew how many settlers were trying to murder him, but there was nothing for them to find about me. But I found out who they were."

ALM 2 -FALLEN AND FELLED FOR GENEVA

The conversation began, "I've been putting this off, now I think it's time we met."

"About what?"

"About soldiers being murdered in the IDF. I'm a soldier who knows things you should know."

The next day, the soldier took a long detour to meet me. For the time being, the only description I'll give is that he is middle-aged. He immediately established his credentials through Mossad name dropping.

"The people who I want to read you will get the message if you precede my information with these two facts. The Mossad recruits hitmen from amongst criminals. One who is doing deep penance is Rabbi Emmanuel Paz of Bet Shemesh, who once operated in Europe. Another European officer was the late Fischel Skornik. He told me how we bungled the rescue of Ron Arad not long after he was captured in Lebanon. The Mossad set up a channel between the Spanish Mafia and their counterparts in Lebanon to buy Arad's freedom. The operation was succeeding but it fell apart when the Mossad negotiator wasn't satisfied with his cut of the operation.

"That should be enough to establish myself where I want to be heard."

The soldier requested a cigarette, sat up and got to the point.

"Remember what happened in Netzarim last October 26? Three soldiers were murdered by a terrorist in their barracks. Two were young women, one an eighteen year old male.

They were disarmed and left helpless the day of the attack. It was done to make certain they couldn't defend themselves. They were murdered in an operation aimed at disbanding Netzarim right after this Geneva Accord is signed.

"The operation was sloppy but they got away with it. The excuses given for disarming the soldiers were ridiculous. The base had run out of funds to supply weapons to the girls and the guy was being transferred for trial so his weapon was removed. The IDF is not running out of automatic weapons and no soldier is allowed to be in a Gaza base unarmed.

"Then came the immediate calls to disband Netzarim in the media because it's too dangerous for our soldiers to serve there. It is if they're being knocked off by the same army they are serving in. The public debate was prepared before the soldiers were murdered. And they weren't the only ones murdered from within the IDF to remove settlements.

"Just off the top of my head, in the last half year or so you had the two soldiers killed near Hebron by an IDF helicopter and the Hebron reserve soldier murdered on the way back from a Shabak interrogation in Jerusalem.

"The first operation worked like this. One of the soldiers, I recall his name being Yehuda Ben Yosef, was an activist behind the building of outposts outside Efrat. His father is a lawyer viewed as an anti-peace troublemaker as well. It was like getting rid of two troublesome birds with one missile. An order was issued to look out for terrorists in IDF uniforms driving a civilan vehicle in the Hebron area. The IAF then blew up their car. The pilot didn't know he was murdering Jews in a covert operation against the settlers. The two killed were not in uniform and their car had a bright insignia on it identifying it as an IDF security vehicle. We don't make mistakes like that.

"Then there was the Hebron reserve soldier active in the building of the Hill 17 outpost outside Hebron. He was taken to Shabak headquarters in Jerusalem for interrogation. On the way home he was shot dead between the eyes. That's not terrorism, that's a hit. His wife delayed his funeral for two days so his body could be examined.

"There is a hit squad in the IDF murdering soldiers who don't like their "peace" plans. To get Beilin's Geneva atrocity through, they are murdering soldiers actively protesting it and ordinary soldiers who can rile public opinion against serving in Yesha.

"I did some checking on Beilin's IDF service. He was a messenger carrying secret communications codes for approval between high-ranking officers. That's all he was, a clerk. And no one would have anything to do with him. He was an outcast in his unit and other soldiers wondered if he wasn't photocopying those codes before they got to their destination. And this IDF pariah wouldn't mind it one bit if there was a murder rampage in the army aimed at getting his diplomacy through. But I strongly doubt he's giving the orders. To find out who is behind this slaughter, you have to follow the millions of dollars being funneled to him and trace which officers are getting a piece of the cake.

"The murders in Netzarim are just stage one of Beilin's plan to destroy the settlements. Netzarim was chosen as the precedent. The government already has a block of land in the Negev all ready for Netzarim's evacuation and replacement. After that operation is completed, the same thing will be repeated with all the targeted settlements and who knows how many soldiers will be murdered until the rest of Yesha is evacuated? This Geneva Accord is being run by criminals and they couldn't care less how many young Jews are eliminated until they get their way."

ALM 3 - "The Secret War Against the Settlers"

Sharon pulled off a coup. Defying his party and supposedly his ideals, he wrangled a Gaza pullout from his government. How did he do it? Through a level of criminality even he is incapable of reaching alone. He had help; the most corrupt and murderous help currently available on the planet.

We begin our understanding of the secret war against the settlers in December, 1993 when a true patriot working in the communications department of a government ministry risked his job and life by letting me read intercepted transcripts of the secret clauses of Oslo, negotiated by Yossi Beilin. He gave the same transcripts to journalists Steve Rodan and Hillel Halkin, but I was the only one to publish the most shocking sections.

The parties agreed to hand over all of Judea, Samaria and Gaza to the PLO and rid the areas of their Jewish residents. The means to this end included increased terror and, this was the most shocking section, the targeted elimination of the population's religious and political leaders. The assassinations began shortly after, with the shooting of NRP leader Rabbi Chaim Drucksman's car, killing his driver and the murder of Moledet leader Miriam Lapid's husband and son in an ambush. The method proved itself when Lapid moved to a new home within the Green Line.

This encouraged the "peacemakers," and the campaign of murder was stepped up. Rabbis throughout the territories fell like kingpins; Shapiro, Raanan, Horowitz, Dickstein, Kahane, Lieberman et al and to pave the way for the Gaza evacuation, Rabbi Yitzhak Arama, the revered rabbi of Gush Katif, was rubbed out in an ambush in 2002. The Israeli hit team gave his location to the Arab triggermen. That is the case in all the targeted murders aimed at demoralizing the Jews from their homes. I mean all.

In December 2003, I had a visit from a career soldier, 27 years in the IDF. He told me that soldiers were being murdered from within the IDF to further political goals. "There was this Yehuda Ben Yosef from Efrat. He was a leader of the hilltop outposts movement. The killers tricked the Air Force into shooting his car with a missile from a helicopter. Then last October 27, they did it again in Netzarim. In the afternoon, the base commander stripped the weapons from three soldiers, two of them women. At night, two terrorists somehow got past base security, which never happened before, and murdered the three disarmed soldiers. They knew exactly where they were sleeping. In a base of over 350 soldiers, that would have been completely impossible without information from our side. The next day the government announced its pullout plan for Netzarim. They murdered three soldiers from the coastal area, two of them young women, none of whom had a chance to defend themselves, just to persuade secular Israelis that it was too risky for their children to stay in Gaza."

Fast forward to May 2004. The Likud Party holds a referendum to decide the future of Gaza. It looks like the Sharon pullout will be defeated. Drastic action was needed. A pregnant mother, Tali Khatuel and her four daughters were slaughtered in their car on the way out of Gaza to participate in a referendum rally. IDF soldiers were not 30 yards away from the massacre and did nothing to stop it. Surely, this ghastly crime would persuade the middle-of-the road Likudniks that it was too dangerous to stay in Gaza. But it did not and Sharon was defeated.

This required even ghastlier atrocities. What what could be better than arranging for the murder of 13 young soldiers and even better, the gleeful mutilation of their bodies. For this operation, the Israeli hit team needed international cooperation and got it. From Arutz Sheva News:

"THE SEARCH FOR BODIES CONTINUES"

"Hundreds of IDF soldiers resumed the search this morning for the remains of soldiers who were killed in the blast of their armed personnel carrier on Wednesday in southern Gaza. The searching soldiers, in lines of ten, are crawling in the sand, combing the area for anything that could prove to be the remainder of their friends. The search is taking place on both sides of the Israeli-Egyptian border,

as the force of the blast scattered pieces hundreds of meters in all directions.

"Military correspondent Danny Shalom of HaTzofeh newspaper noted that Egypt's approval for Israeli searchers to enter Egypt was "given, ridiculously enough, by Egyptian President Hosni Mubarak - who is no less responsible than the terrorists for the smuggling of explosives into Gaza." Israel has often blamed Egypt for "not doing enough" to stop the smuggling from Egypt to Gaza.

"Defense Minister Sha'ul Mofaz said today that ambulances of the United Nations Relief Works Association (UNRWA) had taken remains of soldiers killed in Tuesday's attack to PA-controlled areas. Arab residents of Gaza were filmed gleefully holding and playing with body parts shortly after the attack on Tuesday morning. Though the PA later returned some of the remains, Mofaz demands that UN Secretary-General relate to the fact that representatives of the world body facilitated the abuse of Israeli corpses."

With the help of the UN and Egypt, the Israeli "peace" team got the Gaza massacre and humiliation they needed to exact revenge for Sharon's pullout defeat. The Israeli hit squad is the murder arm of the real powers that be on this wicked planet. Once again we will try and educate a people determined to resist the deep truth and too arrogant to admit their political perspective is all but worthless.

Bush at Bilderberg, a Day After Meeting Pope
Marc Delcour - 31May04
Roughly translated from Metula News Agency article in French.

*The Middle East is soon to be moving under the impulse of **a huge behind-the-scenes agreement between governments of the USA, Israel, and certain components of the Palestinian Authority as well as Egypt and Jordan**. And for the first time these last two countries have accepted* *to play an active role on the side of Israel, coordinated by the Sharon government.*

As this agreement is rolled out of the shadows into the public domain it is becoming clear that the new plan doesn't insist on an end to the Israel-Palestinian conflict but that the partners have a fixed goal now to realize the conditions of the 'road map'.

In other words, it is about the neutralization of armed resistance to Israeli occupation, cessation of violence and an in-depth reform of the Palestinian Authority.

On the Israeli Side, Ariel Sharon has accepted to evacuate the Gaza Strip and to dismantle all Jewish settlements if the agreement is signed.

A reader writes: "I met Charles Bronfman socially last month and told him I live in Gush Katif. He scowled and said that if he had his way, there would be nothing left of my home but sand dunes."

There is a little think tank in Manhattan called the Council On Foreign Relations. The 3800 members are as powerful in America as the Bilderbergers are in Europe. The Bronfman brothers are intimately tied to the CFR and brother Edgar is an executive member of the cabal.

Lately, some CFR members known as neo-cons have been attacked directly by other CFR members like Anthony Zinni and or indirectly by the likes of John Kerry. Incredibly, because they are causing blood to gush in Iraq and claim they are fighting Islamic terror, Israelis and Jews think the neo-cons are their allies. They cannot understand a very simple and clear fact: it is the neo-cons who are behind "the Roadmap," and it is the neo-cons like Wolfowitz, Cheney, Rumsfeld, Perle, Pipes, (every one of them but Rumsfeld CFR members) who are forcing Sharon to pull out of Gaza, even if it requires murdering Jews to make a point. They want for Israel what they've got for Iraq...even foreign troops. Sharon's "disengagement" plan calls for foreign troops taking over lands evacuated by Gaza's Jews.

Allow me to quote a June 3 article from The Jerusalem Post:

BUSH BACKS GAZA WITHDRAWAL

"US President George W. Bush threw his support again behind Prime Minister Sharon's unilateral withdrawal from the Gaza Strip and parts of the West Bank, days before the cabinet is to vote on it.

"Bush: 'His decision provides an historic moment of opportunity to begin building a future Palestinian state.'

"A well-placed source said the administration is trying to help Sharon win cabinet approval on Sunday.

"On Wednesday, senior US officials including Assistant Secretary of State William Burns (CFR) and National Council Middle East Advisor Elliot Abrams (CFR) are scheduled to meet with PA Negotiations Minister Saeb Erekat.

"Bush's White House declaration Tuesday came after a meeting between US National Security Advisor Condeleeza Rice (CFR) and Sharon's bureau chief Dov Weisglass."

Now what kind of man is Dov Weisglass to uproot thousands of Jews from their homes? Why, he is a Mafia hood who wants to get a piece of a casino! Now I reported the Weisglass-Sharon-Arafat etc. casino syndicate two years ago and somehow never got any credit for the discovery.

So I'm going to let someone who never publicly acknowledges my contribution tell the story this time around. I give you, David Bedein:

Plans to give pieces of Israel's land to Austrian Companies

Jews out! Austrians welcome.

"According to the P.A. tourist publication This Week in Palestine, plans are well underway to build a new casino and tourist resort in Southern Gaza. "Is it a coincidence," Bedein asks, "that this is where the Jewish communities of Katif now reside?" PA sources say that the new casino will be owned by the same as those who own the Jericho casino: the PA, an Austrian casino company, the Austrian Bank BAWAG and Martin Schlaff - all of them clients of Weissglass' office. When working for Sharon, Weissglass was engaged in high-level negotiations with PA figures. He also met with American officials regarding preparations for the "disengagement" from Gaza and the evacuation of Jewish towns in Katif.

"Dov Weissglass, who recently resigned as head of Prime Minister Sharon's Office, is still listed as part-owner of a law firm representing PA business interests who wish to build a casino in southern Gaza.

"In January 2003, the Israel Civil Service Commission spokesman affirmed Bedein's finding that Weissglass was still registered in the Israel Corporate Register as part of his law firm, Weissglass-Almagor. The spokesman dismissed its importance, however, saying that Weissglass had divested himself from all financial interests in that firm. The Commission asked him to formally remove his name from the firm, however, and indeed, in April 2003, he did so.

"But, Bedein now reports, it has been confirmed by the Israel Corporate Authority that Weissglass is still registered as the lawyer of record for two other firms that are located at the same addresses and with the same lawyers. One of them, in fact, has the very same name: Weissglass-Almagor.

"On May 11, 2004, the spokesman for the Israel Civil Service Commission wrote that Weissglass had divested himself of his law firm and had sold the shares of his business. Upon examination of the publicly available Israel Corporate Authority records of the Weissglass business, Bedein reports, there is no record of any Weissglass activity

to divest neither from this second law firm nor from his business.

"Two weeks ago," Bedein wrote in Makor Rishon, "Weissglass was asked if he still has contacts with the casino company. His answer: 'No comment.'"

"Bedein lists the following remaining questions:

* What profits did Weissglass' law office and business make from Palestinian Authority interests before and after Weissglass assumed his position?

* What are the current profits of Weissglass' law office and business from Palestinian Authority interests?

* Is there a possibility of a conflict of interest, at a time when Weissglass conducts negotiations on behalf of the state of Israel with all official levels of the Palestinian Authority?

"These questions need to be addressed," Bedein concludes, "by the Knesset, the Attorney-General, the State Comptroller and by the Israel Civil Service Commission." The latter two can be visited at (http://www.mevaker.gov.il/serve/site/english/index.asp) and (http://www.civil-service.gov.il/english/e_index.htm)."

Now, let us recall what I exposed two years ago. As far as I know, I first exposed the Sharon-Weisglass casino mafia. Now everyone is catching up. From Haaretz 5/6/04:

Weisglass pushed Sharon to reopen Jericho casino

Yaakov Katz May. 6, 2004

"During negotiations with the Labor Party in October 2000 over the possibility of the Likud joining a national unity government, Ariel Sharon was asked by attorney Dov Weisglass, today his bureau chief, to speak with then premier Ehud Barak over the possibility of reopening the casino in Palestinian-controlled Jericho, The Jerusalem Post has learned.

20

"The casino is jointly owned by the Palestinian Authority, Casinos Austria, the and Austrian-Jewish businessman Martin Schlaff, a key figure in the ongoing prime minister and his son, Gilad.

"At the time I did not think anything was too strange with Weisglass's request, since at the time we knew that he was an attorney for the casino," said one of the participants at a meeting in October 2000 at the Sharon ranch. "But now, with the allegations that Sharon may have received bribes from Schlaff, the meeting and the request seem suspicious."

"The reopening of the Oasis Casino, which had a daily turnover of some $680,00 before it was closed nearly four years ago due to the conflict with the Palestinians, depends largely on Israeli policy in the territories.

"The owners were reportedly given a franchise to operate the Jericho casino until 2028, with a 10-year tax exemption from the day it opened. BAWAG, like Schlaff, is also eagerly waiting for the government to allow for Israelis to resume gambling at the casino. "Following his victory in the 1999 Likud Party leadership primaries, Sharon went into debt to repay NIS 4.7 million in illegal campaign contributions.

"Gilad Sharon received a $1.5 million loan, originating in Austria, from South Africa-based businessman Cyril Kern in order to repay another loan the family had taken out in order to return the illegal donations.

"The police are investigating the possibility that Kern served as a front man for Schlaff, another friend of Sharon's, and a businessman heavily invested in Israel, who could have made the loan in the hope that Sharon would make decisions favorable to his business interests, including the reopening of the Jericho casino.

"'We met to talk about whether Sharon should join a unity government with Barak, and Weisglass told Arik to pressure Barak into reopening the casino," the source said. 'They agreed that if Sharon joined the coalition, then they would ease restrictions on the Palestinians in Jericho in order to inadvertently allow for the casino to reopen.'

"Shortly after the meeting at the ranch in order to discuss Weisglass's proposal, the national unity talks fell through. After Barak called for elections in December 2000, Sharon, in a landslide victory, was elected prime minister in February 2001 and appointed Weisglass as his bureau chief.

"In November 2002, after Gilad Sharon learned that police were tracking the money transfers, he received two additional money transfers from BAWAG, totaling some $1.5 million."

And two years ago I exposed the ugly fact that Sharon's Bureau Chief, Dov Weisglass was personal attorney to Muhamed Rashid, spelled Rachid below. No conflict of interest here that Sharon's chief aide is on the payroll of the PLO's biggest embezzler. Again, from Haaretz:

"Palestinian Finance Minister Salam Fayyad, a former IMF official who was appointed last year to reform Palestinian finances and end corruption, said recently that his reforms were beginning to bring some order to the murky economic structures created by Arafat.

Last year, the commercial as-sets illegally controlled by Arafat and Rachid were finally trans-ferred to the Palestine Investment Fund. Auditors identified 67 in-vestments in various banks and companies around the world with a total value of $633 million.

"But Khraisheh said the reform had little effect because only the assets were turned over, not the profits from investments, and the tax revenues were not returned at all. In addition, Rachid, who was appointed to head the fund's board of directors, still effectively controlled the assets.

"Khraisheh said the board members had gone to meet Rachid in Cairo, where he now lives, but he 'refused to cooperate in revealing where the money is.'"

SECRET WAR METHODS

Yes, peaceniks everywhere, your "peacemakers" are not interested in peace. No one believes a Gaza pullout will bring peace. Everyone knows it will encourage more such "victories" through terror. Your Israeli "peacemakers" want to launder endless rolls of cash in the casino which will be their reward for the pullout. And the foreign powers are salivating at the thought of even more bloodshed, conflict and best of all, an Israel stripped of its religiosity, patrolled by their troops.

To get their way, they launched a secret war against the settlers. The strategy had several tentacles and it goes on to this day and will until Israel turns into a Sabbataian state or no state at all.

Tentacle 1 - Demoralize Through Ghastly Murder

The list of the dead is too long to even summarize. So I chose three cases where the parents not only refuse to believe me, but have denounced me. If they can be woken up, it would work wonders.

Last week, I was at a political meeting where several Knesset members spoke. Tzvi Hendel was nice to me and we had an extended conversation. But Yitzhak Levy ran from me. When he was Housing Minister, he approved 9000 new units for Judea and Samaria. Shortly after, his daughter was blown up in Jerusalem. A bomb was put on the stairs of her building just before she entered it. He sat at cabinet meetings after with his daughter's real murderers in the same room.

Koby Mandel was a fourteen year old boy butchered with a friend in a cave outside their village near Bethlehem. The boy was barely in the ground before shots went through his teenage sister's bedroom window. Their mother, Sherrie, still thinks this was a coincidence. It was not. It was double-whammy planned terror and "we" told the Arabs where to aim.

Ariel Weiss was the subject of a heart-lifting Jerusalem Post article. Within, was the story of how his mother lifted Nablus troop morale by bringing his platoon some treats. Two weeks later a small uprising was contrived and Ariel was lured into the range of a sniper. The parents refuse to accept this account because they think it makes them guilty. How can they be guilty of anything? How could they have known about the secret war?

Now, time is short. And unless the deviousness of the internal enemy is recognized, all will be lost.

Tentacle Two - Destroy The Opposition

Not long after the second Oslo Accord was signed, a civil insurrection was mounted by Zo Artzeinu, led by Moshe Feiglin. His followers blocked roads with burning tires and posed a real threat to the country's daily viability. This was the only reaction that Oslo deserved. However, a few years ago, Feiglin had a change of heart and decided to join the Likud and "fight from within." And his followers still say, "But look at the effect we're having on the Likud!"

Yeah, look.

Arutz Sheva was the voice of the opposition. So Sharon just shut it down. And nobody did a thing to stop him.

Rabin, Gur, Zeevi, Ben Elissar etc. wanted to shut down Oslo. You know the rest.

Tentacle Three - Bring In The Psychopaths

Netanyahu had just been elected Prime Minister and he was determined to unilaterally pull out of Hebron. Sound familiar? But he was short three votes in the cabinet. In comes a psychopathic soldier named Noam Friedman, fresh from a government hospital psychiatric ward. He shoots up the Hebron shuk in front of the TV cameras and the guilt-ridden cabinet gives Netanyahu his wish.

We will not detail such staged atrocities as the Hebron massacre, Bat Ayin etc. etc. Instead let's look at a picayune incident; the uprooting of olive trees by the settlers of Kfar Tapuakh and Itamar. Now could anything be lower than killing innocent Arab trees? Not in the public eye. Only problem is the uprooters were members of the "peace" team and Kfar Tapuakh and Itamar are on their chopping block.

However, it's not the trees who will suffer as the secret war against the settlers carries on. Jewish families of all political and economic stripes will grieve and grieve until there is no one left to grieve.

ALM 4 - WHY SHARON HAS TO PULL OUT OF GAZA: AND WHAT TO DO ABOUT IT

In October 1999, Leah Rabin went public. She appeared on the IBA channel One 5 PM news program, A New Evening, and recommended my book, Who Murdered Yitzhak Rabin. "The public should leaf through this book," she declared. And then she dropped her bombshell; she supported the reopening of the investigation into her husband's murder.

A year later she was dead of cancer.

Of course, I suspected foul play but kept silent on the matter to negate the response that I see conspiracies everywhere. In the winter of 2001, I gave a lecture at a home in Petakh Tikveh to a national religious group. At the conclusion, a gentleman took me aside and informed me, "I'm an oncologist and I work part of the week at Ichilov Hospital. I saw that Leah Rabin was given the wrong treatment and she was going to die unless that changed. I spoke to the department head and he told me not to butt in."

I did not publicize this conversation because it wasn't corroborated. On Sat. March 20, it was. I attended a small gathering of self-admitted Mapai left-wingers on Perakh Street in East Rishon LeTzion. The hostess asked if I thought Leah Rabin perished before her time. I recounted the testimony I had heard in Petakh Tikveh. She blanched and became very agitated. "My brother is an oncologist at Ichilov and he would not have attended your Petakh Tikveh lecture. He told me the same thing, that Leah Rabin was given nothing more than placebos for her condition. She was murdered by neglect. He also complained and was told to keep his mouth shut if he knew what was good for him."

Recently, the Dutch-Israeli journalist and author of A Trek For Trinnie (Gefen Publishers), Lea Wiesje de Lange made a discovery about the last days of Yitzhak Rabin, which confirmed my published conclusion that Rabin had undergone a transformation and would no longer agree to lead his nation into suicide. That was the primary reason why Shimon Peres was given the go-ahead by his foreign handlers to violently replace Rabin. Rabin made the fatal error of returning to Judaism. Lea's letters to me are self-explanatory:

"Yesterday I heard from a friend who lives in Jerusalem some facts I never heard anywhere, not even from you. It is about Yitzchak Rabin who in his last year became suddenly hungry for Judaism. The man wanted to know, to learn and went, always after sunset, to a yeshiva to listen to shi'urim.

Rather soon his political friends and comrades found him out and told him sternly that this was not done, he went too far. Either he left his monstrous new ways or they would publicize the unspeakable that their hero, their leader was a Jew after all, instead of a nice Mapainik. Not long after those happenings Rabin was killed.

"The rav in question is not one of those Rabbanim who works in the field of returning Jews to roots but gave Rabin an address for the desired shi'urim. The address is "Arachim," a well known institution in Jerusalem. Mossad "Arachim" publishes a journal known all over the Jewish world. Remarkable is that Rabin was found out, resulting in the wrath of the left turning against him 2 weeks before his violent death...

26

"You remember what I told you about Rabin and his sudden craving for Torah? Well I got some more info now. Rabin turned to the Hama'ayan Yeshivat Hanegev in Netivot, to their Rosh Yeshiva, Rabbi Yissachar Meier. It was this Rabbi Yisaschar Meier who advised him to go and study at the Arachim Institution.

"Arachim was established in Israel in 1979 to provide an intellectual response to the thirst of a growing secular Israeli public who were seeking to understand the basic philosophical concepts of Judaism. Arachim addresses basic issues in Jewish philosophy including Science and Religion - Is there an internal contradiction? "The authenticity of the Bible," Practical Mitzvoth- are they relevant in modern society? and many more."

And what was Rabin's reaction to his newly discovered Judaism? He tried first to overturn the worst clauses of the Oslo Accord, and finally to put a stop to the atrocity altogether. Amnon Lord reports in Makor Rishon:

In his last address to the Knesset, one month before his assassination, the late Prime Minister Yitzhak Rabin outlined his concept of defensible borders for Israel.

There were elements that had nothing to do with security but with Israel's national history, e.g., his insistence that Jerusalem remain united under Israeli sovereignty.

He also spoke of the need to retain settlement blocs and the Jordan Rift Valley "in the widest sense of the term." This was Rabin's legacy to the people of Israel.

On March 19, 04, Makor Rishon reported: "Shimon Peres understood after the 1977 elections that he was not electable as prime minister. Since then his strategy has been to work through proxies. He manipulated his current leadership of the Labor Party knowing that he could force Sharon to do his bidding."

And if Sharon doesn't, he will suffer the same fate as Rabin.

Sharon has been ordered to pull out of Gaza and he knows what will happen to him if he doesn't. Like Rabin, he might be willing to sacrifice himself for his country, but not his family. Leah Rabin and her daughter Dahlia demanded that the truth of Yitzhak Rabin's murder be exposed. Leah Rabin was dead within a year and Dahlia is now afflicted with the same disease that killed her mother.

Omri and Gilad Sharon are both fighting corruption charges that could land them in prison. Omri was video-taped accepting bribes, adding, "Maybe this will be enough money to get me out of here." Adir Zik, the courageous journalist who devoted himself to getting to the Rabin murder truth, also sadly, sick with cancer, has traced the framing of the Sharon family to the Shabak and the Oslo Mafia.

At a speech given in Maaleh Shomron on March 24, 04, Zik revealed his investigation of the Cyril Kern bribe, one of the three scandals hanging over the Sharon family. To cover up illegal campaign financing, Omri Sharon with his father's blessing, accepted a loan from a South African businessman named Cyril Kern. Adir Zik told the gathering:

"When Yossi Ginosar died two months ago, he left a billion dollars to his children. You heard me, that's how much he stole from us. A lot of that money came from the Jericho casino he set up with Arafat and the Austrian Martin Schlaff. Omri Sharon and Dov Weisglas had their fingers in the Schlaff's till as well. And guess who else was a partner of Schlaff's; Cyril Kern. Sharon got his fingers in the Oslo crime syndicate safe and they got burned."

For now, Sharon is being kept obedient through legal threats, but if he does not go ahead with the Gaza pullout, the threats against him and his family will turn fatal. He does not want to suffer the fate of Rabin who chose to do the right thing in the end. He will not defy his masters. It will be for others to do that for him. Binyamin Netanyahu's brother-in-law, and I add, my longtime reader, Hagai Ben Artsi went public in Yerushalayim Magazine, March 26, 04, advocating a mutiny in the IDF, resulting in soldiers refusing to obey orders to aid the pullout from Gaza.

Adir Zik told his audience in Maaleh Shomron that non-violent resistance is the best solution. The public will not tolerate their army shooting or beating the nation's leading rabbis.

Ben Artsi and Zik are both wrong. Foolproof plans are being formulated to overcome both contingencies.

The following is the government's plan for the pullout based on public sources, like deputy defence minister Tzvi Hendel, and my own sources.

The army will swoop in completely by surprise and well before the Gaza residents are ready to defend themselves. Disinformation is being spread that the pullout is not imminent In actuality, the pullout could take place, literally, tomorrow.

No soldier likely to disobey orders will be involved in the operation. Ideologically consistent soldiers of the left-wing Nahal Brigade will lead the charge, while foreign troops, reportedly including some 800 Turks, will fill out the ranks. Ben Artsi's call for mass IDF disobedience is an illusion. The army high command isn't as dumb as he thinks.

Adir Zik's plan for masses of resisters lead by the most distinguished rabbis is also not to be. The IDF will block all roads and entrances to the Gaza villages. No one will get anywhere near the pullout. The Jewish villagers will be isolated from the rest of the country.

A convoy of trucks will converge on all the Gaza villages at once and burly soldiers will clear the houses of their contents one by one and quickly. The residents will be forcibly herded into one gathering point, the hotel at Neve Dekalim would serve the purpose, and held physically until the houses and buildings had been cleared. Then they will be blown up until nothing remains of the 30 year old Jewish villages. The residents will then be transported to hotels throughout the country and given at least $180,000 dollars per family to either buy apartments or rebuild their villages in the Negev.

And no soldier will rebel and no civilian will be allowed anywhere near the villages to protest.

If the Gaza Jews are serious about saving their homes, they had better start acting immediately. Their allies have been compromised. Their communications network, Arutz Sheva, has been reduced to organizing a wimpy, barely-attended conference in Jerusalem, while Zo Artzeinu and its once firebrand leader Moshe Feiglin, has been diminished to the status of Likud Party internal squabblers. The Gazan Jews are all alone. No bugle-calling cavalry is going to come to their rescue. If they have any chance of saving their homes, they'll have to take practical steps.

The pullout will take place without any prior warning, so the residents will have to establish their own early warning system based on walkie-talkies since all phone lines will be cut off. When the rumble of the trucks is heard, all vehicles, buses, trucks, vans and cars will have to be rushed to every gate and opening, and parked strategically to complicate the entrance of the military moving vans.

Similar delays would have to be in place outside Gaza, especially on the roads leading to the villages until protesters can arrive en masse. Judging by the crowd of over 200,000 that gathered in Tel Aviv a few months ago to protest the pullout, that many people could be recruited to surround the soldiers and block any entrance into the villages. However, since telecommunications to known organizers will be shut down, those who wish to join the protest will have to be informed in their homes. It will require organization at the highest level to build a communications and transportation network ready for action at a moment's notice, in the middle of the night. And it will help to have insiders within the IDF to provide the correct advance information when they see the convoys assembling, keeping in mind that the operation will likely utilize false starts to wear down resistance.

It will require great attention to detail and motivation from the Gazan Jews to make the resistance work. However, it's the only chance they have to protect their homes and Israel's existence. From my point of view, I don't think anyone's up to it anymore.

ALM 4 - STANDING UP TO AUTHORITY

Within a few days or weeks, thousands of Israelis will no longer accept the authority of the Israeli government. But how many will stand up to it?

Last week I was invited to my friend Sarah's surprise 60th birthday party at Mike's Place, a popular Tel Aviv bar/restaurant. I arrived at 9:30 PM and the strip of restaurants where Mike's was located was packed. I circled the block twice looking for parking and nothing was free. So I settled on a place along the curb opposite the long row of restaurants. It was illegal to do so but it made no sense. There were two dozen vehicles parked along the curb and still there was enough room for a loaded Mack Truck to pass by with ease. And, 6 PM until 7 AM parking is free by city ordnance. What could happen?

At 12:30 AM I was sitting with Sarah when she noticed cars being towed from the curb. She said, "They're at it again. Here come the tow trucks."

I ran out and my car was gone.

This was extortion. The long curb was made illegal for parking knowing that streams of drivers would be forced to. It was a trap. It is a con game played by the mafia running Tel Aviv City Hall.

I walked into the parking lot where my car was being held hostage. Two strong-looking men in their mid-twenties guarded the fortress and processed the suckers in and out. I said to one, "You stole my car and I want it back." He took my details and ordered me to pay 260 shekels for its release.

"Why don't you get respectable work?, "I asked. "How can you live with yourself fleecing people by the thousands? My car wasn't blocking traffic. No one complained about it. At worst I should have received a ticket. There was no need for towing except funding a corrupt city hall through legalized car-knapping and extortion. Do you like being a hood? Are your parents proud of you?"

And on went my harangue. He gave me my receipt and a green slip with it. I asked what the other document was. He said it was a parking ticket. I ripped it into twenty pieces, threw it at him and said, "It's not anymore."

When authority is crooked, there is no choice but to stand up to it. But Israelis haven't learned the lesson yet. They either give in or leave the country by the tens of thousands every year.

June 11, '04, and I'm selling books at the Jerusalem Hebrew Book Fair. I am wearing my Who Murdered Yitzhak Rabin tee-shirt, my sales uniform. I am ascending the steps to my booth when I see President Katsav, surrounded by his entourage of bodyguards and reporters, coming down towards me. I stand in the President's path, forcing him and his entourage to stop. I point to my shirt and say to the President of Israel, "When are you going to tell us who really murdered Rabin?"

The bodyguards tense, ready to spring into action. A stunned Katsav suddenly reacts with a broad smile but does not answer me. I figured I stood up to about as big an authority as the country offered and made my way up the stairs without further incident.

Three hours later, who visits the fair but the former Attorney General, responsible for covering up the country's ruling mafiosi, Elyakim Rubinstein? He is leafing through books at a nearby booth. I grabbed a copy of the Hebrew edition of Who Murdered Yitzhak Rabin and offered Rubinstein the book as a gift. He looked at the title and said, "I don't accept gifts?"

"Why?,"I replied, "Are you too busy protecting criminals? Haven't you covered up Rabin enough?"

Once more, I stood up to authority. I was really getting the hang of it. It's easy to stand up to authority if that authority is a fraud.

Not long after, I see Shimon Sheetrit at a nearby booth. He was Rabin's Economics Minister on the night he was murdered. I offered him the book about that murder and he took it with thanks, probably because he is currently out of authority.

The Authorities Are Back In Action

Now that Sharon has totally caved into his foreign masters and is planning his withdrawals from Yesha, starting soon with Gaza and ending eventually in Jerusalem, the same games are being played as preceded the Rabin rubout.

It began in early July with comments from a Jerusalem rabbi that anyone who uproots a Jewish home is guilty of "din rodef" or persecution. These are the magic words which authorities assured us were in Yigal Amir's mind via his bad rabbis when he shot Rabin. And the rabbi had to have known the significance of this code when he uttered it. Now how did this utterance turn into a national scandal? How many reporters normally attend the seminars of the obscure Rabbi Nebenzahl?

But now the ball is rolling and next to pitch in is Shabak chief Avi Dichter who publicly extolls the dangers of radical religious Jews. Then fifty Hebron children are threatened with foster homes because the courts have deemed their parents too politically extreme to raise their children.

Then the deep shock comes when allies desert the advocates. First, Justice Minister Tsachi Hanebi warns the public that another political murder is on the way. In May 1997, I met Hanegi, then also Justice Minister, at a wedding.

My witness was a Hebrew University student, Brian Bunn. I told Hanegbi that I had documents about the Rabin murder that I wanted his office to investigate. He smiled at me, pointed both hands to his chest and answered, "And I'm going to commit suicide for you?"

Hanegbi knows all about the Rabin murder truth and his current comments show just how deeply the religious and the Right have been infiltrated.

For how long have I warned these communities that Daniel Pipes (CFR) and his board member, one Stephen Plout I believe, are pretenders to your cause? How often have I said that when the chips are down, they will reveal their true colors? And yet, look how surprised one reader is when it finally happened:

The Daniel Pipes Plan for avoiding civil war in Israel
by Yehu Ben Zohar

In the July 6, 2004 internet newsmagazine, World Net Daily, in an article warning of possible civil unrest by Jews unwilling to be forcibly transferred from their homes, there is the following quote, "Daniel Pipes, director of the Middle East Forum, told WND: "Should the government go ahead with the forceable (sic) removal of Jewish residents of Gaza, intra-Israeli violence appears to be a distinct possibility. Which in turn makes me wonder why the Israeli authorities do not take quite a different track and merely stop providing security for them."
There you have it, Daniel Pipes 'simple' solution to the "problem" of Jews being hard headed and stubborn and refusing to be forcibly transferred from their homes. Pull out all the soldiers and leave those pesky "settlers" to the tender mercies of Arafat and his bunch of murderers. No muss, no fuss, let the Arabs do the dirty work and Mr. Pipes and Mr. Sharon, Colin Powell, The EU and the UN can just sit back and not get their hands dirty with the blood of those right

wing "fanatics" who have this crazy, politically incorrect idea that Israel should be for Jews. Mr. Pipes no doubt feels this would ease the unemployment problem as quite a few Arabs would gladly do such work, at minimum wage too, since they would receive the worldly goods, homes and even the womenfolk, to whom I am sure they would be exceptionally gentle.

Mr. Pipes has frequently posed as a supporter of Israel, however on several occasions he has let his true colors show through, this is one of those times. He does not believe Jews have a right to live in Judea, Samaria or in any part of the "west bank."

Mr. Pipes will no doubt be encouraged by the coming persecution of all those who oppose his peace plan.

For those who have followed the years of murder, deceit, and repression, coming in the wake of the 1993 Oslo Accord, they are aware that the Gaza withdrawal is just another trick wrapped in the phoney authority of the state. They know the state has lost its legitimacy and no longer holds authority over them. But will they stand up for their own authority?

The government has turned over the task of the Gaza removal to the police, or so they say. Who believes the government any more? If so, the Gazan Jews have to learn police tactics to protect themselves from the trespassers. Police tactics will involve horses, dogs, teargas and truncheons. The Gazan Jews, therefore, have to stock up on spiked barricades against horses, gasmasks against teargas, helmets, even sports helmets, against the truncheons, and plenty of dog mace. A few karate lessons as defence against arrest would be useful as well.

No one wants to see deadly violence, not the police, not the government and certainly not the residents of Gush Katif. Last winter, over 200,000 people crowded Tel Aviv to protest the Gaza betrayal. If that many people could show up to blockade Gush Katif, the police would be forced to change tactics.

That will mean a siege. All communications lines will be shut down, so other radio media will have to be in place. Some 10,000 outsiders will have to be given a reason to stay in Gush Katif to delay the operation until the mass of blockaders arrive. Water and food will need to be hoarded by the tons. It will not be a short siege. The authorities will not stand down, so their victims will have to stand up.

CHAPTER TWO –
THE PERILS OF POLLARD

ALM 1 - SHIMON PERES IS KEEPING
JONATHAN POLLARD IN PRISON
(The Real Reason Why Pollard Sits)

In early May, '03, I was hired by a group of Israelis now organizing rallies on behalf of Jonathan Pollard's freedom to find out why, defying all reason, he is still sitting in prison. The people who approached me were highly dissatisfied with the official Pollard organization run by Esther Pollard and in fact, suspected her of sabotaging all alternative efforts to liberate her spouse. Since I took on the project, I have noted Esther Pollard's interference with demonstrations, speakers and even one webmaster (www.jonathanpollard.com) working on behalf of justice for Jonathan Jay Pollard.

I don't know what her motivations are, perhaps they are just a personal need for attention, perhaps they are more sinister, but with Esther Pollard at the helm, no new evidence has emerged that could possibly result in Pollard's release. Recent excitement over the revelations that Pollard was sitting for the crimes of master spy Aldrich Ames, as written by John Loftus, are not revelations at all. I discovered the exact claims in a prominent Maariv article from 1995, since repeated often in the Hebrew press.

To sort out the puzzle, I referred to a wide variety of sources and was unfortunate in having a personal expert nearby. He is Joel Bainerman, author of the 1992 classic book on Iran Contra-related felonies, Crimes Of A President. He thoughtfully provided me with relevant text, as well as his rough notes and contacts.

One of his contacts was William Northrup, who lives in a kibbutz near Beersheva and was held in a New York lockup for 10 months on suspicion of illegally selling military hardware to Iran. He insists that the Americans came down hard on Pollard because he exposed the Bechtel Corporation's production of chemical weapons in Iraq.

In the same lockup for the same crime was Ari Ben-Menashe, who wrote a tell-all book called The Profits Of War. He became a primary source for Seymour Hersh and Joel Bainerman, though far from their only one. All have been besmirched by the official Pollard organization but that doesn't mean their facts are all wrong. I use what I have judged to be likely truths.

By the same token, I have utilized many more conventional sources and their basic facts are far from consistently reliable. It was a task just sorting out the dates of the known history. Pollard, himself, insists that he started his spying in July, 1984. Loftus and Aarons have him identifying an arms shipment in April of 1984. That would make the Hersh/Ben Menashe claim that Pollard began his clandestine work in 1981, more plausible.

But once one excuses the inconsistencies, a very consistent story emerges. Pollard thought he was helping Israel protect itself and that his material would fall into honest, trusted hands. Sadly for him, it fell into the grimy paws of Shimon Peres and he used it to create a crime empire, broadly called Iran Contra. It is the fear of exposing Peres and his cronies, that is the real reason why the Israeli government has made no sincere effort to free Joanthan Jay Pollard.

It's a fairly complicated story and I will lead you through it by way of other people's research. When I comment you will see three stars *** at the beginning and end of the commentary. For instance:

*** In 1987, a government commission of inquiry headed by Abba Eban issued its report on the Pollard Affair. It concluded that the man most responsible for the fiasco was Shimon Peres, who became Prime Minister in late May, 1984. He was not only apprised of Pollard's intelligence, he read it daily. Receiving smaller portions of blame were Defence Minister Yitzhak Rabin and Foreign Minister Yitzhak Shamir.

This long buried report is, naturally, long forgotten because Peres spent a good week denying every word in it and arranging the end of Eban's political carrer. But let us not forget, the official investigation conducted by the Israel government concluded that Peres was the chief culprit.***

LEADING THE COVERUP

Amir Oren, Haaretz, 1998: *"Shimon Peres was almost as concerned about domestic policies as he was about the American reaction. He was proud of the fact that he, Rabin and Shamir refrained from mutual recriminations and how that prevented the media from turning it into an Israeli Watergate. Peres worked hard to prevent public discussion..."*

Zeev Segal, Haaretz 24/10/95: *"One body that studied the subject was a committee headed by then MK, Abba Eban. In a report published in May, 1987, the committee...totally rejected the claim of the government of Israel, which stated that the Pollard affair was a 'rogue' operation."*

Washington Report On Middle East, Jan/Feb 2003: *"Eban disappeared from political life after 1987 (for) a report criticizing Labor Party leaders Shimon Peres and Yitzhak Rabin for using American Joanthan Jay Pollard to spy on the United States. Both rebuked him and the next year his name was left off the candidates for parliament."*

Seymour Hersh, The Samson Option, Random House, 1991: *"The Israeli Officials most tarnished by the scandal were Rafi Eitan and Aviem Sella, but Eitan did not suffer financially. He was subsequently named to a high administrative position with Israel Chemicals, the largest state-owned enterprise in Israel. His surprising appointment was authorized by none other than Ariel Sharon, who had been named Minister of Trade and Industry in 1984."*

And Sharon is not the only high present official involved in the coverup. Attorney General Elyakim Rubinstein was the legal attache to the Washington Embassy Pollard was ejected from, and later tried out a coverup tactic that Washington attorney Leonard Garment found odious. Such details must be presented in a wider-ranging future report. For now let us get to the heart of the matter at hand...Iran Contra.

IRAN CONTRA

Federal Government Watch Discussion List: *"The back channel came alive under Vice-President Bush from 1984-91. The channel was used to direct the laundering of American money to the PLO. Although Pollard didn't know it, when he warned the Israelis that a PLO arms shipment was going through Greece in 1984, he inadvertantly blew the whistle on the White House's first transaction of arms to Iran...In the summer of 1984, Pollard noticed a pattern of vessels going back and forth from Greece to Yemen, where the PLO had a major base. Pollard passed the tip to the Israelis. In the summer of 1984, the Israelis tipped off the Greek authorities who seized an entire shipload of arms believed destined for the PLO. Neither Pollard nor the government of Israel was aware that they had smashed George Bush's first shipment of arms to Iran. Pollard never realized that he had busted the most secret White House operation of modern times. The summer of 1984 Greek shipment was a dagger over George Bush's head."*

Loftus, Aarons, The Secret War Against The Jews: *"Pollard notified the Israelis, who passed word to the Greeks, who raided the arms ship. None of the players knew that this shipment was directly connected to an event two months previous, in which US hostages had been kidnapped in Lebanon. The ship had not been commissioned by Arafat but by US Vice-President Bush and was ultimately destined for the patron the of Lebanese kidnappers, Iran. The shipment marks he true beginning of the infamous Iran Contra scandal."*

Winston Mideast Analysis And Commentary 8/13/99: *"Pollard inadvertantly exposed the first shipment of arms-for-hostages in what became the Iran Contra scandal. As he was in the Naval Intelligence Anti-Terrorism Unit, he saw this shipment, one year earlier than is generally known, and believing it to be arms for the PLO or Iraq, revealed it to the Israelis. This alone would make it imperative for the Iran/Contra planners to keep him locked up forever."*

***Enter Peres. Pollard provided the data that exposed Bush's arms for hostages operation. Of course, a moral Prime Minister would have demanded that Bush put an end to this arming of Israel's worst enemies. But Peres is not remotely moral, so he saw the bigger potential of this nascent crime. He wanted in and the crime expanded into what we know as Irangate.

How do we know this? Because when Pollard discovered the arms ship, Israel had no role in paying America's enemies off with arms for releasing hostages in Lebanon. But by September, Peres had sent a team to Washington consisting of Yaacov Nimrodi, the former Ambassador to Iran, Al Schwimmer, former head of Israel Aircraft Industries, and David Kimche, chairman of the Israeli branch of the Council On Foreign Relations.

After that, Israel was right in the middle of the operation. This is basic indisputable logic. Israel joined the operation only after Pollard's intelligence exposed the existence of it. That means Peres wanted a piece of the pie and must have used Pollard's data to get his cut of the action.

41

The easiest way in would have been threatening to expose the arms for hostages operation and bring down Bush and his team. We call such a threat, blackmail. And that's how Pollard's good intentions were used. And not for the last time.

Shortly after Pollard's capture on Non.22/85, the Peres team of Kimche, Schwimmer and Nimrodi all quit the operation. In laymen's terms, they hauled ass out of there. But Peres didn't want to give up all the goodies that came with Iran Contra. So in January 1986, he replaced the team with his anti-terrorism advisor Amiram Nir. He was murdered in 1989 in Mexico shortly before he was to testify to the Senate Committee investigating Irangate.

Lest one think Iran Contra wasn't worth the trouble, look how much just one member of Peres' team brought in for his effort and then consider what Nir knew. Finally, note who else quit his post in the wake of Pollard; the American National Security Advisor, Bud McFarlane, who resigned in Dec. '85.***

Joel Bainerman, Crimes Of A President, SPI Books, NY, 1992, raw notes and final text: *"In June 1991 an Israel police investigation was opened to determine if Nimrodi withheld profits from the sales from the Defence Ministry. A month later Nimrodi made a public declaration in a Tel Aviv court stating that he had acted on his own behalf in his arms dealings with the Iranians and thus all the profits from the deals were his. He claimed he earned $37 million from the Iranians, but after paying for the missiles and other expenses, he says he took a loss on the deal of nearly $750,000. (Inside Israel, August, 1993)*

Those same bank records in Switzerland could have become a nightmare for some Israeli government officials, namely Prime Minister Peres, even shedding light on why the Israeli government never allowed Nir (or Schwimmer and Nimrodi) to testify before Congressional investigations. Was Peres perhaps worried that Nir would disclose that it was his role in the diversion of money from the Iranian arms sales to the Contras or that he personally authorized the establishment of the fund to initiate covert anti-terrorist operations?

I ndeed Nir knew a great deal about U.S. and Israeli arms sales to Iran because he was the roundabout via everyone's activities passed through. He must have known who set up the Swiss accounts, who controlled them, and how much went to the Contras and how much to middlemen like Ghorbanifar and Secord's pockets? He sat in on crucial meetings in Teheran, Frankfurt, Washington, Tel Aviv and London. He knew of all covert operations and where the money originated from to fund them.

In an interview with YEDIOT ACHRONOT after leaving office in March l987 Nir said that Shamir went out of his way to protect his name and reputation, in Israel and in the U.S., while Peres simply 'left him to the dogs' adding that "the moment you need support from him (Peres), he vanishes."'

DID POLLARD HAVE HELP?

Codevilla, MENL 24/7/00: "He gave them that part of the flow of US intelligence which they used to receive regularly, but which the US cut off in 1981...This consisted of intelligence 'products.' It was satellite pictures, reports of all kinds, electronic directories and so forth."

John Loftus, Moment, 6/03: "Jonathan Pollard didn't have the 'blue stripe' clearance according to intelligence sources I spoke with. That was the bombshell that would clear him of any possible connection to the deaths of our Russian agents."

Codevilla, ibid: "Jonathan Pollard could not have provided codes, because he did not have any access to codes."

Ari Ben-Menashe, Profits Of War, Sheridan Square Press, 1992: *"McFarlane, in fact, had been providing computer access codes of intelligence reports to Rafi Eitan, according to Eitan. Sitting in Tel Aviv, Eitan would request computer access codes for certain items he was interested in. A representative in Washington, a woman named Iris, would pass the request to McFarlane. He would then give her back the specified access codes. She would give the codes to Pollard."*

Consortiumnews.com 8/6/03:: *The issue was brought to the high court by former national security advisor Robert McFarlane who claims he was libeled by a 1991 Esquire magazine story linking him to the Jonathan Pollard spy case...Both courts ruled that McFarlane failed to show that Esquire displayed a reckless disregard for the truth."*

***Now we move into stage two of the exploitation of Jonathan Pollard. Pollard was assigned to receive and analyse satellite photos of ship positions and look for aberrant routes. That would have made the discovery of Bush's arms ship natural. But for the next piece of Peres blackmail, he would most likely have needed help.

Pollard uncovered a crime the equal of Iran Contra: the American corporation Bechtel was making chemical weaponry for Saddam Hussein. And Peres instinctively knew he could milk this discovery for all it was worth because Defence Secretary Caspar Weinberger was a VP of Bechtel before choosing public service and Secretary of State George Shultz was a former Bechtel CEO.

I have no doubt that Pollard passed the Bechtel gas data to Israel but how he got it is still in dispute. Perhaps he received satellite photos which exposed the factories, but it seems more likely that he was given intelligence much higher than he was entitled to receive. For that he would have needed help from one of the few entitled to receive top secret access codes and Robert McFarlane as National Security Advisor was one those few.***

BECHTEL AND CASPAR WEINBERGER

Codevilla, MENL 24/7/00: *"This memo contained the lie that Pollard caused the deaths of countless US agents. It also reportedly said the Israelis sold part of that information to the Soviet Union. All of these things are not only untrue, they were known by Weinberger not to be true...The policy was building up Iraq, a policy to which Weinberger and much of the rest of the US government sacrificed true American interests in the 1980s. We supplied Saddam Hussein with not only arms but with intelligence and forbearance...The main thing is we permitted, licensed and financed large American corporations to build plants there. The infrastructure that is being bombed in Iraq right now is mostly American-built. Now we get to the deeply embarassing part. One of the companies involved was Bechtel, with whom Caspar Weinberger and George Schultz, Secretaries of Defense and State, had close personal relations."*

Federal Government Watch Discussion List, Yahoo, message 631: *"As Jonathan Pollard discovered to his horror, the German nerve gas factories constructed in Libya and Iraq are using the identical formulas used on Jews at Auschwitz... President Bush Sr. was good friends with Saddam's Deputy Foreign Minister and made personal phone calls to one of his former Yale classmates to obtain American funding for Bechtel's oil pipeline in Iraq...The Bechtel corporation was even building Saddam Hussein a chemical factory he could use for poison gas production."*

Counterpunch.org, 9/4/03: *"Schultz worked at Bechtel, so did Caspar Weinberger.Bechtel was listed by Iraq in its report to the UN weapons inspectors as one of the companies that helped supply Saddam with equipment and* knowledge for making chemical weapons. Bechtel in the 1980s was prime contractor on PC1 and 2, two petrochemical plants constructed in Iraq which had dual use capacity. So I guess the bottom line is that the Bush-Cheney-Rumsfield squad are now holding Saddam Hussein accountable for chemical weapons of mass destruction - the same weapons which these same officials ignored in pursuit of the Aqaba pipeline project."

IRAQ PIPELINE

Barry Chamish, The Fall Of Israel, Canongate, Edinburgh, 1992:"By 1985 Syria had closed down Iraq's pipeline to the Mediterranean and Iran was blockading the Persian Gulf.Iraq wanted to build an alternative pipeline to Aqaba, Jordan's Red Sea port, and the American corporation Bechtel agreed to construct this multi-billion dollar project, but only if it received assurances that Israel would never blow it up, not even in wartime. American Attorney-General Edwin Meeese approached Peres who agreed in return for $70 million a year to be transferred to the Israeli Labor Party. When word of the bribe leaked, Meese was forced out of office, but, as usual, scandal escaped Peres."

Joel Bainerman, Crimes Of A President, Notes And Final Text:

"Pipeline deal. To be built by the Bechtel company. It would feed 300,000 barrels of oil each day from Iraqi oilfields to a terminal at the Jordanian port of Aquaba. As part of the arrangement, then Israeli Prime Minister Shimon Peres's Labor party would receive up to $1 billion over a ten year period in return for a pledge not to bomb the pipeline in the event of a war.

"McFarlane was also the major White House backer of the Iraqi pipeline deal. To bebuilt by the Bechtel company it would feed 300,000 barrels of oil each day from Iraqi oilfields

46

to a terminal at the Jordanian port of Aquaba. As part of the arrangement, then Israeli Prime Minister Shimon Peres's Labor party would receive up to $1 billion over a ten year period in return for a pledge not to bomb the pipeline in the event of a war"

"Originally, it may have been intended to have this money come from the Pentagon's budget. When John Poindexter took over from McFarlane as National Security Adviser in December 1985 he killed a plan his predecessor had come up with to have secret payments made to Israel out of a heavily disguised National Security Counsel-controlled appropriation in the Pentagon's budget. (Washington Post, March 5th, 1988) "The idea was for it to come out of the defence budget on an installment basis," one source was quoted as saying. "It was, to be a payment to the Israelis to be good." (Washington Post,February 25th, 1988) .

"It may be nothing but a mere coincidence, but Israel's spy in Washington, Jonathan Pollard, was operating throughout McFarlane's period as National Security Advisor. A month after Pollard was arrested, McFarlane resigned. Yet six months later he is leading a delegation on a secret mission to Teheran. Why didn't National Security Adviser Poindexter go?

"McFarlane's ties to Rafi Eitan, then the Prime Minister's Anti-Terrorism Advisor and who would later be named as the Israeli intelligence agent behind the masterminding of the Pollard affair, also need to be investigated"ch.org, 9/4/03: "Bechtel and the State Department were having trouble getting the right degree from the Israeli Labor Party that the pipeline would be off limits to attack. Bechtel and Reagan administration officials were trying to get complete assurance from the Labor Party that the pipeline would absolutely not be attacked."

***So here's what the Peres government did with Pollard's intelligence: they put the squeeze on Bechtel and that meant on Caspar Weinberger. The threat was simple enough: if you guys at Bechtel don''t find a way to funnel me a lot of money, $700 million will do, we'll expose the Iraqi gas plants and sabotage your pipeline deal. Hence, the insurance policy excuse was formulated under great duress.

When a very peeved Weinberger discovered that it was Pollard who was passing Peres his blackmail weapons, he showed no mercy. He intervened with Pollard's judge and made sure he got life for a five year crime knowing the Israeli government could put no stop to him or risk its own massive exposure.

Weinberger is home free. In 1992, President Bush pardoned him for all Iran Contra-related crimes. Shimon Peres was just chosen as head of the Israeli Labor Party. And unless this little piece of the whole truth is thoroughly investigated, Jonathan Pollard will sit for good in his cold, cold cell.***

ALM 2 - BROKEN PROMISES

My recent piece proving that the Israeli government under Shimon Peres badly exploited Jonathan Pollard's intelligence and encouraged his continued incarceration led to a blizzard of mail and new information.

One intelligence insider verified most of my findings but disputed one. In fact, the Israeli government under Peres' successor as Prime Minister, Yitzhak Shamir, did try to buy Pollard out of prison for a fair exchange.

The person who gave me the story is a retired London commodities broker, Johnny Lancaster, whose first person book character is named Aaron Goldman.

He sat in prison for three years as a result of an ill-fated plot to free Terry Waite, a Brit held hostage in Lebanon. He claims he was a victim of a Mossad sting, in retaliation for their broken promise to him, which led to still another American broken promise over Pollard.

I had a long conversation with Lancaster, following which he faxed me 8 pages of documents verifying his story. These included an airfare receipt from Salzburg on the day he claimed he was there arranging one of the great intelligence capers of the century; and a Tel Aviv Hilton hotel memo signed by the Mossad agent he claims betrayed him.

Lancaster wrote a book describing his journeys into the netherworld of covert operations called Forbidden Yesterday. He insists all stock was bought out by the Mossad and his publisher persuaded not to reprint. But he does have a site to look at: www.forbiddenyesterday.co.uk

This is the letter he sent me. *You're not going to understand it, but I'll sort it out after you've looked at it:*

It is lesser known that on August 9th 1985, a London born Jew, (later code-named 'Johnny Lancaster' by Mossad), a branded Jeans import-exporter turned entrepreneur, whom by God's will or chance was invited to Israel's London Embassy by a Mossad Agent (Alon) posing as an Agricultural Attache' ...'Johnny Lancaster' left the Israeli embassy naively agreeing to help Israel gain an edge to trade in West Africa by recruiting a well-placed West German associate (AB) The deal was confirmed with Mazel un Brocheh, a most revered and cherished binding Hebrew promise affirmed with a handshake, which according to learned Rabbi was handed down from God to Abraham.

The London Embassy meeting led to Munich, Salzburg and the infiltration of Germany's largest exporter of electronics weapons and 'Operation Prairie Fire', the Pentagon's code name for the controversial naval-raid on Libya, the USA first encounter of smart-weapons, due to the well-placed West German who passed over the secret Libyan defence codes in Salzburg the 1st and 2nd February 1986 to Mossad agents.

It is little know that Caspar Weinberger secretly met with his Israeli counterpart Ehad Barak prior to 'Operation Prairie Fire'..The far-reaching meeting/agenda remains unpublished

despite the US Supreme Court ruling for them to be dislosed. Consequently, the America Sixth Fleet picked up the gauntlet for the Free World to cross Gadaffi's self-imposed 'Line of Death' in the Gulf of Sidra 24th March 1986 to curb terrorism.

It is well known that Mossad keep their most successful operations secret. To this day Mossad have not claimed credit for their part in covertly securing the Libyan defence secrets when breaching German and Austrian Sovereignty: 1st & 2nd Feb 1986 and prior to. Is it because Israel traded them for Jonathan Pollard spying, not to be cut off from all military and monetary aid by the USA, which enabled the US Sixth Fleet to cross Gadaffi's battle-ready 'Line of Death' without fear of loss of ship, plane nor man from the Hi-Tec German installed defence system of the day? It is also little known: that the American Sixth Fleet jammed the Libyan defence system and homed-in the F1-11 bombers that took off from the UK to bomb Tripoli and Benghazi the follow April.

One wonders at the historical raid's, gagging order that swept the the action of the President Reagan under the carpet to allow the long-arm of the USA to be forgotten/not realised. Possibly the 'Eleventh' would not have happened if 'Operation Prairie Fire' had been proclaimed from the top of the Twin Towers instead of being swept under the carpet to appease and to cover-up the truth?

Further, it is known to but a few, that Johnny Lancaster perused the broken promise in the Holy Land when he met with a ranking Mossad officer (MP, Alon's direct boss) in the Tel Aviv Hilton late December 1986 and Ist January 1987 when and where the Mossad officer revealed that Israel was obliged to trade the secret Libyan defence codes for the indiscretions of Jonathan Pollard so Israel would not to be cut off of all military and monitory aid by the USA.

It is lesser known still, that Mossad blatantly duped and reneged on the deal thrice sealed by Mazel un Brocheh and indeed thrice threatened the naįve' Johnny Lancaster' life: but settled on setting him up to go to jail..

Seventeen years on, Jonathan Pollard remains in jail regardless of the agreed plea bargaining with the US Government and the World-wide call and indeed a British MP for Jonathan Pollard's release.

Now, I'll try and explain what happened. I spoke with Aaron at length and took notes. But I'm still not entirely comfortable with all the facts. Aaron has sent me his book and that should do the trick. Meanwhile, this is what I gleaned from our conversation:

BC: So how did you get involved in a Mossad operation?

JL: I was a comodities broker dealing in residue oil contracts and I had contacts all over Europe. I had one contact in Yugoslavia who mentioned he befriended a real character at Siemens in Germany named Alex Becker. The guy installed the radio air defence systems for Nigeria and Libya and knew their codes. He was a miserable alcoholic and was shooting off his mouth about that.
   I told the story to Uri Raz, a friend and neighbour and he arranged a meeting at the Israeli embassy with someone named Alon, who claimed he was an agricultural attache. This was in August '85. He was highly interested and the talks began. In the end it was agreed I would get $5 million to be divided between Becker, my Yugoslavian contact and me. My cut was $1.2 million. We shook on it. In December '86, I met with Becker in Salzburg. He gave me the Libyan radio frequencies and codes and I gave him his check. I flew back to London to get my share and Alon suddenly didn't know me. An intermediary, Manny Levy, told me the name of the game was not to pay me.

BC: Is there anyone to turn to when this happens?

JL: Remember, I wasn't entirely helpless. I had first hand evidence that the Mossad breached the sovereignty of the

UK, Germany and Austria. I had a few high cards. So I flew to Tel Aviv and met a Mossad officer there, Michael Perry. I'll fax you his signature on a hotel memo. He told me that since Pollard was caught, the Mossad was forbidden to pay foreign nationals. It was politically too hot. He was sorry but I was out.

Then he told me what was done with the codes. Ehud Barak was given them and told to fly to Washington to meet Caspar Weinberger. Remember, Barak was Peres' damage-control man from the day Pollard was captured. He was on the first flight to Washington. He cut a deal with Weinberger: the codes for Pollard. It was Israel's way of saying sorry and Weinberger took the offer.

Next month a nightclub is blown up in Berlin and American servicemen are killed. The US traces the bombing to Libya and in March they launch two air raids on Tripoli. They kill Khaddafi's adopted daughter and almost get him. In retaliation, Libya blew up Pan Am 103 over Lockerbie, Scotland. So my little operation had consequences I never imagined, nor wanted.

And for all that, I wasn't paid and my handlers split the money. They all bought new flats when they were done with me. And Weinberger betrayed Barak and kept Pollard in prison. Both sides were crooks and Pollard and I were the main victims.

BC: Have you told this to anyone else?

JL: I contacted Esther Pollard and she cold-shouldered me. I'll fax you her letter. She actually writes that my medicine might be worse than the cure, whatever that means. I was flabbergasted at her refusal to take advantage of my information. Then I turned to John Butterhill, a Member of Parliament who is Vice Chairman of the Free Pollard Committee here. He told me there is no working with this Esther Pollard and he had given up trying. But she had made herself the only channel to Jonathan Pollard, so it was futile for me to reveal my information through her organization. I have documented proof of Pollard's betrayal and it's in the American government records that are being sealed by court order. If that order could be challenged, we'd have the proof that the American Secretary Of Defense promised the Israeli government to free Pollard in return for the Libyan codes and frequencies and then reneged on its promise. That should be enough to set Pollard free.

***

Then came correspondence with Susan Rosenbluth, editor of the New Jersey Jewish Voice And Opinion:

Barry, you are really on to something. As a journalist, I listen for "chords" to see if things sound right, and with the Pollards (really it's only Esther, and she claims to speak in Jonathan's name--maybe she does), things are as discordant as they can be. From personal experience (no second-hand stuff here), I can tell you there is something very, very wrong with their entire story.

For sure, the US government lied to Pollard--no one agrees to a plea bargain only to have the book thrown at him. Many people claim Jonathan is now nuts--and who are we to cast stones. Maybe any and all of us would be nuts after spending 16-17 years in prison. My own experience with the Pollards has shown that they are not interested in doing everything and anything possible to secure his release. ..

For reasons of his own, Luchins wanted very much to help the Pollards at that time. Luchins said he would come to the meeting (which was supposed to be at my office, where Esther had been before) alone. If the meeting went well, he said he would bring to the next meeting Joe Lieberman, Pat Moynihan, and possibly Hillary Clinton.

While I was not delighted at the prospect of Hillary's helping Pollard and thus becoming a heroine to the Jews, I really did think it might have been a solution to the Pollard issue. If Hillary wanted Pollard pardoned, Pollard would have

53

been pardoned--and Luchins just might have been able to pull it off.

But we will never know if it could have happened. Esther flat out refused to meet with Luchins--she would have liked to meet with the Senators and the First Lady, but, in fact, Luchins was probably the only Jewish leader with the connections and the clout to arrange it, and Esther would not meet with him.

I was--and still remain--flabbergasted. I could not imagine a loving wife refusing to meet with anyone who might be able to help her poor imprisoned husband--especially since she was not being asked to do anything else except meet with Luchins. She didn't have to agree to do anything in advance, and goodness knows, she could have had any number of advisors to make sure she didn't do anything she would have regretted later. Had she gone to the meeting, it's just possible--although nothing is for certain--that Pollard could have been freed.

In her position, I imagine, a loving wife would meet with Satan himself if it might help her husband. Instead, Esther has insulted personally so many people who might be of help to Jonathan. Now, it is possible Esther really does want Jonathan Pollard freed, but the question must be asked: If she wanted him to remain behind bars, how would she behave differently?

Pollard could have been released but his "wife" and her lawyer seem more interested in his continued incarceration. Now we have to ask why. Is it because his imprisonment is good for business or are they being encouraged by certain authorities to ensure that Pollard never has a chance to set the record straight?

CHAPTER THREE –
THE SYNDICATE THAT MURDERED A CONGRESSMAN

ALM 1 - EDGAR AND THE TERMINATOR

The intended objective of this article was to examine the activities of the hidden powerbrokers of and against Israel. My readers supplied invaluable information, and though they don't know each other personally, produced a strange cycle beginning with Egdar Bronfman and connecting, finally, with Arnold Schwarzenegger. Here is how Edgar meets the Terminator. It begins in early August when Bronfman of the Council On Foreign Relations (CFR), co-writes a letter to President Bush with Lawrence Eagleburger (CFR), a vice-president of Henry Kissinger (CFR) Associates. Bronfman is self-appointed head of the World Jewish Congress and his Israeli executive member is Isi Leibler. He wrote an open letter to Bronfman published in the Jerusalem Post, in a building so dismal its own writers fear to enter, then owned by Conrad Black of the CFR.

I will separate my own commentary with those of my readers and the material they sent with three stars *** at the beginning and end of my intrusions, like this:

*** We preface the scandal with Bronfman's ties to the Vatican, which will make the rest of his treacherous activities almost understandable. ***

You've been warning us for a while about Edgar Bronfman, most recently in the piece about the Vatican:

October 1991

On October 12th, the head of the World Jewish Congress,

Edgar Bronfman, is appointed head of the International Jewish Committee of Inter-religious Consultation to conduct official contacts with The Vatican and the State of Israel.
****

Well, check this out, from JTA via IMRA, URLs included:

http://www.imra.org.il/story.php3?id=17904
Wednesday, August 13, 2003

JTA: Bronfman suggested Palestinians murder "only" settlers

"If the Palestinian suicide bombers only went to the settlements and told the whole world they were wrong, then the whole world would have had a case against Israel and there would be a two-state solution by now," he said. "Instead, they sent them into Israel proper, which is ghastly."

BEHIND THE HEADLINES

Bronfman letter on fence revives debate on Jewish criticism of Israel
By Joe Berkofsky
http://www.jta.org/page_view_story.asp?intarticleid=13083 &intcategoryid=4

NEW YORK, Aug. 12 (JTA) - An uproar over Israel´s security fence is provoking an unusual public scuffle in a major Jewish organization and reviving the longtime Diaspora debate on the propriety of publicly challenging Israeli policy.
The spat between the World Jewish Congress´ president, Edgar Bronfman, and the group´s senior vice president, Isi Leibler, erupted last week when Leibler wrote a newspaper column demanding that Bronfman apologize or resign for urging President Bush to pressure Israel and the Palestinians to follow the "road map" peace plan.

Bronfman also called the security fence Israel is building to keep out terrorists - which Palestinians describe as a land grab - "potentially problematic."

After a flurry of letters and news articles, Bronfman told JTA that he will ask the WJC leadership to oust Leibler, setting up a battle of wills between two of world Jewry´s wealthiest public figures. The fight broke out when Leibler wrote an "open letter" to the Jerusalem

Post on Aug. 6 urging Bronfman to apologize or resign for the letter he sent Bush on the eve of a White House summit with Israeli Prime Minister Ariel Sharon.

In the wake of Leibler´s article, Singer said more than 150 WJC members had acked Bronfman´s letter, which he co-wrote with Lawrence Eagleburger, who was secretary of state in the administration of George H.W. Bush and today is chairman of the International Commission on Holocaust-Era Insurance Claims.

Among Bronfman´s supporters is former Israeli Prime Minister Shimon Peres. "Clearly, issues that are open for debate in Israel, are also open for discussion in the jewish world," Peres wrote to Bronfman and Eagleburger. "The Jewish people hould never be taken for a rubber stamp. Such a role would enfeeble the Jewish people and undermine the people of Israel." Eagleburger, a longtime friend and neighbor of Bronfman´s, did not return calls seeking comment. Bronfman continued to defend his letter, saying he did not write on WJC stationery or use his WJC title.

Bronfman said he would ask the WJC executive committee to strip Leibler of his title at the group´s next meeting. The leadership meets twice yearly, but the next meeting has not been set.

Leibler, who founded a chain of Australian travel agencies before moving to Israel, vowed to continue challenging Bronfman, the former owner of Seagrams. The struggle is largely to establish clear rules in the WJC, Leibler said. "Nobody wants to take on Edgar Bronfman; he´s an extremely powerful personality," Leibler said. "But I will take on this battle if it means we have a man who has the title of World Jewish Congress president and who lobbies against the security interests of Israel."

The dispute threatened to get messier when Bronfman began discussing Palestinian political aims and his longtime opposition to Jewish settlements in the West Bank and Gaza Strip.

While "murder is murder and mayhem is mayhem, no matter where," Bronfman said, he felt a "more effective" Palestinian tactic would have been to launch attacks only against settlements, which do not enjoy international support, rather than inside pre-1967 Israel.

"If the Palestinian suicide bombers only went to the settlements and told the whole world they were wrong, then the whole world would have had a case against Israel and there would be a two-state solution by now," he said. "Instead, they sent them into Israel proper, which is ghastly."

Leibler called the statement "outrageous" and "obscene."

"There seems to me an implicit suggestion that there is a difference between Jews over the Green Line and behind the Green Line," he said. "Are you telling me that the president of the World Jewish Congress said to you that had the Palestinians concentrated on Jews over the Green Line, that would have been more acceptable?"Bronfman said his point was different.

"It would not have been more acceptable," he said, "it would have been smarter on their part."

***Recall later that Bronfman's partner in outrage is Lawrence Eagleburger, chairman of the International Commission on Holocaust-Era Insurance Claims. This will soon tie Edgar to the Terminator. And when we arrive there, forget not that it was Bronfman and his WJC which, for the past decade, has led the fight against the Swiss Banks to release their assets stolen by the Nazis from Holocaust victims and deposited in Switzerland. And begin wondering why almost none of these monies ever reached the hands of their rightful owners.

But first, let us have a look at another insider we barely know, PM Sharon's chief advisor, Dov Weisglass.***

DOV WEISGLASS

As reported in the previous article, Sharon is being set up for his upcoming all, in order to pave the way back for Shimon Peres to the Prime Minister's office, by way of a series of financial and long-past military scandals. The attorney-general and media are busy dredging up anything that can be used to oust Sharon from office. Yet somehow the following scandal will never be mentioned. You see, Sharon's appointments organizer, Weisglass, and his son Omri, met the PLO's security minister Muhamed Dahlan in Austria a while back in order to get a piece of the action in a casino run by the PLO in Jericho.

Haaretz, Jan. 10, Page 1B

"It is not clear why $1.5 million were transferred from South Africa to somewhere else, to a bank in Austria via a bank in New York, until they finally landed in a branch of Discount Bank in Tel Aviv. Why this circuitous route?

"What is known, however, is that Omri Sharon and attorney Dov Weisglass (the director of the Prime Minister's Bureau) visited both Austria and the United States together this past year. Austria is the domicile of Martin Schlaff, one of the owners of the casino in Jericho and a partner in the Bank of Austria. Schlaff is a client of attorney Weisglass."

So you would think that Weisglass is acting on behalf of Sharon and the Right, right? So why is he representing Labor party member Dahlia Rabin and her brother Yuval, both the children of slain Labor party leader Yitzhak Rabin? And what is his role in the coverup of the murder?

Here is a weird quote from a Roni Kempler interview on the website you reference in your latest email:

http://www.geocities.com/freepages4all/index.htm

INTERVIEWER: Have you ever met with Dalia Rabin?

KEMPLER: "The day before the videotape was shown on television, I was supposed to meet with Dalia Rabin and Yuval Rabin at the office of attorney Dov Weisglass. They said that they wanted a meeting and they didn't give any reason why. A short time before the meeting was due to take place, they sent word that the meeting was canceled - without giving any explanation."

*** My reader wisely observes, "Weisglass seems to be at the center of everything. I don't think you've focused on him enough... from the Ginosar scandal to Rabin, Peres and Sharon. Seems he's the common denominator to everything."
Indeed he may be, because when you're negotiating oil pipelines with the Iranians, you're in the loop. My reader asks a good question:"Do you think he got paid in Swiss currency for negotiating the Eilat-Ashkelon Pipeline Pipeline deal with the Iranians and the Portuguese World Bank?" ***

http://www.iranexpert.com/2002/israeliraneapc31october.htm

The offer was made to Adv. Dov Weissglass before he was appointed director of the Prime Minister's Bureau. A Russian company is also interested in Eilat-Ashkelon pipeline Co. (EAPC).

The Iranian government recently held negotiations to sell its 50% stake in Eilat-Ashkelon Pipeline Co. (EAPC) to the Portuguese World Bank.

Adv. Dov Weisglass represented the Portuguese World Bank before he was appointed director of the Prime Minister's Bureau. Weissglass notified various government offices several months ago about the negotiations. Weissglass declined to comment on the report.

The Portuguese World Bank, which had received an offer from the Iranian government sources, sent a message through Weissglass that it and other foreign investors conditioned the acquisition of EAPC on the Israeli government also selling its 50% holding.

The Israeli-Iranian partnership was created in the late 1960s. EAPC was set up to build an oil pipeline from Iran to Israel, and thence to Europe, in order to bypass the Suez Canal, which was closed at the time, in the wake of the 1967 Six-Day War. EAPC eventually became one of Israel's largest energy companies, benefiting from benefits and tax breaks not granted to its competitors, thanks to its partial Iranian   ownership.

A Russian company has also reportedly show interest in recent months in acquiring EAPC, in order exploit its international pipeline.

A British correspondent puts the pieces together connecting Shimon Peres and his toy "rabbi", Michael Melchior, to a suspicious coalition of British Arabs and Jews, leading to a Tory MK forced to resign in disgrace, David Mellor. The bold letters are his way to emphasize the ugly circle of "friends" and their direct ties to the embezzlement of the "palestinian" Authority.

"RABBI" MICHAEL MELCHIOR
Up to his kippa in crime.

http://news.ft.com/servlet/ContentServer?pagename=FT.com/StoryFT/FullStory&c=StoryFT&cid=1059478773013&p=1012571727132

MEDIA EYE COMMENT - "RABBI" GLUCK WAS THE PERSON WHO, A YEAR AGO, ON 18 AUGUST 2002 ARRANGED WITH HIS FRIEND "RABBI" MELICHOR, THEN DEPUTY ISRAELI FM TO FLY THE PLO FINANCIER, JAWAD (AL) GHUSSEIN, TO LONDON FROM GAZA. THE UK HOME OFFICE DENIES THAT THE FINANCIER EVER ATTEMPTED TO ENTER THE UK DESPITE THE ARTICLES IN THE TIMES, THE JERUSALEM POST AND THE LONDON JEWISH NEWS CONFIRMING HIS ARRIVAL .

THE INTERESTING ASPECT OFTHIS IS TWOFOLD.

ONE, THE UK HOME OFFICE IMMIGRATION DEPARTMENT DENY HIS APPLICATION FOR ENTRY CLEARANCE AND REFUSE TO ENTER IN CORRESPONDENCE OVER THIS

THE SECOND IS THAT GLUCK'S INVOLVEMENT BEGAN WHEN HE MET GHUSSEIN'S DAUGHTER, THROUGH THE NEXT CENTURY FOUNDATION, PARTLY FINANCED BY THE UK FOREIGN OFFICE. THE DAUGHTER IS THE WELL KNOW MONA BAUWENS WHO HAD ASSOCIATIONS WITH THE EX TORY MINISTER AND ANTI SEMITE DAVID MELLOR!(SEE BELOW REPORT FROM JERUSALEM POST)

Beyond Belief

By Michael Skapinker Published: August 8 2003 18:10 | Last Updated: August 8 2003 18:10

Rabbi Hershel Gluck bustles through the streets of the east London borough of Hackney, pausing only to accept a fellow Orthodox Jew's congratulations on the birth of his first grandchild. He turns the corner and bounds up the stairs of the local Muslim community centre, where he is admitted with a flurry of handshakes and shouts of "Rabbi!" from a group of young men hanging around the entrance hall. Rabbi Gluck is at home here. He strides into an inner room, tosses his black hat onto a chair, revealing his skullcap underneath, and greets two friends - Ismael Amaan, a Muslim community leader, and Mohamed Munaf Zeena, head of the Council of Indian Muslims. The three men are leading lights in the Muslim Jewish Forum, which they boast is the most tightly-knit example of co-operation between the two faiths anywhere in the UK, and, Rabbi Gluck claims, in the world. The grey-bearded Rabbi Gluck and the black-bearded Amaan are photogenic local celebrities, having appeared on a much-discussed BBC news programme about how Muslims and Jews can live as friends in the same community.

The two are considering a national tour, in which they will appear together in Muslim communities that have never seen a Jew and Jewish communities that know few Muslims, as well as large areas of the country that have never seen either group. "There are many parts of the UK where a Jew or Muslim is considered a mythical character, both by each other and by the country at large," says Rabbi Gluck, who enjoys telling stories about the sensation that Jewish and Muslim friendship creates. "I remember meeting a senior Muslim cleric. When we kissed each other the taxi driver said he thought he was dreaming."

Jawid Ghussein, a Palestinian multi-millionaire who ran the PLO's finances for 12 years, has fled from Jerusalem to London. Palestinian security officials accuse Ghussein, 71, of embezzling $7 million.

Ghussein, who was the head of the PLO's National Fund, a body that supervises the Palestinian economic institutions and social welfare projects, had been under house arrest in Gaza ever since he was abducted from his hospital bed in Cairo by PA security agents last January. The National Fund is in charge of hundreds of millions of dollars that are transferred to the PLO by Arab states as part of their pledge to support the Palestinian struggle.

His daughter, Mona Bauwens, and his son, Tawfiq, both of whom live in London, have been waging a campaign to secure his release and hinting that he knows enough to blow the lid off PLO corruption.

Bauwens shot to fame a few years ago after David Mellor, the Tory minister, and his family accepted a holiday in Marbella at her expense. She arrived in Jerusalem last week and accompanied her father to London.

While Melchior likes to help embezzlers escape to London, a Belgian correspondent helps clear the mystery of why his country is so focused on disgracing Israel.

KING ALBERT I OF BELGIUM

"If you've been wondering why so much anti-Israel venom passes through the corridors and courts of Brussels, here's the answer. We have another royal family which believes it owns title to Israel:"

We think that Belgium only colonised Congo, but our country was also active in the Middle-East. Under Leopold I (the first Belgian King in the period of 1830 on.) there was already a mighty Arab lobby in our country. For instance

Acec, the financial group around baron Ampain, had founded in the most important cities in the former Ottoman empire, among them Cairo, Istanbul and Damascus- water and electric utilities and metrolines. There was a lot of Belgian capital in the cotton business, while on the Egyptian beer bottles of Stella there is still the star of Congo. During the WW I, Palestine was claimed as a colony by the Belgian Ministry of Foreign Affairs, referring to Godfried of Bouillon, the first king of Jerusalem, who's natural successor was Albert I. (Godfried of Bouillon had the status of "Fisherking", which means a direct descendent of the Temple priests in the time of Jesus or a natural descendent of Jesus himself. When it became clear that the Germans were about to loose WWI, the French and the English started the partition of the Ottoman Empire. They couldn't get to an agreement on Jerusalem and from French side there was pressure to assign the holy places to Belgium, mainly to keep the British away from there. Also the Vatican supported the Belgian claim, because the pope chose Belgium, rather than the British Protestants. He believed that the Belgian, Catholic monarchy would protect the holy places. But when the British, together with the allied troops marched into Jerusalem in 1917, the Belgian dream collapsed.

THE TERMINATOR

Did anyone notice that Arnold Schwarzenegger and his new political partner, Warren Buffet took a trip together to a Rothschild estate in England this week? (International Herald Tribune, Aug. 18). There is more to the Terminator's new political career than meets the eye. Follow closely the connections back to Edgar the Bronfman:

At the bottom of my latest post, you will find some information regarding Warren Buffet and Arnold

Schwarzenegger which I feel is important to get out to Jewish communities.

As you probably know already, Buffet is the Chairman of Berkshire Hathaway, the Insurance Monolith. He's openly backing Arnold in order to crush California and Washington's HVIRA Laws, which would require disclosure of unpaid policies belonging to Holocaust victims.

General Re will probably save billions through this move, with Jews once again becoming the victim.

(SACRAMENTO) – Attorney General Bill Lockyer took another major step in defending the constitutionality of California laws that allow World War II-era slave laborers and victims of the Holocaust to seek compensation from private companies that were enriched by their forced services and unpaid insurance claims.

"The California laws under attack seek basic justice for victims of the Holocaust who have insurance claims pending and for World War II-era slave laborers who were deprived of wages as slave labor victims," Lockyer said. "The California laws address state issues while avoiding foreign relations and foreign policy. The laws are narrowly tailored remedies for abuses by businesses that unconscionably enriched themselves by using slave labor or by failing to pay insurance   claims."

www.insurance.wa.gov/news/dynamic/newsreleasedetail.asp?rcdNum=354

OLYMPIA, Wash. — The U.S. Supreme Court struck down California's Holocaust Victims Insurance Relief Act (HVIRA) today effectively leaving in question Washington state's own similar law passed unanimously in 1999.

"The Court's decision severely impedes states' ability to protect their citizens," said Kreidler. "With an average of 10 Holocaust survivors dying every week, surely we owe them a chance at pursuing restitution – despite what the federal government   thinks.

***My correspondent puts most of the puzzle together but

66

misses one piece:*"'Ten Holocaust survivors dying every week. Holocaust victims have been a thorn in the side of insurance companies for decades. They want what's owed to them, and the Insurance companies refuse to pay. They've been in court forever. By putting their muscle behind Arnold, Buffet and company are trying to crush the unpaid insurance claimants and former slaves once and for all.*

Note that the AIA is one of the principals in the lawsuit. The sadists are hoping they can stall in court until all the people they victimized are dead.I guarantee that if Arnold wins, Holocaust victims lose, and California support for the rights of Holocaust victims who were screwed by insurance companies will be a dead issue. Gee, this really helps the Bush family too doesn't it?

After all, Prescott Bush used Jewish slaves at Consolidated Silesian Steel in Poland, who were slave labor contracted by CSS from the Nazi conglomerate IG Farben. Farben ran Auschwitz for Hitler, which is where the Bush family's slaves came from. So now you have some idea who Arnold is working for, and what some of these people want. Protection from liability for either their participation in or profiteering from the Holocaust.

Still think it's irrelevant that Arnold comes from a Nazi family?"

*** Certainly, it is worth more than mere noting that Bush's grandfather and Schwarzenegger's father were enthusiastic supporters of Naziism. But look even more closely at how the circle closes. Edgar Bronfman's letter writing partner is Lawrence Eagleburger, the government's international director for Holocaust insurance claims.   The Terminator's political partner is obsessed with having these claims wiped out in California.

Apparently opposing Schwarzenegger and Buffet's nefarious goal of depriving Holocaust victims of ompensation would be Bronfman. The Terminator, if he has his way, will have to go through Bronfman's co-signator on the Bush letter, Lawrence Eagleburger.

But Edgar couldn't care less about dead Jews if they don't support his politics or live where he thinks they should. And the money he supposedly helped release from Swiss banks to Holocaust victims has not reached their hands. Just the way the Terminator wants things to be.***

ALM 2 - CRIME!!!!

Look what happens when you participate in crime: Carmi Gillon, head of the secret services (Shabak), plots numerous deadly misdemeanors with Shimon Peres, including the murder of Yitzhak Rabin, and Judge Meir Shamgar covers them up in the gritty halls of justice.

Now, when guiding your children to be law-abiding, consider by example, the wrong path you are setting the little ones on. Carmi Gillon is ran for head of the city council of Mevasseret Tzion, a well-off suburb of Jerusalem, he won the race. Meanwhile, Shimon Peres is about to receive one whale of a Hollywood 80th birthday party, featuring as many celebrities as he can persuade. Will somebody please inform these beautiful people that the only cake Shimon should be getting from them is one with a file baked in it?

Like zeidy like nekhed. Like grandfather, like grandson. Look what the scion of the Peres crime empire got caught doing last week:

Peres' grandson Nadav Peres (21) was arrested today by police together with a known criminal trying to steal overnight a motorbike in Ramat Hasharon. He is in police custody now.

As for Shamgar, I don't even think you'll believe this one. Someone decided to fund him his very own Israel Democratic Institute. Yup, the man who brought us the Hebron, Rabin and Kishon coverups, and who as state attorney general, sent Amos Baranes to life imprisonment to cover for a Shabak murderer, is going to teach us dumb Israelis about democracy.

Here is the link to the Israel Democratic Institute
http://www.idi.org.il/english/article.php?id=20707f8f6729db83a376afc3088c92f

This   is   list   of   supporters
http://www.idi.org.il/english/departments.php?did=76

This link to a message from its president.

Now, let's just look at the A's of the institute directory. I'll add comments in brackets:

Justice Meir Shamgar, Former President Former of the Supreme Court Mr. Ami Ayalon (Shabak head deeply enmired in the Rabin murder coverup and much, much more).

MK Taleb Asana (Arab Knesset member which means he will destroy Israel from within). Former Justice Edna Arbel, Attorney General (Former attorney general who closed the criminal files of Avishai Raviv and is implicated deeply in the coverup of the Rabin murder).

Prof. Uzi Arad, Department of Political Science, Haifa University (Netanyahu's aide who brags on his bio sheet that he is a past member of the Council On Foreign Relations).

Prof. Asher Arian (Never heard of him).

Attorney Yoram Aridor (The Finance Minister who was hired to destroy Menachem Begin by raising inflation to 500%. Later rewarded for wrecking the economy with post as Israeli UN ambassador).

MK Prof. Moshe Arens (Who sits on the CFR's International Affairs Council).

And that's just the A's. Look how the B's start:

Dr. Yossi Beilin

The man speaks for himself, doesn't he? What a combo, Beilin and Shamgar, the Oslo liar and the Rabin liar, teaching us ignoramuses all about democracy. If it wasn't so bitterly pathetic, it might even be cute in the absurd sense. So what happens when criminals are our democracy teachers? Well for one thing, the people get ruled by practising felons and no one else.

Shall we look at some crimes? I'll preface my comments with the usual *** at the beginning and ending of the observations, like this:

Liberman denies the following story and says he never even met Martin Schlaff. But we'll publish this anyway because my readers know I've been exposing the Austrian connection to Omri Sharon, Dov Weisglass, Muhamed Dahlan, and Yasir Arafat for a year now. Odd that everyone else is just catching up. If the following report is right, then here is another darling of the Right caught in the Austrian trap.

Police suspect transportation minister of illegal business ties

http://www.haaretz.com/hasen/pages/ShArt.jhtml?itemNo=33 4029&contrassID=2&subContrassID=1&sbSubContrassID=0 &listSrc=Y

28.8.2003 | 07:36
Baruch Kra
The police have been conducting a lengthy inquiry into suspicions that Transportation Minister Avigdor Liberman has an illegal business relationship with Austrian businessman Martin Schlaff, who has substantial business interests in Israel.

An Austrian court recently approved an Israeli request to conduct its investigation in Austria, allowing investigators to take depositions from various people and to examine bank accounts suspected of being connected to the affair. The court decision followed a lower court ruling denying the Israeli request.

Haaretz has learned that several years ago, during a special session of an Austrian parliamentary committee investigating that country's intelligence services, information came up regarding business connections between Martin Schlaff, the Austrian businessman who is believed to own 50% of the Jericho casino, and Liberman, and how money was transferred to the political party Liberman established, Yisrael Beitenu.

As in the Sharon-Cyril Kern affair, the Liberman case also began in the wake of a State Comptroller's report on party financing. The report, which came out in 2000, was conducted mostly because of its examination of non-profit organizations that funneled funding to former premier Ehud Barak's election campaign in 1999. But the public interest in the millions that went to the Barak campaign distracted attention from some other scandals that appeared in the report, even though, as in the case of the Barak campaign contributions, the attorney general ordered police inquiries.

The comptroller said that Yisrael Beitenu received a million dollar credit line from a bank in Israel, using a bank guarantee from Vienna for the credit line. The Viennese bank, said the report, was given a personal guarantee of the million dollar guarantee by a foreign resident.

But Liberman also refused to name the businessman who backed the million dollar credit line and only said it was a "personal friend" from Austria. Liberman said that he met the "friend" after leaving the Prime Minister's Office (where he had been the bureau chief for former premier Benjamin Netanyahu) and went into business in eastern Europe. He emphasized that at the time he had no business ties with the Austrian, "who did not want his name published."

A few months later, close to the Camp David summit of 2000, Liberman, then an opposition MK from the far right, met in London with Mohammed Rashid, Yasser Arafat's financier, who was known for his business relations with Schlaff as a partner in the Jericho casino.

A few months later, Rashid and Schlaff met in Vienna with Dov Weisglass, who represents Schlaff's interests in the Middle East, Omri Sharon and Eitan Bentsur, a former director general of the foreign ministry. Then-prime minister Barak charged that Liberman urged the Palestinians not to strike a deal with the Labor-Meretz government but to wait for a right wing government with which they could get a better deal. Liberman refused then to comment on the connection between the meeting in London and the one in Vienna.

Look who is visiting the patsy's brother! Now what could be so important that the nation's attorney general would want a few words with the Rabin "murderer's" brother Hagai Amir?

AG Visits Chaggai Amir

07:42 Aug. 12, '03 / 14 Av 5763

(IsraelNN.com) *During a visit yesterday in the Ashmoret Prison, Attorney General Elyakim Rubinstein met with Chaggai Amir, the brother of convicted Rabin assassin Yigal Amir.*

The attorney general regularly makes unannounced visits to prisons to get a first-hand look at prisoner conditions. During the visit, Amir complained about his conditions.

Following is a letter from a reader who suspects another person who knew too much was conveniently removed permanently from her position.

Barry, what do you say about the murder of Etty G'alyah last winter? She was a senior economist with Bank of Israel, in charge of inspection of ten banks. She was brilliant and

72

incisive and very capable of knowing where all sorts of bones were buried. She was murdered in the terrorist attack at Tzomet Rimonim on the way to Kochav Hashachar. The roadblock was taken down for a few months and she was the only casualty.

***I have been long claiming that part of the campaign to destroy Israel's moral backbone includes murdering its rabbis, especially those foolish enough to live in Judea and Samaria and actually claim they do so because God and history gave them the unarguable right to do so. The last Jerusalem bus bombing claimed the lives of three more rabbis, as undoubtedly, it was supposed to. Add to the list which includes Rabbis Lieberman, Shapiro, Dickstein, Urama, Kahane etc.

Rabbi Shmuel Volner
Rabbi Shalom Mordechai Reinitz
Rabbi Eliezer Weissfish

So look who've become pals! Ami Ayalon and a relative newcomer to the game, Sari Nusseibeh. For those who recall my reports on the murder of former Utah Senator Wayne Owens, Nusseibeh was his ally, being set up to take over the leadership of the PA. So it's no surprise, with so much murder to cover up, they'd be drawn together in good works.***

Since the Owens murder and Sari Nusseibeh's excommunication from the PA, Sari has resurfaced to become buddies with Ami Ayalon who knows most about the Rabin murder after Carmi Gillon. They're gathering a petition.

http://web.israelinsider.com/bin/en.jsp?enPage=ArticlePage&enDisplay=view&enDispWhat=object&enDispWho=Article%5EI2447&enZone=Diplomacy&enVersion=0&

In the very first chapter of my last book, Save Israel, I explain that, as part of the psychological battle to remove Jews from Judea and Samaria, people who have lost loved ones to terrorism are struck again to compound the impact. Now they're arresting a father who lost a baby to a sniper,along with someone who lost his brother in a similar way, claiming they were plotting revenge together. Wanna bet this Jewish Department provocation won't make it to court? It doesn't have to, as a correspondent in BOLD letters and deep anguish explains.

Last update - 23:53 21/08/2003
W. Bank settler detained as suspected underground member
By Nadav Shragai, Haaretz Correspondent
The Shin Bet security service arrested late Wednesday night a West Bank settler suspected of involvement in planning attacks on Palestinians in the territories.
The suspect, David Libman, is the brother of Shlomo Libman, who was killed by terrorists on the settlement of Yitzhar a few years ago. He is not being allowed to meet with his lawyer.

***Now this Pollard affair just keeps getting weirder. Let's start with the bizarre report in Maariv last week, in which Esther Pollard claimed to be so poor that she cannot afford Israeli health insurance, so has to fly to Canada for cancer treatments. I wish her a full recovery but those with low incomes pay about $20 a month for health coverage in Israel and a flight to Canada is $900.

My research on the subject concluded that the Israeli government under, who else, Shifty Shimon, in 1984 abused Pollard's intelligence and turned it into a crime empire headed by the Godfather of Israeli crime, the selfsame, Shifty Shimon. I added that those involved in the coverup of Pollard, including Sharon and Rabin were rewarded with revolving shifts as prime minister. So why don't we add another future prime minister to the list?***

Demand That Barak Reveal Involvement in Pollard Affair

October 20, 1999 - Ma'ariv - Ben Caspit
[Translated from Hebrew]

Documents newly-obtained in the USA show that the senior Israeli official who met with American Intelligence officials right after the arrest of Jonathan Pollard in 1985 was none other than the Prime Minister himself, then head of AMAN, IDF General Ehud Barak.

According to the documents which reached Ma'ariv, Ehud Barak was the senior official in the team that traveled to Washington at the end of November 1985 that met with, amongst others, the director of American Military Intelligence.

One of the documents recently obtained by a Pollard source in Washington, reads: "The DR will meet with General Barak (Israel Defense Forces) next week and needs to be briefed re: Pollard."

And now on to the CFR. Two weeks ago, I reported CFR executive Edgar Bronfman's ties to the Vatican, and hinted he is doing the dirty work for the Papal cabal. A reader informs me that I had just scratched the Bronfman Catholic connection.

Dear Barry,

Please let me share with you some information about EDGAR BRONFMAN.

What I am stating below are facts and the deductions from these facts.

75

EG got himself elected to a very prestigious position amongst American Jewry, making him the leader of American Jewry. It would be logical that such a person would look out for the interests of Jewry, and by extention, of Israel, due to the obvious linkage of Israel and Jewry.

EG is Jewish, but is the interests of Jewry (and Israel) uppermost with him ?EG's son is married to a South American practicing Catholic. EG's granchildren are not Jewish. All of EG's friends are either assimilated Jews or Gentiles.

EG knows that he is the last Jew in his family. Does this bother him ? No !!! Therefor, a man with his surroundings CANNOT have the welfare of Jewry in his mind. He is an American, and his descendants will all be (and are) Americans (non-Jewish), so where is his connection to Israel ?

Is it any wonder ??

Thank you, and you have my permission to quote me, all or part.

Still another reader discovers yet another disturbing CFR machination.

You may already be familiar with the Atlantic Council, -yet another proxy for the CFR, -still, you might be surprised by the following document. A short read, then onto the final page for an alarming listing of those involved.

http://www.acus.org/publications/policypapers/AtlanticCooper ation/ArmsTransfers.pdf

And now for those of you who still think the CFR is a friendly gathering of concerned citizens, with no ill intent towards Jews... The CFR was founded with Rockefeller, Carnegie and Harriman money and influence. And they set in motion the biggest, ugliest crime in history. Read Edwin Black, surely one of the premier historians at work today, on what the organization Jews like Bronfman, Siegman, Pipes, Lauder and Zuckerman are so proud to be members of, were up to before they joined.*

Hitler made eugenics famous, but he took it from United States

By Edwin Black

WASHINGTON, Aug. 28 (JTA) — Hitler victimized an entire continent and exterminated millions in his quest for a so-called "Master Race." The world thought Hitler was mad and barely understood his rationales. But the concept of a white, blond-haired, blue-eyed master Nordic race was not Adolf Hitler's. The idea was created in the United States at least two decades before Hitler came to power.It was the product of the American eugenics movement.

Eugenics was the racist American pseudoscience designed to wipe out all human beings except those who conformed to a Nordic stereotype. The philosophy was enshrined into national policy by forced sterilization, segregation laws and marriage restrictions that were enacted in 27 states.

Ultimately, eugenics coercively sterilized some 60,000 Americans, barred the marriage of thousands, forcibly segregated thousands more in colonies and persecuted untold numbers in ways we are just learning.

Only after eugenics and race biology became entrenched as an American ideal was the campaign transplanted to Germany, where it came to Hitler's attention.

Hitler studied American eugenic laws and rationales and sought to legitimize his innate race hatred and anti-Semitism by medicalizing it and wrapping it in a pseudoscientific facade. Indeed, Hitler was able to attract many reasonable Germans by claiming that science was on his side.

While Hitler's race hatred sprung from his own mind, the intellectual outlines of the eugenics Hitler adopted in 1924 were strictly American.

Eugenics would have been little more than bizarre parlor talk had it not been for massive financing by corporate philanthropies, specifically the Carnegie Institution, the Rockefeller Foundation and the Harriman railroad fortune.

They were in league with America's most respected scientists from prestigious universities such as Harvard, Yale and Princeton. These academicians faked and twisted data to serve eugenics' racist aims.

The Carnegie Institution effectively invented the American movement when it established a laboratory complex at Cold Spring Harbor, on Long Island. This complex stockpiled millions of index cards on ordinary Americans as the movement carefully plotted the removal of families, bloodlines and whole peoples.

From Cold Spring Harbor, eugenics advocates agitated in the legislatures of America as well as in the nation's social service agencies and associations.

The Harriman railroad fortune paid local charities, such as the New York Bureau of Industries and Immigration, to seek out Jewish, Italian and other immigrants in New York and other crowded cities and subject them to deportation, confinement or forced sterilization.

The Rockefeller Foundation helped found and fund the German eugenics program, and it even funded the program that ultimately sent Josef Mengele into Auschwitz.

The Rockefeller Foundation, the Carnegie Institution, Cold Spring Harbor Laboratory and the Max Planck Institute — the successor to the Kaiser Wilhelm Institute — all gave unlimited access and unstinting assistance in the course of this investigation. These organizations all have worked hard to help the world discover their pasts and have set an example of philanthropic openness.

The Jews of Israel and the world still have no idea that their leaders have been totally corrupted by the CFR and the Vatican. They will blindly walk into a new eugenics program funded by CFR honorary chairman David Rockefeller, or throw a swinging Hollywood bash for the dashing monster Peres. The utter ignorance of these Jews, and their fawning deference to these crooks, that, that is the most despicable crime of them all.

ALM 3 - WATCH THE GINOSAR SCANDAL GO AWAY

On December 4, '02, Maariv broke the biggest scandal in years in the biggest way in years. On Thursday, there was a massive front page promo for the Ginosar revelations about to appear in the weekend edition. On Friday, the big newspaper day in Israel, it was front page all over again in Maariv, followed by four *more pages of* expose and commentary. Wouldst that Rabin's real murder had received only 1% of the coverage.

And with all this razzmatazz in the country's second largest circulation newspaper, my readers were very excited. This was the scandal that would lead to the Rabin assassination and Oslo. Here's a pretty typical example of the hopes this scandal was engendering:

Barry,
I think this might be it. If this scandal really breaks and the public demands justice... then you can ride the wave of all the economic corruption in the Oslo deal including Peres, Gillon and Rubin's foreign accounts! Follow the money. It should all lead to the assassination of Rabin.

If Ginosar was financially vested in the Oslo windfall, along with his business partner Yasir...What would happen if Rabin threatened to pull the plug? Yasir would lose a lot of money in his personal bank accounts... which were controlled and skimmed by Ginosar. Couldn't Yasir have told his buddy Yosi and his mentor Shimon to get rid of Yitzhak or else he would blow their cover? Didn't Yasir and doesn't he still have information so damaging to Ginosar and Peres to motivate them to commit the crime? Why look to the Europeans and CFR?

Shimon and Yosi could easily solve their woes with their history of shenanigans and their contacts within the Shabak.

What about opening up a class action civil suit to sue Ginosar on behalf of the taxpayers of Israel. If it's not done in civil court, but in criminal court, Peres will make sure Ginosar is the lone patsy. Why is Maariv breaking this story?

Dear reader, it's just not going to happen that way. The government is going to bury the story and has already started. Did you notice that at both the Likud and Labor primary conventions, not one candidate mentioned Ginossar? Have you seen how TV coverage of the scandal is becoming nearly non-existant? Here is the test of Israel's political and media honesty: if Yossi Ginosar becomes Avishai Raviv, we have double proof of the depths of corruption within the Knesset, Courts and Media.

For those unacquainted, here's the Ginosar Scandal. Yossi Ginosar was deputy head of the General Security Services (Shabak) until 1986 when it was discovered that he lied to a government commission of inquiry into the early killings of two terrorists in what is known as the Bus 300 Scandal. It should really be called The President Herzog Is A Crook Scandal because the then-Israeli president, Chaim Herzog pardoned Ginosar from his perjury crimes, (there was another one involving the false imprisonment of an IDF officer, Izat Nafsu for espionage), thus tainting the Herzog name forever.

But did Ginosar's double-perjury to the IDF and government disqualify him from public service? Not at all. After being sacked by the Shabak, then-Trade Minister Ariel

Sharon, appointed Ginosar to head the Israel Export Institute. When his tenure there ended in 1992, then-Housing Minister Binyamin Ben Eliezer appointed him head of the public housing corporation, Amidar.

1993 was a turning point. Yitzhak Rabin was forced by President Bush at a meeting in Kenebunkport Maine, on September 17, 1992 to begin what became known as the Oslo process. By the next year, the "peace" process was rolling in high gear and Rabin appointed Ginosar his special envoy to the PLO.

Now why did Rabin choose such a slimeball for this sensitive post? Maariv provides an answer; "Ginosar threatened Rabin that if he didn't have his way, he'd spill the beans about everything. As a result, Rabin's daughter Dahlia would have nothing to do with him."

It's a fair bet that Ginosar received Herzog's pardon and Sharon and Ben Eliezer's cushy jobs because he threatened them the same way. If you were once deputy head of the internal security services, it's not surprising what information you'd pick up along the way. Whatever Ginosar knew, it was strong enough to risk extortion charges against one president, one serving and one future prime minister, and one future head of the opposition. And more kingpins were to follow, but for slighty different motivations. The carrot would replace the stick.

That is because Ginosar exploited his position as the emissary to the PLO to create a crime empire with Yasir Arafat. Perhaps the first offer was to arrange to have a casino built in Jericho, with everyone scraping away lots of the profits. But it didn't take long for Ginosar to expand his and Arafat's holdings. He offered to open up a secret Swiss bank account for Arafat and lots of straw companies to launder the funds through. Ginosar hired General Ehud Barak's paymaster Ozrad Lev to arrange the banking formalities and Arafat summoned his paymaster, Muhamed Rashid to work hand in hand with Lev. Eventually over $300 million of monies stolen from Arafat's people entered the account. Some of the money was invested in Israeli companies contracted to the PA in return for kickbacks, some went to offshore corporations which existed only to launder Arafat's stolen cash. But all the money came from either international aid or Israeli tax rebates to the PA.

Last August, Rashid emptied the account and no one has any idea where the $65 million he removed is today. This particular scam ended for Ginosar and he was at least $10 million richer for it, according to Rashid. However, Ginosar's downfall lay in wait. Ozrad Lev now had the time to consider what he had done. While much of the money went to buying new villas for Arafat and his cronies and other such expenses, at least some of the money might have been used to finance terrorism.

Ozrad used the word "might," we will say "did." Ginosar and Lev were financing the mass murder of their countrymen and endangering the viability of the state.

And a week after the facts came out, the attorney-general and police are debating whether there is any basis for opening a criminal investigation against Ginosar and Lev and the media is slowly killing the issue.

And here are two reasons why: Barak and Peres. Of Barak, he was so fond of Ginossar that he wanted him to be a representative at the Camp David "Peace" Talks under the "honest" tutelage of William Clinton.

But Attorney-General Elyakim Rubinstein, the same one we're stuck with today, forbade Barak appointing him a member of his delegation because Ginosar refused to sign a declaration detailing his business ties with the PLO. So, now get this, it's rich, Barak persuaded Clinton to invite Ginosar to be a member of HIS delegation. And Clinton agreed. Ginosar now sat in the inner corridors of Camp David as a member of the American team. No kidding, this really happened.

And what was Barak's pretext for excusing Ginosar? He claimed that Mossad chief Danny Yatom told him Rubinstein was wrong. According to a 1996 article in the London

Observor, PM Netanyahu appointed Yatom head of the Mossad in return for his silence about the true Rabin murder.

Let's ignore Barak's flimsy excuse and start asking real questions. So here we have, negotiating away Israel's security, both Arafat and his business partner Ginosar. Why would Barak really agree to this arrangement when Rubinstein informed him precisely what the problem was? Maariv provides us with two hints. Just after Barak was elected, Lev and Ginosar drove to Ramallah to meet the PLO leaders, probably all getting a cut of the action by now. Ginosar told Lev, "You were Barak's paymaster. They want to know everything about him from you and they'll pay you well for the information." Lev claims he rejected Ginosar's proposal with disgust.

But what do we make of this insight from Maariv? A few months later Ginosar phoned Lev and said, "I just had a meeting with Barak. He's completely nuts, you know."

Though nuts, Barak likes to earn money through fraud and extortion. The second biggest recent scandal, after the Rabin murder, that the government has managed to squelch, is Barak's illegal campaign funds. His cronies collected many millions of dollars from unwary foreign donors, assuring them that the money was not going to be used to defeat Netanyahu but to defeat poverty and ignorance. Naturally it all ended up in Barak's back pocket.

And why is Barak so reluctant to answer congressional questions about how he persuaded Clinton to pardon Marc Rich? The answer is the same one as why Barak appointed Ginosar to Camp David: he was getting a cut of Ginosar and Arafat's action. And Clinton got a payoff.

Why else?

And now we go back to 1995. Rabin is dead and Peres takes over as prime minister. It doesn't take very long before he appoints Ginosar his special envoy to the "Palestinian" rulers. As my astute reader pointed out at the beginning of this explanation, Rabin wanted out of Oslo and that would have been very costly for Ginosar. Was he in on the Peres assassination team? If he isn't investigated, we'll never know.

Peres got a cut of Ginosar's deals and we know that because Peres, through the Peres Center For Peace, owns a 3.1% share of Arafat's telephone company, Paltel. The Bin Laden family of Saudi Arabia owns the lion's share. This was another revelation made initially by Maariv, some two years ago.

Now we look at the list of directors of the Peres Peace Center. What do you know, Yossi Ginosar is on Peres' board.

No, my hopeful readers, this scandal will be buried because it will take down Peres and Barak for starters and then spread throughout the Israeli and "Palestinian" leadership, finally exposing the Oslo "Peace" Process as a model of statesmanship by graft and embezzlement.

ALM 4 - BURYING GINOSAR ALIVE

So here's how you bury the Yossi Ginosar scandal. You create an even better one. Like clockwork, before every national election, the Attorney General or State comptroller recommends indicting Likud politicians for sundry crimes. In 1992, this strategy helped put Rabin in power.

In 2003, the strategy resumed with new urgency. It served the double purpose of trying to put Labor back in power and covering up the scandal that can destroy its very existence   forever;   the Ginosar/Arafat/Muhamed/Lev/Barak/Peres/Beilin embezzlement of the Oslo "peace" process.

This week, 2/4/03, Attorney - General Elyakim Rubinstein discovered vote buying at the Likud primaries and within a nanosecond ordered the police to open an investigation. The media hopped on board in half a nanosecond and voila, the public is talking about such steamy issues as the selling of sex for Likud votes. Meanwhile, the Attorney General has not ordered an investigation of Ginosar and the media are forgetting this infinitely more felonious crime.

Not that the public is completely blind to the farce. Reports I received from inside the Feiglin camp confirm the charges against the Likud. But everyone knows that Labor invented vote buying and this year was no different than any other. So, Rubinstein announced that he has directed the police to investigate Labor too. That should hog the headlines until the election and shunt Ginosar aside until his crimes no longer interest the public.

And while the Likud's corruption is guaranteed to grab most of the reporting space, look what Rubinstein forgot to investigate:

- Gad Zeevi is finally being indicted for massive fraud. To follow this side scandal, do a search at www.globes.co.il As I recently reported, Zeevi and Haifa mayor Amram Mitzna were just a bit too buddy buddy over the past years. Mitzna handed Zeevi prime municipal real estate for a song to build huge shopping and residential complexes. So why aren't Mitzna's ties to international bunko artist Zeevi being investigated by Rubinstein?

- And look who is number ten on the Labor list. Why it's none other than Isaac Herzog, son of the president who pardoned Ginosar for his blatant crimes of perjury in 1987. Isaac was head of Ehud Barak's campaign team which defrauded innocent, well-meaning foreigners with scam charity projects whose donations went straight into Barak's wallet. Rubinstein ordered this scandal investigated two years ago and subsequently Herzog took the Fifth with the cops, revealing not a word about his illegal activities. Now why did Labor put him into their top ten charts?

Rubinstein's strategy to hush Ginosar may not work because this scandal is just so filthy. Knowing how the government covered up the real Rabin murder, we shouldn't be too hopeful. Yet there are signs.

For one thing, new information was published by Maariv last Friday. An owner of the original Jericho casino explained how Ginosar got wind of the project and had a little talk with the PLO's intelligence chief Jibril Rajoub. He turned up at the building site with his goons and gave the workers twenty minutes to clear out. He then took over the casino with his partner Ginosar.

And the plot thickens. Ginosar planted himself in the Defence Ministry and persuaded its Minister, Binyamin Ben Eliezer, not to attack the casino. So while the intifada burned, the casino's profits kept rolling in, then to be skimmed by Ginosar and Rajoub. And while reported income was a mere $50 million monthly, the actual take was closer to an astounding $800 million. This was a money laundering apparatus par excellence. Only when the terrorists used the casino building to attack the IDF did the army put an end to its operation.

Now why, oh why, did Ben Eliezer agree to Ginosar's protection request? Could it be money, money, money? In his pocket, pocket, pocket?

ALM 5 - GINOSAR CLAIMS FIRST AMERICAN VICTIM: THE MURDER OF WAYNE OWENS

Here is why Rep. Wayne Owens was murdered in Tel Aviv. He is the latest victim of Shimon Peres' decades old murderama. Let us begin with some background from the Washington Post before we sort out the murder:

Friday, December 20, 2002; Page B07

"Wayne Owens, 65, a Utah Democrat who had represented Salt Lake City in the House of Representatives for eight years and who was a founder of Washington's Center for Middle East Peace and Economic Cooperation, was found dead Dec. 18 on a beach in Tel Aviv.

A State Department spokesman said that the cause of death was unknown but that there were no signs of foul play. His death came at the end of a congressional delegation visit with leaders of Syria, Egypt, Qatar, Oman, Saudi Arabia and Israel and representatives of the Palestinian Authority.

On the House's Foreign Affairs and Permanent Select Intelligence committees, Rep. Owens was an advocate of improved Middle East relations. Since leaving Congress in 1993, he had served as president of the Middle East Peace Center.

He co-founded the center with Slim Fast Foods Chairman S. Daniel Abraham in 1989 and worked with Middle East leaders to promote peace through economic development. He was present at the September 1993 White House peace summit at which then-Israeli President Yitzhak Rabin and Palestinian leader Yasser Arafat shook hands. His interest in international relations sprung chiefly from his work on the Foreign Affairs Committee. In 1989, he held a controversial meeting in Tunisia with Arafat, during which he raised congressional concern about Palestinian-sponsored terrorism. Still, the visit raised the ire of some Israeli activists."

Now let's introduce the characters:

Yossi Ginosar - Deputy head of the General Security Services until 1987 when he was forced to retire after two serious perjury scandals. Nonetheless, he was appointed special emissary to the PLO by Prime Ministers Rabin, Peres, and Barak. In early December 2002, the newspaper

Maariv exposed Ginosar's embezzlement scam with Arafat and Arafat's paymaster Muhamed Rashid. The scandal was destined to lead to the kickbacks and payoffs that reached the pockets of Peres, Barak and Pres. Bill Clinton, but it has been effectively covered up by the Israeli media. Member of the board of the Shimon Peres Center For Peace.

Hani Masri - Partner of Owens and Daniel Abraham. With the help of Clinton and Owens, he swindled the American people of $60 million, supposedly aimed at increasing economic activities in the PA, but which has subsequently disappeared.

From OPIC.GOV
West Bank / Gaza & Jordan Fund
Capital Investment Management Corporation Canceled
West Bank/Gaza and Jordan at least 60% in West
Bank/Gaza 60 Equity investments in basic service and
manufacturing companies.
Contact Information for West Bank / Gaza & Jordan Fund
Organization Title Name Address Telephone Fax
International Capital Advisors Scott Stupay 6862 Elm
Street, Suite 720 McLean, VA 22101 703-847-0870
703-847-3068"

Here is a transcript of the founding of the fund:

http://www.usembassy-israel.org.il/publish/peace/archives/1997/me1117e.html
Needless to say, Masri sits on the board of the Peres Center For Peace.

Daniel Abraham - Leading donor to the Peres Peace Center. Most prolific moneyman behind the Oslo "peace" process. Member of the board of the Peres Center For Peace.

Stephen P. Cohen - American professor, leading American Jewish advocate of Oslo process. A steady contributor to the editorial pages of such august journals as the New York Times. Was exposed by Maariv two weeks before Owens' murder as a partner in the Ginosar/Arafat embezzlement scandals. Ginosar's partner Ozrad Lev, who spilled the beans to Maariv, claimed Cohen had large stakes in phoney companies founded to launder the nearly $350 million Arafat stole from his people, which Ginosar and Lev deposited for him in a Swiss bank. He is now under investigation by Israel Police for his part in the Ginosar scandal. Go to Owens own website and look at his "Business Development Organization" file. What do you know, Owens' business organization was set up by Stephen P. Cohen and Daniel Abraham! Member of the board of the Peres Center For Peace.

Here is what Peres has to say about Cohen and Abraham on Owns' site:

"In all likelihood, much of what Dan Abraham and Wayne Owens have done, working through the Center, to help Israel normalize relations with her neighbors will never be fully appreciated. I began counseling with them regularly ten years ago and we have become close friends as a result. Then, as now, they constantly asked questions, tested ideas, and carefully passed along messages between the region's leaders. Now the Center must expand in order to undertake new projects that could lead to significant diplomatic and economic benefits to the Middle East. The potential here is enormous."
                                                    Shimon Peres

Now for more damning information from the website. The comments in brackets are not mine, but those of my brilliant correspondent D. M:

"The Center for Middle East Peace and Economic Cooperation was established in 1989 by Slim Fast Foods Chairman S. Daniel Abraham and Utah Congressman

Wayne Owens. A World War II combat veteran, Mr. Abraham had experienced the horrors of war and committed himself to the prevention of future conflicts. When he met Congressman Owens, who served on the House Foreign Affairs and Select Intelligence Committees, the two men recognized that they shared a determination to achieve a peaceful resolution to the Arab-Israeli conflict.

"In 1990, they recruited Dr. Stephen Cohen to join the Center and bring his experience in unofficial diplomacy and conflict resolution to the organization. Ms. Sara Ehrman, long time peace activist and former Senior Political Advisor at the Democratic National Committee, became Senior Advisor at the Center in early 1997.

"Since its founding, the Center's officers have traveled extensively and regularly throughout the Middle East. We have also sponsored numerous fact finding missions to the region for Members of Congress, government officials, and private citizens to meet with Middle East leaders. Visiting Israel and more than 20 Arab countries, the Center has enabled American decision makers to witness first hand the challenges facing leaders who seek peace in the region.

"During these visits, the Center was able to open unprecedented [read, "illegal"] channels of communication as it formed close relationships [read "payoffs"] with the leadership of all parties involved in the Arab-Israeli conflict. Through the discussions with Middle Eastern leaders, it became apparent that there is a role for the private sector to play in promoting and protecting the Middle East peace process. [Raking in millions of dollars in business deals]

"Each year, the Center sponsors a Consultation on the New Middle East. The Consultations bring groups of business leaders and policy makers together for private, off the record meetings [so no one will know about the illegal business dealings and payoffs] which seek to create an environment that encourages the prospects for peace in the Middle East. The Center also conducts an annual Retrospective on the Peace Process—a

public forum where leading policy makers from the Middle East and United States exchange fresh ideas on the peace process.

"Over the past eight years, the Center for Middle East Peace and Economic Cooperation has sponsored numerous activities aimed at bringing policy makers and influential leaders in the private sector together to foster the atmosphere necessary for the promotion and protection of Middle East peace [by bribing them and then holding them hostage to blackmail in the future].

"As a result of these efforts, the Center has become an address for leaders seeking a dialogue among government officials and the private sector."

Now here is how Owens most likely died:

Barely a fortnight before, Rep. Owens learned the Ginosar scandal broke in Israel. He was either terrified or furious. It's a tossup. If he was terrified, it was because it wouldn't be long before his direct ties to Stephen Cohen would implicate him deeply in the scandals. If he was furious, it was because he finally learned how badly he had been scammed by Peres, Abraham, Masri and Cohen.

Either way, he threatened to blow the whistle on the Peres Peace Center. He was poisoned at dinner and dead on a beach by 9 PM. Rep. Owens is now another notch on Peres' gunbelt.

ALM 6 - WE'VE GOT A SUSPECT IN THE WAYNE OWENS MURDER - AVI GIL

In the previous expose of the murder of Wayne Owens, we surmised that Owens was poisoned at dinner and died a couple of hours later on a Tel Aviv Beach. All we needed was to find out who Owens' dinner guest was and we have; the man Haaretz's Akiva Elder constantly refers to as "an

Oslo architect," Avi Gil. As we shall soon see he had the means and the motive.

But first, a summary: On Dec 11, the wide circulation newspaper Maariv broke "the Ginosar scandal." Yossi Ginossar was, until 1987, deputy head of the General Security Services (Shabak). He was forced to resign because of two perjury scandals but somehow became the personal emissary to the PLO for Prime Ministers Rabin, Peres and Barak.

Using his position, Ginosar opened a secret Swiss account to hide over $300 million that Yasir Arafat had stolen from his people. Ginosar appointed Ozrad Lev to take care of the banking and Arafat appointed Muhamed Rashi to oversee the account with Lev. It was Lev who broke the story to Maariv.

Meanwhile Ginosar opened a variety of phoney and barely legitimate straw companies to launder Arafat's embezzlements. He appointed an American academic, Prof. Stephen Cohen to head some of these companies, adding a bit more legitimacy to the enterprises, and Cohen was paid well for his services.

The scandal was destined to implicate Peres, Barak and Pres. Clinton in massive payoffs and kickbacks but Peres was the most vulnerable since Ginosar and Cohen are both members of the board of the Peres Center For Peace which had invested deeply in Arafat and Ginosar's corporations. And if Peres went down, so would Daniel Abraham, a member of his board, and like Stephen Cohen, a business partner of Wayne Owens' own Middle East Peace Center.

Finally, to the uninitiated, most Israelis do no believe their government's version of the Rabin assassination. Here are the results of a poll undertaken this week by Autuz Sheva. Admittedly, the majority of respondents were right wing but still:

Do you feel that there are serious unanswered questions regarding the
Rabin assassination?

Yes 78.69 % (2068)
No 21.31 % (560)
Total Votes: 2628

Then, if so many Israelis disbelieve the government's version of Rabin's murder, what version do they accept? As a result of a great deal of evidence gathering, the other version of Rabin's demise has Shimon Peres and then-Shabak chief Carmi Gillon plotting it. I certainly subscribe to this version as accurate and proven.

Now, on to Avi Gil.

http://www.haaretzdaily.com/hasen/pages/ShArt.jhtml?itemN o=244362&contrassID=2&subContrassID=5&sbSubContrass ID=0&listSrc=Y

Death of a peace negotiator
by Akiva Eldar

Wayne Owens died suddenly last week on the beach in Tel Aviv, one of the places most beloved by the former U.S. congressman from Utah. Eleven years ago, in early summer, Owens arrived in Jerusalem straight from Damascus on board a plane owned by his friend, businessman and philanthropist Danny Abrams.
Few know that Owens brought the tidings of the peace process that began at Madrid, continued in Oslo, and reached where it has reached. Owens and his partner

Steve Cohen invited me, at the time, to the King David Hotel in Jerusalem to tell me that then-Syrian president Hafez Assad had decided to accept U.S. President George Bush's invitation to an international peace conference. Syria's participation was one of the preconditions set at the time by then-premier Yitzhak Shamir for Israel's participation in what would become the Madrid Conference.

Owens never gave up pressing Arab leaders. The doors to the offices of Jordan's King Hussein, Egyptian President Hosni Mubarak, and the Saudi Arabian crown prince were open to him, and Israeli leaders regarded him as an emissary of goodwill. Last week, he came to Israel with two Democratic Party congressmen. They told Sharon and Peres about their meetings with Syrian President Bashar Assad and Gulf state leaders.

Avi Gil, until recently the director general of the Foreign Ministry, met Owens at the Hilton Hotel in Tel Aviv a few hours before Owens' body was found on the beach. Gil said Owens spoke about ways the peace process could be pulled out of the quagmire. He said Owens believed the Israelis and Palestinians would have to find their own way to a solution to the conflict. Gil said he hopes that more people of goodwill, like Owens, will be found, ready to devote their lives to shorten that route to peace and help end the suffering.

So who is Avi Gil, who shared Owens' Last Supper? Here is his bio as compiled by the government.

http://www.israel-mfa.gov.il/mfa/go.asp?MFAH0k370

Ambassador Avi Gil served as the Director-General of Israel's Ministry of Foreign Afairs April 2001 until November 2002. Prior to this appointment, Mr. Gil served as the Director-General of Israel's Ministry of Regional Cooperation.

A longtime confidant of Israel's Minister of Foreign Affairs, Nobel Prize Laureate Mr. Shimon Peres, Ambassador Gil held a number of key governmental positions during the last 13 years. From 1996 to 1999, Mr. Gil held the position of Deputy Director-General of the Peres Center for Peace. Mr. Gil also served as the Prime Minister's Chief of Staff, Media Advisor to the Minister of Foreign Affairs and the Minister of Finance, and Executive Policy Advisor to the Minister of Foreign Affairs.

In his years with Mr. Peres, Ambassador Gil was closely involved in Israel's policy-making and peace efforts, including the negotiations that led to the Oslo Accords and the peace treaty with Jordan.

Note that Gil was Carmi Gillon's deputy at the Peres Peace Center when Gillon was director of the center from 1996-99. That he was working for two of the plotters of the Rabin murder, Peres and Gillon, is probably significant but so far we haven't found direct links to the Ginosar scandal. We will, but first let's establish ties to another financial crime. Last March, Yoav Yitzhak of Maariv and David Bedein of Makor Rishon revealed that Peres had given his Norwegian pal Terje Roed-Larsen $100,000 to persuade his buddies on the Nobel Prize committee to award him a peace prize along with Rabin and Arafat.

www.jewishmediaresources.com/article/426/

Thus after the cabinet voted in December not to permit Arafat to attend Christmas ceremonies in Bethlehem, Foreign Ministry Director-General Avi Gil ordered Israeli diplomatic missions not to defend the decision. A month later, Gil declared that the Foreign Ministry finds it "increasingly difficult to defend government policy," including its insistence of seven days of quiet prior to negotiations and its classification of the Palestinian Authority as a terrorist organization. The Foreign Ministry didn't, and Israel was effectively left without any defense in the international arena.

Some will attribute the Foreign Minister's independent foreign policy to financial conflicts of interest. Lending credence to such claims was his impassioned defense of Terje Roed-Larsen, after the latter proclaimed that Israel had lost "all moral standing" as a result of its actions in Jenin. Larsen and his wife, the Norwegian ambassador to Israel, were recipients of a $100,000 undeclared prize from the Peres Center. Not coincidentally, one suspects, the Peres Center, which exists primarily to pay large salaries to old Oslo hands, like Ron Pundak and Uri Savir, was itself the beneficiary of a $1,000,000 gift from Norway. Yes, the same Norway that refused this week to allow the import of Israeli produce.

***

Needless to say, Gil's treasonous behaviour did not go unnoticed:

http://www.freeman.org/m_online/dec02/weinberg.htm

5. Promptly fire anybody in the Shimon Peres-Avi Gil Foreign Ministry that can't or won't bring himself to vigorously defend Israel's tough anti-terror and proud foreign policy line. Especially bureaucrats who leak nasty gossip about Netanyahu. The people paid to be our diplomats, especially abroad, and the academics sent abroad on speaking tours by the ministry, should hew to the government hasbara line, or pack it in. From experience, I know that there is significant house-cleaning to be done.

http://www.cdn-friends-icej.ca/isreport/dec01/bethlehem.html

Only six months ago the world was still prepared to accept his declarations and promises, despite the terrorist campaign

he initiated 15 months ago. The American administration and even some of the EU leaders now know that Arafat is a pathological liar. The process of delegitimizing Arafat, who succeeded in persuading the world that he was a real partner for peace for Israel, is now bearing fruit. It seems that only in Israel does Arafat still have uncritical supporters, led of course by Foreign Minister Peres and his director-general, Avi Gil. If the more than 1,000 Israeli and Palestinian fatalities and the thousands of injured on both sides have not succeeded in convincing this pair, as well as the politically blind Yossi Sarid and Yossi Beilin, that Arafat by any standards is a war criminal, nothing will convince them.

http://198.65.147.194/English/News/2001-12/24/article1.shtml

Peres, and his ministry director, General Avi Gil, have held talks with the speaker of the P.A. legislative council, Abu Ala, and Mohammed Rashid - Palestinian Authority President Yasser Arafat's top financial advisor - as well as Mohammed Dahlan, the head of Preventive Security in Gaza, about the proposal.

Despite his oft-repeated pledge not to conduct negotiations under fire, Sharon has been aware of contacts between Peres and senior Palestinian officials with whom the foreign minister has been hatching his plan.

And now we have it, Gil dealt directly with Arafat's embezzlement director Muhamed Rashid. Yes, Virginia, Gil was in on the payoffs. And so was Mohammed Dahlan, who was handed over exclusive rights to Israeli industrial monopolies in the PA by Arafat. It's not a big step to understand that the meetings just described included Gil's organizing of the monopolies.

The next site wouldn't open. So we can only contemplate the significance of Peres and Gil meeting Rashid in Rome:

*- ... **Peres** met in Rome over the weekend with Mohammed Rashid, the top financial adviser to Arafat, and sent **Avi Gil**, his director general at the Foreign Ministry ...*
http://www.eindtijd.com/laatst022.html

Wayne Owens was a member of the board of the Peres Peace Center and worked hand in hand with Peres, Cohen and Abraham...and Gil. When the Ginosar scandal broke, he knew these ties would ruin him forever and would likely send him off to the big house to his dying days. Had he had any decency in him he would have threatened to tell all he knew about the Peres Peace Center.

It seems he was on his way to doing the decent thing when someone poisoned his dinner. Avi Gil was his dinner companion two hours before his death. Owens' parting saved Gil the humiliation of being exposed as an active partner of the Peres/Arafat Oslo peace extortion, graft, embezzlement and murder scams.

For now.

ALM 7 - NOW THE GREEK ORTHODOX FALLOUT FROM GINOSAR

Following quickly upon the Ginosar scandal, came PM Sharon's appointment of a terror-advocating priest, Irineos 1 as head of the Greek Orthodox church in Israel. Now who would believe that this mistaken judgement call by Sharon could possibly be associated in any way with the use of Yossi Ginosar as interlocutor for the $350 million intended for the Treasury of the PA that Yasir Arafat stole from his people?

But it is, it is. The route is somewhat precarious, so let us save me the effort of summarizing the Irineos/Sharon background by directly quoting Arutz Sheva.

More Scoops On The Israeli-Greek Near-Tragedy

Arutz-7 continues to reveal more of what went on behind the scenes in the decision not to appoint Arafat-ally Irineos I as head of the Greek Orthodox Church in Israel. It will be recalled that Prime Minister Sharon was in favor of the appointment, but backed down at the end of last week in the face of strong opposition from some of his ministers.

Evidence of Irineos' anti-Semitism was provided by a letter he wrote Arafat on July 17, 2001, stating, "You [Arafat] are aware of the sentiments of disgust and disrespect that all the Holy Sepulchre fathers are feeling for the descendants of the crucifiers of our Lord... actual crucifiers of your people, Sionists [sic] Jewish conquerors of the Holy Land of Palestine." Irineos' letter asks Arafat for his support, promising that if he is elected head of the church, "rest assured, Mr. President, that the rights of our most beloved Palestinian people on the Holy City of Jerusalem will find the most 'hot' supporter."

Arutz-7's Shimon Cohen has now learned that Irineos tried unsuccessfully to pull off an underhanded trick that would have gained him legitimacy in the eyes of the Israeli Cabinet. Atty. Gilad Sher - who served as bureau chief to Prime Minister Ehud Barak - conducted a correspondence on Irineos' behalf with Justice Minister Meir Sheetrit regarding a deal between the Greek Orthodox Church and the State of Israel. The deal would involve the granting of a 150-year lease to Israel for Church-owned lands on which stand properties such as the Knesset, the government complex, and the residences of the President and the Prime Minister. Irineos then sent Sher a letter of approval for the idea - but did not include his official stamp and signature. Also "overlooked" was the fact that the Greek Orthodox Church cannot make any real estate deals without the signatures of all 18 members of its highest religious authority, known as the Synod.

Irineos' plan apparently was to present the deal to the Synod only after it was approved by the Israeli government; the Synod would likely not have approved it, but Irineos would thus present himself as a "moderate" and a "friend of Israel." When Attorney-General Elyakim Rubenstein learned of the ruse, he sent a letter to Justice Minister Sheetrit saying that the procedure he and Atty. Sher had begun was illegal, because of the Synod requirement of 18. The trick to "purify" Irineos was thus nipped in the bud.

To begin this tale, we must return to the late '90s when Ehud Barak was prime minister.

The Seattle Times (Seattle, WA),
Dec 31, 2000 pA4.

There are still behind-the-scenes efforts to keep the flagging negotiations alive. Barak's chief of staff, Gilead Sher, has been meeting with the Palestinian negotiator Saeb Erekat. The Palestinian parliamentary speaker, Ahmed Korei, who has been an outspoken critic of the Clinton proposals, is said to be ready to meet with U.S. officials in Washington and has reportedly been secretly meeting with a frequent go-between for Barak, Yossi Ginosar, a businessman.

The Independent (London, England), July 21, 2000 p13

Other members of the Israeli PR team reveal the khaki tinge of Mr Barak's circle: they include the former chief of the Israel Defence Force's northern command, Major-General Yossi Peled and Amram Mitzna, the mayor of Haifa, the IDF's former head of central command.

We note that the same Gilead Sher, who along with Yossi Ginosar and Amram Mitzna were members of Barak's intimate "peace" team, was the chosen emissary to trick

100

Sharon into approving Irineos' appointment as Greek Orthodox church head. Now what interest did Sher have in promoting Irineos? Or more to the point, who was he representing? As the following connections reveal, Sher was upholding the standing of one of the embezzlement partners of Arafat/Peres Inc.

Another time saver:

For a transcript of Maariv's historic expose of the Ginosar fraud, visit:
http://memri.org/bin/opener.cgi?Page=archives&ID=SP4530 2

_Let us recall that Yossi Ginosar and Hani Masri are both members of the board of directors of the Shimon Peres Center For Peace. Let us recall still that Daniel Abraham and Prof. Stephen F. Cohen are also members of that illustrious monument to money laundering. Let us further recall that the former Utah Congressman Wayne Owens was also a member of the board of Peres' Peace Center and ran his own peace center in Washington. His business organizers were Daniel Abraham and Stephen Cohen. And a very close associate of Owens, Cohen and Abraham was Hani Masri. Working hand in hand with his peace partners, Masri managed to get the American government to cough up $60 million to promote business projects in Arafat-land. The funds were handled by the Capital Investment Management Corporation of Maclean, Virginia.

Now look at the Greek Orthodox Connection to this Clinton-era scam:

http://www.qatarbusinesscouncil.org/bio.html

Immediately before his appointment to Qatar Ambassador, Patrick Nickolas Theros served as Deputy Coordinator for Counterterrorism, responsible for the oordination of all U.S. Government counterterrorism activities outside the United States.

101

In September 1999 the Greek Orthodox Patriarch of Jerusalem, Diodoros I, appointed Ambassador Theros as his representative in the United States.

Upon retiring from the Foreign Service in December 1998, Ambassador Theros assumed position as Director for International Projects of Capital Investment Management Corporation, a McLean, Virginia investment firm.

Now isn't this a sweet coincidence? Theros, merely second in charge of American counter-terrorism operations, retires and soonafter becomes director of Capital Investment Management Corporation, which bilked the US government of $60 million by way of Owens, Peres, Arafat, and Ginosar partner, Hani Masri. And who appointed him their personal representative in America; why the Greek Orthodox Patriarch of Jerusalem.

Yes, it's true. The Greek Orthodox Church was all tied up in the Ginosar scandal and indirectly, so far, in the subsequent murder of Wayne Owens.

We now return to 1997 when Stuart Eisenstadt and William Daley inaugurate the Masri initiative:

http://www.usembassy-israel.org.il/publish/peace/archives/1997/me1117e.html

November 17, 1997

Doha -- Secretary of Commerce William Daley said November 17 that the signing of a protocol for a new $60 million equity fund that will invest in the Gaza, West Bank and Jordan, backed by the Overseas Private Investment Corporation (OPIC), "demonstrates the commitment of the United States to furthering the cause of peace in the region (and) will also directly lead to expanded commercial *cooperation between American firms throughout the West Bank, Gaza and Jordan."*

It is now with great pleasure and honor that I will introduce the United States secretary of Commerce, the Honorable William Daley, who will then be followed by Undersecretary of State Mr. Stuart Eizenstat and Mr. Hani Masri, Chairman of the Capital Investment Management Corporation, who will each make a few comments about this event today...

Last but assuredly not least, I especially want to commend Mr. Hani Masri, the chairman of Capital Management Investment Corporation. Mr. Masri is the kind of fund manager who will get results for this fund because of his own expertise and because he cares for the people of the region. As a Palestinian American, he has a particular interest in seeing that the Palestinian people experience what they have not experienced so far: The fruits of peace, so long overdue. As you can see today, Mr. Masri has already made this fund into a going concern.

This is a perfect example of what has been a centerpiece of this Administration's international economic policy, mainly private-public partnerships. OPIC has provided a two-for-one match for the generous investment which Mr. Masri has made. Mr. Masri, thank you for your contribution and for the participation,
*   I know, of a partner from Qatar. We are very proud to be here with*
*   you.*

But all the great hopes turned to ash, when one Bernard Bucheit blew the whistle on this great experiment in Middle East bunco artistry.

http://www.house.gov/ethics/Traficant_Transmittal_Letter.htm

Finally, as noted, Count X of the SAV charges Representative Traficant with engaging in a continuing pattern and practice of official misconduct, through which he misused his office for personal gain, and which

103

comprised the following instances of conduct, or any combination thereof: the instances of conduct alleged in each of Counts I, II, III, IV, V, and VII of the SAV, separately and inclusive; and/or the course of conduct in which Representative Traficant agreed to and did perform official acts on behalf of Bernard "Pete" Bucheit, for which Bucheit and companies he controlled agreed to and did provide Representative Traficant with things of value. On behalf of Bucheit, Representative Traficant intervened with United States government authorities with respect to a contract dispute between Bucheit's company and Prince Mishaal of Saudi Arabia, and/or with respect to an investment in the Gaza Strip.

http://www.americanmafia.com/Feature_Articles_189.html
http://www.wkyc.com/news/morelocal/cleveland/020828trafic
ant.asp
http://www.jmcc.org/media/report/99/Sep/5b.htm
And this interesting excerpt from the link above:

The first American-owned company to invest in Gaza has been awarded a $15 million judgement against the Cairo Amman Bank for misappropriating a US government loan. United States district judge Kathleen McDonald O'Malley ruled in August that the bank's "pattern of racketeering activity" had caused the failure of Bucheit International, Ltd's precast concrete plant in Gaza. The Cairo Amman bank is one of three banks permitted to do business in Gaza and frequently handles donor funds. "Our family has decided that the Palestinians don't deserve our money and time as long as a 'racketeering Enterprise' exists in Gaza," says company owner B.J. Bucheit, Jr. in a response to questions. Bucheit has appealed to Congress to hold out on funding designated for the implementation of "Wye 2" as long as corruption has not been cleaned up. "The real losers, as usual, are the people of Palestine," he wrote. -Published 29/9/99 (c)Palestine Report

And there it is, wrapped up in one package. The Greek Orthodox Patriarch of Jerusalem appoints Theros its American representative while Theros is the head of the corporation running the Masri scam. Hence, weren't Masri, Peres, Arafat, Ginosar, Owens and The Greek Orthodox Church of Israel all tied up together in the scheme to bilk the US government of $60 million? And wasn't Gilead Sher pushing for a pro-Arafat Greek Orthodox church head at the behest of this ungodly cabal of "peace" crooks?

It appears that the timing of Irineos 1's attempted takeover of the Greek Orthodox Church in Israel so quickly after the exposure of the Ginosar scandal was not all that coincidental.

***

My readers are the most perceptive of anybody's. I defy anyone to prove otherwise. Here are a few vital addendae sent to me regarding the Ginosar crimes. First, observe that the Greek Orthodox Church in Israel is involved in at least, one other fraudulent scheme:

Judge investigated for false affidavits
By Arnon Regular, Ha'aretz Correspondent

A land dispute in the western Galilee from several years ago has turned into a national fraud squad investigation into whether a magistrate judge from the north, while working as a private lawyer prior to becoming a judge, filed false affidavits to the court.

The police investigation, currently in the preliminary stages, involves examining allegations brought to the police by the losing side in the case. The land dispute centered around ownership of rights to develop land owned by the Greek Orthodox Patriarchy in the village of Samia.

The police is remaining mum on the issue, except to say it is handling the complaint. The court system says that the case is in the hands of the police, "and the judge was not aware of the police examination until the question was raised" by Ha'aretz.

According to the complaint, the lawyer-turned-judge represented a group calling itself the Greek Orthodox Council, which received permission from Greek Orthodox patriarch Metropolitan Irenios I, to develop the land as a tourist and pilgrim center. But an investigation conducted by private detective Suheil Haddad, a former police officer, commissioned by Yusuf Nasser of Samia, who lost the case on the rights issue, allegedly turned up evidence of the fraudulent affidavits.

Nasser is now calling for a police investigation to prove the documents were falsified, so that he can reopen his claim to the land. Nasser claims to have received permission from Diodoros I, the previous Greek Orthodox prelate, for the development rights.

Now take in another betrayal by Ginosar as he worked hand in hand with Arafat to bank and launder the monies that the PA President For Life stole from his unwary followers. Moshe Dayan once made some off the cuff comments that the capture of the Golan Heights in 1967 was an act of greed lust. He asked that the comments never be published. Ginosar made sure they were and in doing so, further aided the cause of the enemy:

Rocky Mountain News (Denver, CO), May 4, 1997 p70A.

Title: ISRAEL TOOK GOLAN HEIGHTS FROM SYRIA IN 1967 WAR OUT OF GREED, DAYAN SAID 1976 INTERVIEW,

Those and other of Dayan's thoughts were set down on paper in 1976 by Rami Tal as they sat in Dayan's Tel Aviv garden. Tal, now a senior editor at the publishing house for

the newspaper Yediot Aharonot, asked permission to record Dayan's words.

Dayan agreed on condition that they not be published without his permission. Tal, who printed them in Yediot Aharonot's Passover supplement this week, said that after Dayan died in 1981, the transcripts sat in a drawer for 15 years.

Last year, he showed them to Yossi Ginossar, a former high official in theShin Bet security service and a confidant of Dayan's who urged that they be published.

One observant correspondent noted, for whatever it means, that Stephen F. Cohen, the director of Ginosar's front companies for Arafat, is a member of the Council On Foreign Relations.

Stephen Frand Cohen

Birth: November 25, 1938 in Indianapolis, Indiana, United States

Occupation: political scientist, historian, educator, author, broadcaster

Source: The Complete Marquis Who's Who ^{TM}. Marquis Who's Who, 2001.

Source Citation

Family: s. Marvin Stafford and Ruth (Frand) C.; m. Katrina vanden Heuvel; children: Andrew, Alexandra, Nicola.
Education: B.S., Ind. U., 1960; M.A., Ind. U., 1962; Ph.D., Columbia U., 1969; cert., Russian Inst., 1969. **Civil/Military Service:** Bd. dirs. NYU Ctr. for the Media. **Memberships:** Mem. Council Fgn. Relations, Am. Polit. Sci. Assn., Am. Hist. Assn., Am. Assn. for Advancement Slavic Studies.
Addresses: Home, 340 Riverside Dr Apt 8B, New York, NY, 10025-3436.

And who else is behind Geneva, but the eminent crook, Stephen Cohen?

"However, one of the architects of the Geneva Initiative, Dr. Stephen Cohen, introducing himself as a paid advisor to the US State Department, spoke at a conference of the Brit Tzedek V'Shalom conference in Boston on November 19th, in which he stated that the funder of the Geneva Iniative was the Swiss Government. Cohen stated in answer to a question in the audience that he did not know of any major Jewish contributors to the Geneva Initiative."

Shall we recall who this criminal is? Remember the Ginosar scandal of March '02? Former GSS deputy head Yossi Ginosar arranged the illegal transfer of $300 million stolen by Yasir Arafat from the PA's treasury to Swiss bank accounts. Along the way, numerous straw companies were created to blur the money trail. And who was chosen to be CEO of these companies? Why Dr. Stephen Cohen. When former Utah Congressman Wayne Owens threatened to expose Cohen and Ginsosar, he was murdered and his body was thrown on a Tel Aviv beach.

One correspondent discovered the coverup of Cohen's felonies:

"In my frustration I decided to check out Wayne Owens' peace center site.
www.centerpeace.org
They had decided to revamp their site. Well, the new version is up and guess what? They seem to have purged any reference to Stephen P. Cohen. Remember the Yossi Ginossar henchman? "I had nothing to do with the missing millions."
Well their newsletters and conferences were full of Stephen Cohen, and now all that stuff is off the website. (However the

pages are still there with the info on their webserver). You would never know that Cohen had anything to do with the center."

ALM 8 - Why The Likud Isn't Fighting Back- SHARON AND GINOSAR

The setting: There was a fine casino in Jericho until two years ago. It was supposedly majority-owned by the Palestinian Authority in a limited partnership with a group of experienced Israeli casino owners led by Reuven Gabrieli. But Shimon Peres' special envoy to the PA, Yossi Ginosar got wind of the plan and had a few ideas of his own. He convinced his buddy Jibril Rajoub, the PLO warlord of Jericho, to stop construction of the casino complex, and what better way than to shoo off the construction workers at gunpoint? Now a new group of owners took over and they reportedly understated earnings by at least a billion dollars a year. The casino became a hub of extremely lucrative money laundering. Arafat would pillage the PA's treasury, while Ginosar and his cronies would hide the money. In 1997, Ginosar opened a Swiss bank account for Arafat and around $350 million stolen from Arafat's peasant class found a safe haven there. Ginosar's cut for his trouble was around $10 million. For full details of the Ginosar scandal, contact me and I'll send a package of my five previous investigations.

INTERIOR - DAY - BANQUET HALL BAT YAM JANUARY 8, 03

I am sitting at a table at a brit mila celebration. To my right is Likud candidate Moshe Feiglin. To his right, Herut Knesset member Michael Kleiner. The Likud has been victimized by still another scandal and is on the way to losing the elections. Watch out for Prime Minister Mitzna. The latest scandal concerns a $1.5 million loan Sharon's sons took from a businessman named Cyril Kern. It looks like the knockout punch. I explain the Ginosar scandal in depth to Feiglin and Kleiner, up to the murder of Wayne Owens. I point out that Barak and moreso, Peres are up to their ears in Ginosar and the money involved will make the Kern loan seem like loose change.

But they pretend not to hear. Feiglin tells me the country isn't ready for this kind of scandal. Kleiner changes the subject and talks about when we first met some fifteen years ago. What is going on? Why are they ignoring Ginosar and taking all the punches to the jaw with fatalistic abandonment?

On my left is Prof. Hillel Weiss. He says, "Don't you know Sharon is deeply involved in the Ginosar affair? Who do you think negotiated the deal for Arafat's casino?"

HATSOFE, Jan. 10, Item From, The Weekend Magazine:

"The Ginosar Affair has been forgotten. Could there be a connection between the government's neglect of the scandal and the fact that a high ranking official of Sharon's office conducted negotiations with the same Palestinians involved with Ginosar? This is even more serious than Ginosar's role, because he wasn't an official government employee, while the one we speak of holds a very high-ranking position in Sharon's office."

A BIT LATER - DAY - BANQUET HALL

Hillel Weiss turns to me and answers his own question; "Dov Weisglass and Omri Sharon were the assigned Israeli negotiators with the Austrians who ran the casino."

The blow was immediate. Weisglass is Sharon's Office Director and his son Omri is his special emissary to the PLO. And they were getting a cut of the stolen Arafat money too!

Haaretz, Jan. 10, Page 1B

"It is not clear why $1.5 million were transferred from South Africa to somewhere else, to a bank in Austria via a bank in New York, until they finally landed in a branch of Discount Bank in Tel Aviv. Why this circuitous route?

"What is known, however, is that Omri Sharon and attorney Dov Weisglass (the director of the Prime Minister's Bureau) visited both Austria and the United States together this past year. Austria is the domicile of Martin Schlaff, one of the owners of the casino in Jericho and a partner in the Bank of Austria. Schlaff is a client of attorney Weisglass."

Which Answers A Lot Of Questions

Like why Arafat permitted the constructon of the casino despite the murderous protests of his religious opposition. Like why other Ginosar beneficiaries like Barak and Peres used all their political influence to keep Arafat solvent no matter how many Jews he ordered murdered. Like why Omri Sharon was so buddy-buddy with Arafat and his hoodlums. And like why Ariel Sharon is using all of his political influence to keep the lid on Ginosar and cover up the murder of another gang member, former congressman Wayne Owens of Utah.

**

ALM 8 - SHARON, GINOSAR, PERES AND THE LATE WAYNE OWENS

Of my previous bulletin, a reader notes:

"Nothing new in what you wrote: it is public knowledge that Duby Weisglass was Rashid's lawyer - so all you need to do is put 2 and 2 together."

My reaction: if it is public knowledge that Sharon's Office Manager Dov Weinglass is attorney for Muhamed Rashid, who ran the $300 million plus bank account opened by Yossi Ginosar to hide money Yasir Arafat stole from his people's Treasury, then why hasn't the public put two and two together? That little Sharon connection to the Ginosar scandal has remained buried deep. So let's exhume it for our masochistic pleasure.

****We begin with the great idea of opening a casino in Jericho to launder Arafat's pilfered treasure. The best plot of land in town was already owned, so Yasir decided to expropriate it by force:***

10 May 2000
The Scotsman

Mr Hamdouni had bought 40 acres of land in the desert outside Jericho. He had built a petrol station and planned a housing development.

Then the reality of Yasser Arafat's rule hit Mr Hamdouni. Accused of the capital crime of treason 18 months ago, he was freed from jail only after he signed over his land to the Palestinian Authority.

Within months, a front company for Mr Arafat had taken a secret 28 per cent sta ke in a casino built on what had been Mr Hamdouni's land. The casino now makes $9 million in monthly profits, but Mr Hamdouni sits at home, chain-smoking and lamenting the destruction of all the hopes he had for his people once the long Israeli occupation had ended.

"Who can help me when my land is taken by the 40 thieves? I mean, Arafat is Al i Baba," says Mr Hamdouni, who lost #3 million on the petrol station and land. "We are under Palestinian economic occupation."

The dream of a Palestinian state, which sustained the people here through occupation and intifada, has become a nightmare. The state which Mr Arafat promises to declare in September has all the trappings of independence, from uniformed police to postage stamps, but it is run as a fiefdom by a mafia of corrupt officials.

*** The dream of Jewish/Arab cooperation in money-laundering for Arafat was almost derailed by attorney-general Rubinstein and Weisglass was hopping mad. **

Israelis may be barred from casino in Jericho
Jewish Telegraphic Agency

JERUSALEM - The recently opened gambling casino in Jericho could face a major shortage of customers if Israel's attorney general has his way. Elyakim Rubinstein determined this week that Israelis, the casino's prime source of customers, should be barred from gambling there.

In his decision, he cited a regulation that authorizes local courts to try Israeli citizens for offenses committed in the Palestinian self-rule areas. Gambling is illegal in Israel.

Dov Weisglass, the lawyer representing the Austrian state-run firm that built and operates the casino, said Israelis already gamble in Turkey, the Red Sea resort of Taba as well as at illegal gambling houses within Israel. Weisglass said he hoped the attorney general would reverse his decision in light of what he called the oasis of "peace and friendship" operating in the West Bank town.

"The attorney general has the authority not to enforce the letter of the law" when it is considered in the public interest to do so, Weisglass told Israel Radio. "I hope he will use his judgment to let this (remain) a place of peace, cooperation and friendliness."

*** Criminal cooperation with Arafat or not, the master terrorist just murdered so many Jews that Jericho was blockaded. Shimon Peres didn't like that one bit and he got the blockade lifted after a good talk with Muhamed Rashid, the gangster Arafat chose to safeguard the Ginosar account in Switzerland. **

25 April 2001

The Jerusalem Post

Peres said lifting the Jericho blockade is part of a policy to let Palestinians lead normal lives despite the violence.

"In the Jericho area, $700 million was invested in different industries... this plus the tourism... Everything has been paralyzed," Peres told Israel Radio. "Our position is to allow for a normal lifestyle unconditionally and without receiving anything in return... We don't want to harm innocent people."

Palestinian officials welcomed Peres's statements. One source said the reopening of the casino and easing the closure on Jericho, which is a tourist resort, was discussed between Peres and Arafat's financial adviser, Mohammad Rashid, last Thursday, and not as reported in the Israeli press between Peres and Palestinian negotiator Saeb Erekat.

*** However, all the ill-gained profits just couldn't stop Yasir from practising his art of mass murder. So the casino got itself shut down. At this point Ariel Sharon involves himself personally with Yossi Ginosar. Sharon meets with Weisglass, his son Omri and Ginosar, all of whom have personal financial stakes in the casino. The subject of the tete-a-tete had to have been how to reopen their gold mine, terrorism or not. To Sharon's credit, his position was opposed to reopening the gambling joint until Arafat's murders stopped. ***

http://www.israelinsider.com/channels/diplomacy/articles/dip 0026.htm
Attention was also directed to an alleged connection between the Prime Minister's son Omri Sharon and the idea

to reopen the casino. Omri Sharon reportedly discussed the reopening of the casino at a meeting with Palestinian officials before the elections.

Attending recent negotiations with Sharon was former GSS agent Yossi Ginossar, who allegedly has a financial interest in the casino. Sharon was also accompanied by Israeli lawyer Dov Weisglass, who also serves as attorney for one of the casino owners.

*** The pressure on Sharon was too much to bear. ***

Casinos Austria "knew nothing" – Foreign Ministry not informed.

25 January 2001 19:02 GMT
APA News Service English

(c) 2001 APA NEWS SERVICE

Israel has not had an ambassador here since February 4 last year when he was withdrawn in protest at the right-wing Freedom Party (FP) joining the Austrian government. Casinos Austria meanwhile denied it had been involved at all. Spokeswoman Bettina Stroblich said she knew nothing of the meeting. The Austrian foreign ministry also said it had not been informed. Earlier, Israeli reports said Sharon had sent three envoys to Vienna for private contacts with a top Palestinian official and an Austrian-based businessman. Sharon's three envoys were his son and election campaign manager Omri, lawyer Dov Weisglas, and ex-foreign ministry general secretary Eytan Bentzur. According to the Israeli radio and TV reports, the envoys were to meet Arafat's economic advisor, and also millionaire businessman Martin Schlaff, who has a share of the "Oasis" casino.

In Israel, Sharon's press spokesman Rannan Gissin said the aim of the mission was to take up contact with an influential personality close to Arafat, and thus to show Sharon was willing for a dialogue with the Palestinians. Until recently, the "Oasis" casino in Jericho was one of the main sources of income for the Palestinian Autonomy Authority, and also a lucrative source of profit for Schlaff. It was closed last October when fighting broke out between Israelis and Palestinians. Weisglas represents Schlaff's business interests in the region. He is reported to be sueing the State of Israel for the forced closure of the casino, and for damage to the building caused by gunbattles.

*** Not at all to his credit, Sharon mixes diplomacy with Ginosar and sends his son and Weisglass to Austria to conduct "peace" talks. This is reality in Osloland, where the lives of Israelis and Arabs are determined by the flow of illicit funds from their region to Europe. That being so, here is why Sharon set up Naomi Blumenthal to be dismissed: ***

JTA Dec 11.

BEHIND THE HEADLINES

New financial scandal could hurt both Arafat and Israel's Labor Party
....
"Shortly after the story [about the Ginossar scandal- DM] was published in Ma'ariv, Sharon instructed the Mossad to check whether the Swiss accounts were used to finance terrorism.

Naomi Blumenthal, deputy minister of infrastructure from Sharon's Likud Party, demanded the establishment of a state inquiry commission that would examine not just the Ginossar affair but "all those who took part in the negotiations with the Palestinians."

*** Blumenthal knew all about Sharon, his son Omri, Weinglass and their ugly ties to Ginosar and just how deeply they are involved in formulating policy. She can count herself lucky she didn't suffer the fate of Wayne Owens. Look at the list of people who decide how much money Arafat is to get from Israel. ***

Oct. 15, 2002 - Jerusalem Post

On the eve of Prime Minister Ariel Sharon's visit to Washington Tuesday, Israel and the US reached an understanding to enable the transfer of some NIS 2 billion in frozen tax revenue to the Palestinian Authority, a senior source said. The US has recently applied heavy pressure to release the remainder of the funds as a way of easing Palestinian hardships.

Israel's position has been that it would only release the funds when it is convinced a supervision mechanism is in place that would assure the money does not fund terror organizations.

A senior source in the Prime Minister's Office said that the mechanism was set up at a meeting Monday of Palestinian Finance Minister Salaam Fayad, Prime Minister's Bureau chief Dov Weisglass, Foreign Ministry Director-General Avi Gil, Finance Ministry Director-General Ohad Marani, US Ambassador Dan Kurtzer, and Maj.-Gen. Amos Gilad, coordinator of government activities in the territories. The source denied the agreement was an attempt to "give" the US something prior to Sharon's visit Tuesday.

The new mechanism will reportedly require the Palestinian Authority to deliver a list of who is on its payroll to American and European officials, who will monitor finances from inside the Palestinian Finance Ministry.

Here is the "mechanism:"

* Ozrad Lev, Ginosar's partner who spilled the beans to Maariv, served in IDF intelligence, served as aide to Amos

117

Gilad, the office director of the commander of military intelligence, who was Ehud Barak at that time.

* Daniel Kurtzer is the CFR's American Ambassador to Israel and the first foreign backer of Amram Mitzna for PM.

* Dov Weisglass has deeply implicated Sharon in the Ginosar affair.

* Avi Gil was Shimon Peres' Foreign Ministry director and the last man to see Wayne Owens alive.

WHAT THE GINOSAR REVELATIONS COST WAYNE OWENS BESIDES HIS LIFE

The Jericho casino wasn't where the real big money was going. The biggest scam of all was the "peaceful" use of water. Wayne Owens was the head of "Middle East Energy and Water Resource Institute."

Read
http://www.meweri.org/Documents/2000%20Report.doc

And his company won the tender to build Israel's first major desalinization plant. This was no tiny operation:
"A decision by the Israeli Ministries of Finance and National Infrastructure to issue an International Tender for private development of a 50 million cubic meter per year sea water desalination facility expandable to 100 million m3/yr (November 5, 000)."

Arafat was persuaded not to sabotage the plant:

" A formal decision by President Arafat to separate West Bank water right claims from the need to proceed

118

immediately with large-scale sea water desalination in Gaza (April 2000). Efforts started in 1995 by the founders of the Institute and added to significantly by the Institute helped bring about this decision (April 26, 2000). "

And why was Arafat so kind to this enterprise?

"(He) influenced a policy decision by USAID to commit full funding ($75million) for full and fast-track development of a Gaza Water Carrier, arguing that this commitment would in turn stimulate the needed private investment interest a large-scale desalination facilities for Gaza (July 2000)."

Now look who gets to supply special projects for the plant?:

"To magnify opportunities, credibility and effectiveness during its first 16 months, the Institute, partnered with its two parent organizations the Center for Middle East Peace (the Center) and the International Arid Lands Consortium (the IALC) on most of its projects. Together with the Center and the IALC, the Institute also formed strategic partnerships for specific projects with NGO's Green Cross International (whose President is Mikhail Gorbechev) and the Peres Center for Peace (the NGO team)."

Yes, you read it properly. The Shimon Peres Center For Peace had its grimy paws in the honeypot. To remind us all, members of the board of the Peres Peace Center included Wayne Owens, Yossi Ginosar and Owens' own business partners Daniel Abraham and Stephen Cohen. But let us look at the board structure of the water corporation:

Appendix B. Board of Directors:

The Honorable Wayne Owens, Chairman
President and Co-Founder, Center for Middle East Peace
and Economic Cooperation
Former member of Congress from Utah

Mr. S. Daniel Abraham
Chairman and Founder, Center for Middle East Peace and
Economic Cooperation
Former Chairman, Slim Fast Foods, Inc. and Thompson
Medical Corporation

Ms. Sara Ehrman
Senior Advisor, Center for Middle East Peace and
Economic Cooperation
Former Senior Political Advisor, Democratic National
Committee
Co-Founder, Americans for Peace Now

Dr. Richard Schoell
Vice President for Research, New Mexico State
University
Founding Board Member, International Arid Lands
Consortium

Dr. Kennith Foster
President, Member of Board of Directors, International
Arid Lands Consortium
Chairman, Board of Directors, Multilateral Middle East
Initiative
Director, Office of Arid Lands Studies, University of
Arizona

Mr. Sabih T. Masri
Chairman, of Astra Investment Company (Jordan)
Chairman, Palestinian Economic Development and
Investment Company (PADECO)

The Honorable Shimon Peres
Chairman, The Peres Center for Peace
Former Prime Minister of Israel

Mr. Jean Frydman
Prominent French/Israeli/Canadian businessman
Senior advisor to Prime Minister Ehud Barak

The Honorable Paul Simon
Chairman, U.S. Institute for Peace
Former U.S. Senator from Illinois

Dr. Fu-Tong Hsu
Prominent U.S./Taiwan businessman
Chairman, Taiwan Vision Council

Dr. Shiang Kueen Hsu
Congressman, The National Assembly of Taiwan, ROC
Director-General, Taiwan Resources Bureau
Chairman, Chinese Taipei Committee, ICID

The Honorable John Rhodes, III
Special Counsel, Hunton and Williams
Former member of Congress from Arizona

STRATEGIC PARTNERS:
* "Economic Cooperation Foundation" - Yossi
Beilin.

* Mikhail Gorbachev

Just look who got to skim off the cream from this watery

gold mine! Owens organized the scam and his partners included Peres; Jean Frydman, who financed the Rabin murder for Peres; Sabih Masri, relative of Hani Masri of the Peres and Owens' peace centers boards, who headed a scam which bilked the American government of $60 million intended to boost the PA's economy; Daniel Abraham, of the board of Peres Peace Center and business organizer of Owens' peace center; and his assistant, Sarah Ehrman, head of Peace Now - America. Somehow Yossi Beilin and Mikhail Gorbachev also received baby-sized bites of the pie.

Look what Owens stood to lose by the Ginosar affair! No wonder he was unconsolable. No wonder he had to be hushed up.

The Oslo Peace process was nothing but a huge embezzlement scam exploiting Arafat and Peres' unquenchable criminality and the naivete of government do-gooders in Europe and America. Sharon had a cut of the crime through his son Omri and his Office Director Dov Weisglass. They had nothing to do with the desalinization plant where the real money lay, nor did they murder Wayne Owens. But they stood to profit from the Oslo crimes and Sharon has chosen to protect them by covering up the Ginosar scandal any way he can.

Even if it costs him the election.

And Israel, its soul.

ALM 10 -THE OWENS SCANDAL IS BREAKING

A brave Salt Lake City radio station is breaking the Wayne Owens murder. For once, there is a feeling that this lonely work of mine could result in an official investigation. I exposed the murder on the Barbara Jean Show three days ago was invited to talk about Owens for two hours on Monday, Feb.1, 03 at 11AM MST on the same station.

"The Jim Dexter Show"
Mondays & Tuesdays,
11:00 AM to 1:00 PM (Mountain)
KTKK-AM 630 -- The Voice of Utah
http://www.k-talk.com
Past shows archived @
http://www.mindcleaner.com

I promised Jim Dexter that I would update my research for his program and I remained true to my word.

OWENS' LAST DAYS

FORMER Utah Congressman Wayne Owens was murdered on Dec.18 in Tel Aviv at the end of a factfinding mission shared with House Representatives David Price and Jim Davis. Price prepared a summation of the mission, noting early on that, "Wayne Owens had few illusions about the obstacles to getting peace negotiations back on track."

He continued: "We met in Cairo with Chief of Intelligence General Omar Seuliman regarding the next round of cease-fire talks to be brokered by Egypt among Hamas, Fatah, and possibly other groups.

"We then visited chief Palestinian Authority negotiator Abu Mazen on the day it was determined that he would personally attend this second round. "We met with Palestinian Authority Finance Minister Salam Fayyad regarding financial and budget reform, where there has been enough progress to allow the U.S. to broker the release of a first installment of Palestinian Authority revenues impounded by   Israel.
"We talked with Sari Nusseibeh, head of Jerusalem Affairs for the PLO, about the back-channel, unofficial peace initiatives undertaken by him and others."

By Akiva Eldar (Ha'aretz)
Dec. 20, 2002

Palestinian Authority Chairman Yasser Arafat has taken over responsibility for the Jerusalem portfolio by deposing prominent Palestinian peace activist Prof. Sari Nusseibeh. Nussibeh, president of Al Quds University, hammered out a peace plan with former Shin Bet chief Maj. Gen. (res.) Ami Ayalon earlier this year. A senior Palestinian official who asked to remain unnamed said that Nusseibeh's removal and the establishment of the two committees appear to be part of a pattern of eccentric behavior exhibited by Arafat. The official mentioned, for example, Arafat's announcement that East Jerusalem publisher Hanna Siniora would be the PA's ambassador in Washington, but when the prospective envoy arrived in the U.S. capital, Arafat backed down from the appointment. Recent visitors to Arafat's office in the Muqata said his behavior has become strange. They said he was not focused, spoke in a confused manner, and his lips are shaking again. His doctors attribute the shaking lips to neurological damage that followed an airplane crash in the Libyan desert that Arafat survived. During the past year, Nusseibeh and Ayalon worked out a draft peace plan based on the 1967 borders without a right of return for palestinian refugees. The paper was presented publicly a few months ago at a modest ceremony in Athens attended by former U.S. president Bill Clinton and the Greek foreign minister. Yesterday, however, Nusseibeh issued a statement saying that in protest of the arrest of Musa Balawneh, a former militant-turned-peace activist in Nusseibeh's "People's Peace Campaign," which hopes to get one million signatures on the Nusseibeh-Ayalon plan, Nusseibeh is ceasing his peace activist work in the Palestinian community, his dialogue with Israel, and his efforts to transform the armed intifada into a non-violent civil disobedience campaign - until Balawneh is released.
Balawneh was arrested Wednesday night at a checkpoint

near Nablus while on his way to a meeting of peace activists in Ramallah. According to Nusseibeh, Balawneh has not been accused of anything nor informed of the reason for the arrest. Balawneh's travel permit, according to the Nusseibeh statement, was issued by Israel at Nusseibeh's request and with Israeli understanding that he would not be intercepted or arrested.

THE PLOT SO FAR

1. ON December 17, Owens' group met with Sari Nusseibeh, the Palestinian Authority's Jerusalem Affairs minister and Finance Minister Salam Fayyad.

2. On Dec.18, Owens met with Avi Gil, Shimon Peres' deputy director, for dinner. Owens was found dead on a Tel Aviv beach two and a half hours later.

3. A short time after Owens' body was discovered, Nusseibeh's political partner, Ibrahim Musa Mussalam Balawneh, was arrested by IDF troops.

4. On Dec.19, Nusseibeh condemned the arrest of Balawneh who was travelling on a special permit that he personally arranged.

5. Also on Dec. 19, Arafat stripped Nusseibeh of his Jerusalem portfolio.

And jumping ahead:

6. On Feb.15, under American pressure, Arafat agreed to share power with Salam Fayyad.

If no one minds, I'm going to give away the motive for murder. I may have been underestimating Owens. It seems that he was plotting behind Arafat's back with the, possibly, untainted Nusseibeh. The goal was to replace Arafat's criminal regime with one run by Nusseibeh and Fayyad. If that happened, a lot of crooks headed by Arafat and Peres were going to lose hundreds of millions of dollars, if not billions.

I am not going to rehash my previous articles at this point. I will send them to those who so request. But I had put Owens in the middle of an enormous Oslo embezzlement cartel whose members included Arafat, Peres, Muhamed Rashid, Hani Masri, Yossi Ginosar, the Greek Orthodox Patriarch of Jerusalem and a host of sundry American, Arab and Israeli politicians, all taking their cuts of the peace pie. Now we must ask if Owens was attempting to destroy this extended crime family.

I was asked by Salt Lake City radio hostess Barbara Jean if there was any chance that Owens didn't know about the crimes being run through his and Peres' peace centers. I answered that after 13 years in the Middle East peace business, Owens had to have been a willing participant. The latest evidence more than suggests that either he was used all these years or he had a change of heart and decided to do the right thing and end the Arafat/Peres crime syndicate. This betrayal would have constituted a strong motive for murder.

ENTER USAID

READERS will recall that at the time of his murder, Owens was the CEO of a desalinization project and Peres was the project's NGO director. USAID provided $128 million of American taxpayer's money to fund the enterprise. Following is a press release from the US Consulate in Jerusalem from April 4, 2002 announcing, "The U.S. Government to finance construction of a seawater desalination plant and water carrier pipeline in the Gaza Strip."

http://www.uscongen-jerusalem.org/DOCS/PressReleases/PRUSAID040402.html
"Congratulating Minister Sha'ath and Chairman Sharif, U.S. Consul General Schlicher remarked, "The Palestinian Authority is to be complimented for taking the steps

necessary to introduce desalinated water on a large scale for the people of Gaza. This agreement will result in an increased supply of water while also protecting the ground water quality in Gaza." USAID Mission Director Garber added that, "USAID financed a pilot desalination project in Gaza with superior results. We are pleased that MOPIC and the PWA have asked us to help them with these historic desalination and water distribution projects that will bring healthier lives to people throughout the Gaza Strip."

SO who is the USAID Director Larry Garber? Here is a bit of background found, guess where? On Wayne Owens own web site. Why is Larry Garber's bio on Owens site? Because they invited him to speak at the Center for Middle East Peace and Economic Development on January 29, 2002.

The topic was "Challenges Facing the Donor Community" http://www.centerpeace.org/events/02-01-29Garber.htm

Here are some key points from his talk:

* The West Bank and Gaza are among the top five recipients of U.S. assistance in the world and are probably the largest recipients of per capita aid other than Israel.
* Congressional legislation prevents USAID (and the United States) from providing any funding directly to the Palestinian Authority; it only provides grants to NGOs and commercial businesses, whose programs are overseen and audited by USAID.
* Before September 2000...The Peres Center for Peace was working with USAID on developing an information technology park in Tulkarm, and USAID was in the third phase of developing its wastewater treatment program.
- *In response to the deteriorating situation... Border industrial zone and local government projects have been suspended, but rule of law and civil society programs continue, as do*

127

some infrastructure projects, such as a
desalination plant and water carrier in Gaza
and a wastewater treatment facility in Hebron.

●

NOW what do we notice here? We learn that USAID, and its billion dollars invested in the region so far, only work through NGOs; and who is NGO director of the biggest project of all, Wayne Owens' desalinization plant? Why it just happens to be Shimon Peres. But recall that Arafat's NGOs also received $75 million from USAID to construct a water carrier in Gaza, we must believe, to transport some of the desalinized water to him for sale to his people.

But of course, a good chunk of the dough will finance terror and Peres and Owens, unless they were completely blind, had to have known that when they arranged it for him.

Owens, however, had an out. USAID had a director in the region who was responsible for auditing the funds. His name was Larry Foley and he was murdered:

Lawrence Foley who was the most senior USAID employee
based in Amman Jordan. Unfortunately he was assassinated
on   October   28,   2002.
http://news.bbc.co.uk/2/hi/middle_east/2367311.stm

NOW who would have benefitted from this murder? You can be sure, for starters, everyone involved in the Owens desalinization project. For instance, the builders:

Desalination To Meet Shortfall After Water Import Deal Setback

National Infrastructure Minister Avigdor Lieberman said on
11/28 that Israel would have to build a new desalination plant
for 50 million cubic meters of water a year if the government
fails to follow through plans to import water from Turkey.
Lieberman made the comment following the tender's
cancellation by an inter-ministerial committee. The only two

bidders - Universe Waters and Anatalia - said a clause in the tender that would allow the government of Israel to cancel the project without compensation for up to a year after the contract is signed was unacceptable. The companies said they could not afford to invest tens of millions of dollars in refitting oil tankers for water transport without receiving compensation if the project is scrapped. Water experts say that even if the import of water from Turkey goes forward, the panel's decision would set the project back by up to two years and leave the country short of 50 million cubic meters of water a year. A senior ministry official said that if a desalination plant is built in place of importing water from Turkey, it should be constructed south of Ashkelon, where plans are already afoot for such a plant that is to be built by the VID consortium, composed of Dankner Elran Investments, Engineering & Desalination (part of Israel Chemicals) and Vivendi, the world's largest desalination company. The government has the option of asking the consortium to increase its production from 50 million cubic meters of water a year to 100 million cubic meters. But David Gershonovitz, chair of the central committee for desalination, said last week that if an additional facility is to be constructed, the contract will not be automatically given to VID but would be subject to an international tender. (Ha'aretz 11/29/01)

AFTER sabotaging the Turkish water project with an option no company could accept, desalinization carried on, full steam ahead:

The tender for the construction of Israel's first seawater desalination plant ended this week with a surprising price - 52.69 cents per cubic meter - the lowest ever price offered worldwide for seawater desalination. The group that was awarded the project is V.I.D. Desalination, comprising Dankner-Elran investments (25%), Desalination Engineering

(50%) and Vivendi (25%), which is the world's largest water company and is French-American owned.

THE tie here which should raise alarm bells is Vivendi. In July 2000, the Seagrams Group, founded and controlled by the Bronfman family, bought Vivendi. Charles Bronfman is a member of the board of The Peres Center For Peace. He is, along with Daniel Abraham, Owens' business partner, the leading contributor to Peres' center and to Peace Now. Sarah Ehrman, on the board of both Owens' peace center and water project, was director of Peace Now - America. And the ties get deeper and deeper.

Let's cut to the chase. Did the Bronfman family decide to go into the water business in July 2000 because of the guaranteed prospect of building a $150 million desalinization plant in Ashkelon and other projects funded by USAID? How much of USAID funds to "peace" went into the hands of other nepotists and insiders for "peace?" How much funded the murders of Israelis for "peace?"

THE FALLOUT SINCE THE OWENS MURDER

Jerusalem Post
Feb. 5, 2003

Palestinian Finance Minister Salaam Fayad confirmed Tuesday that Israel earlier this week transferred to the Palestinian Authority almost $60 million in taxes (some NIS 280m.) collected from Palestinian laborers and businesses, the single largest payment since the fighting began.

A senior diplomatic official said Israel is satisfied that with a new US-backed supervisory mechanism in place, the money is not being funneled to fund or support terrorism. Some NIS 100m. of this amount is not merely tax payments due the PA from the previous month, but comes from the more than NIS

2.5 billion that has been frozen since the early days of the violence. "There is an expectation that Israel will make the payments regularly now," The Associated Press quoted Fayad as saying. Fayad, according to one senior Israeli official, is "giving us hope that at least in the financial sphere some reform is being done. He is trying to do what he can." The transfer of the funds was made possible after the establishment of a supervisory mechanism to ensure that the money is not misused. The main component of the supervisory mechanism is the placement of officials from the US Agency for International Development inside the PA Finance Ministry to train auditors and help monitor the money flow.

USAID is now firmly in charge of auditing funds to the PA. And Fayad is sharing power with Arafat. It seems Owens got his way after all.

But look at one of the conditions for releasing new funds:

http://www.usaid.gov/procurement_bus_opp/procurement/an nual_pstatements/wb_aps2942002021.html

"Prior to the second intifada, the PLO agreed to cooperate with our requests for information available to them that could shed light on the status of U.S. nationals known to have been held by the PLO or factions thereof in the past. Currently, we do not have an ongoing relationship with the PLO on these matters."

NOW who are these Americans held by the PLO? Could they have been USAID workers who got in the way and had to be persuaded not to report anything that would upset the Arafat/Peres crime syndicate? Presumably they got off cheaper than Foley and Owens.

CHAPTER FOUR –
FROM THE FINE FOLKS WHO BROUGHT
YOU THE INQUISITION

ALM 1 - THE GRAND ILLUSION
OF THE ROADMAP

It's an illusion, this Roadmap To Peace. President Bush's trip to Roadmap summits in Sharm El Sheikh and Aqaba this week were to further the illusion that he is personally committed to peace for Israel. Most people did not see through this illusion; in fact, except for some of my readers, especially one in Ontario, no one saw through the illusion. But then, most people are under the illusion that they have a choice of leadership when they vote. If PM Sharon has done the Jews only one favor lately, it is that he has finally shattered that illusion for good.

The hard reality behind the illusion is that the Roadmap is one more ugly Vatican manoever to place those unwanted Jews in a deadly trap. Now if anyone dares doubt that Bush is being guided by Rome and its Spanish outpost, please read the following reports and try to draw another conclusion.

I will add not another word until you finish reading:

ACTIVITIES OF SECRETARY-GENERAL IN SPAIN, 6 - 10 APRIL

Secretary-General Kofi Annan departed New York on 6 April and arrived in Madrid, Spain, on Sunday, 7 April, to begin a weeklong visit to Europe that would also take him to Rome and Geneva.

On Sunday evening, he and Mrs. Annan attended a private dinner hosted by King Juan Carlos and Queen Sofia at the Palacio de la Zarzuela on the outskirts of the Spanish capital.

In the afternoon, the Secretary-General visited the Madrid-based World Tourism Organization and then addressed a ceremony to mark 160 companies signing up to the Global Compact. (See Press Release SG/SM/8193.)

Also on Tuesday, the Secretary-General conferred with his Special Coordinator for the Middle East Peace Process, Terje Roed-Larsen, in advance of his meeting the following morning with members of the so-called "Quartet" on the situation in the Middle East.

At that meeting on Wednesday morning, the Secretary-General discussed the escalating crisis for over an hour without aides at Madrid's Palace of Moncloa with U.S. Secretary of State Colin Powell, Spanish Foreign Minister Josep Piqu? representing the rotating presidency of the European Union, High Representative for European Union Common Foreign and Security Policy Javier Solana, and Russian Foreign Minister Igor Ivanov.

Immediately after the press conference, the Secretary-General departed Madrid for Rome, Italy.

http://www.cluboffrome.org/archive/publications/Presidential_Address_long_version.pdf

New World Order without Ideologies

by HRH Prince El Hassan bin Talal (Jordanian Prince, Uncle of King Abdullah of Jordan and present President of the Club of Rome.)

Hours after the five-week standoff at Bethlehem's Church of the Nativity ended, Israeli Foreign Minister Shimon Peres arrived in Rome for talks with Premier Silvio Berlusconi and top Vatican officials. Peres met with Vatican Secretary of State Angelo Sodano and Vatican Foreign Minister Archbishop Jean-Louis Tauran. During his visit Peres said Italy would be a good venue for a peace conference.

Israel's Prime Minister, Ariel Sharon, said: 'We have excellent relations with Rome and my personal relations with Prime Minister Silvio Berlusconi are great.'

Saturday, May 03, 2003

MADRID, Spain — Pope John Paul II (search) began a whirlwind visit to Madrid on Saturday, testing his frail health and seeking to reinvigorate those Spanish Catholics who have strayed from their once-dominant church.

The pontiff, who turns 83 this month, arrived at Barajas airport outside Madrid aboard an Alitalia jetliner. King Juan Carlos and Queen Sofia greeted him at the VIP terminal as he began his first visit abroad in nine months.

King Juan Carlos, speaking before the pope, praised the pontiff as "a tireless fighter for the most noble causes."

"This will probably be this pope's last visit to Spain, although you never know," the archbishop of Madrid, Cardinal Antonio Maria Rouco, said in an interview published Saturday in the newspaper El Mundo.

http://www.news.com.au/common/story_page/0,4057,65106
36%255E1702,00.htm
Powell To Meet Pope

US Secretary of State Colin Powell will visit Pope John Paul II next week to discuss the Middle East peace process and rebuilding post-war Iraq, US and Vatican sources said today.

The meeting on Monday will be the first high-ranking face-to-face talks between the US government and the Vatican since the US-led war in Iraq, which the Pope vehemently opposed.

http://www.watch.org/showart.php3?idx=44842&rtn=/index.ht
ml&showsubj=1&mcat=1

Pope Meets with Colin Powell, Calls for a Palestinian State

Again, Pope John Paul II takes a position regarding God's covenant land that is not biblical.

As a reminder, PLO Chairman Yassir Arafat had nine meetings with Pope John Paul II at the Vatican since the signing of the Oslo I Agreement on September 13, 1993.

Vatican Signs Agreement with the Palestinians over Jerusalem

The Vatican and the Palestinians signed an agreement on February 15, 2000, stating the following:

An equitable solution for the issue of Jerusalem, based on international resolutions, is fundamental for a just and lasting peace in the Middle East, and that unilateral decisions and actions altering the specific character and status of Jerusalem are morally and legally unacceptable; Calling, therefore, for a special statute for Jerusalem, internationally guaranteed, which should safeguard the following: (a). **Freedom of religion and conscience for all.** *(b). The equality before the law of the three monotheistic religions and their Institutions and followers in the City. (c). The proper identity and sacred character of the City and its universally significant, religious and cultural heritage. (d).* **The Holy Places, the freedom of access to them and of worship in them.** *(e). The Regime of "Status Quo" in those Holy Places where it applies.*

The Israelis responded by saying, "Israel expresses its great displeasure with the declaration made in Rome by the Holy See and the PLO, which includes the issue of Jerusalem, and other issues which are subjects of the Israeli-Palestinian negotiations on permanent status. The agreement signed by these two parties constitutes a regretful intervention in the talks between Israel and the Palestinians."

POWELL HAILS ITALY'S US SUPPORT

US Secretary of State Colin Powell has been holding talks with Italian Foreign Minister Franco Frattini in Rome. He said Italy was the US's best friend and ally and that President George W Bush was grateful for Italy's contribution during the war with Iraq. Mr Powell also met Pope John Paul II in the Vatican to discuss Middle East peace efforts and the reconstruction of Iraq. It was the first high-level meeting between the US and the Vatican since the Iraq war. During the audience, the Pope spoke of his hopes for the United States-backed 'road map' for Middle East peace. He said he hoped that Israelis and Palestinians would be able finally to enjoy the same security and the same sovereignty.

Source: *WorldWatch*

http://story.news.yahoo.com/news?tmpl=story&u=/nm/20030424/ts_nm/mideast_usa_dc_4

U.S. Ready to Put 'Shoulder to Wheel' on Mideast Peace 2 hours, 16 minutes ago Add Top Stories - Reuters to My Yahoo!
WASHINGTON (Reuters) - The United States on Wednesday called for quick confirmation of a Palestinian cabinet and vowed to put its "shoulder to the wheel" to implement a long-delayed Middle East peace plan.

President Bush discussed the developments and his plans to release the road map by phone with British Prime Minister Tony Blair and Spanish Prime Minister Jose Maria Aznar.

http://story.news.yahoo.com/news?tmpl=story&u=/usatoday/20030318/pl_usatoday/4956670
Bush's ultimatum recalls post-9/11 remarks
Tue Mar 18, 6:27 AM ET

Judy Keen USA TODAY

Bush spent part of Monday rehearsing. He was up before dawn, as always, and made phone calls to his most steadfast allies : Blair, Aznar and Spain's King Juan Carlos.

http://www.euobserver.com/index.phtml?aid=11301
Bush on 'axis of weasel' tour
EUOBSERVER / BRUSSELS - *US President George Bush will embark on a week-long day visit to Europe on Thursday which will take in Berlin, Moscow, St. Petersburg, Paris, Normandy, and Rome.*

Mr Bush will meet with the three leaders of what some have dubbed the "axis of weasel" for their opposition to the war on Iraq - German Chancellor Gerhard Schroder, French President Jacques Chirac and Russian President Vladimir Putin.

Mr Bush will also meet with the Pope, not named a member of the axis, but strongly anti-war.

http://www.guardian.co.uk/US_electi...,393341,00.html

Victory is in the blood for 'aristocratic' Republican
The Guardian
Press Association

The Republican George W Bush will be elected US president on November 7 because he has more royal blood than his opponent, it was claimed today.

Mr Bush has direct descents from William the Conqueror, Henry II and Charles II, according to Burke's Peerage.

He also scores better than his father, who lost the office of president to Bill Clinton, because of his mother's well-to-do ancestors. Barbara Pierce Bush's royal connections include French Bourbon and several Scandinavian monarchs, as well as members of the Russian, Spanish and German monarchies.

http://search.news.yahoo.com/search/news/?p=spain+easter&ei=UTF-8

Vatican Moves Emperor Near Beatification
Sat Apr 12, 9:57 PM ET

VATICAN CITY - The Vatican (news - web sites) moved the last emperor of Austria-Hungary on the path to beatification Saturday, decades after the monarch died in exile.

Charles I *was a man of "moral integrity and solid faith," the Vatican said, adding that he "always sought the well-being of his people and was inspired by the social doctrine of the Church in his government actions."*

http://www.haaretzdaily.com/hasen/spages/291756.html

Danish foreign minister hints at sanctions if road map stalls

By Arnon Regular, Haaretz Correspondent

Danish Foreign Minister Per Stig Moeller said Saturday the foreign ministers of the international Quartet (the UN, United States, EU and Russia) had prepared various means of applying pressure to force Israel and the Palestinians to implement the road map for a solution to their conflict.

Moeller, whose country, Denmark, headed the EU presidency when the road map was put together, was speaking on the eve of the arrival in the region of U.S.

Secretary of State Colin Powell. He had been asked what sanctions could be imposed by the EU and the Quartet on any side that failed to implement the road map.

"We have a series of measures we will come out with at the appropriate time," Moeller said at a conference of peace activists from Israel, the Palestinian Authority, Egypt and Jordan that was organized by the Jordanian Foreign Ministry. "I won't expose them now because if I were to do so, they would lose their effectiveness; but we are ready to use them if we are required to do so," he added.

Delegates at the conference included Haim Ramon, MK (Labor), former Labor lawmaker Uzi Bar'am, **representatives from the Peres Center for Peace,** *Fatah activists from the PA and Jerusalem, and members of Jordanian and Egyptian peace movements.*

http://www.euobserver.com/index.phtml?aid=11344

EUOBSERVER / BRUSSELS – Ahead of a key Israeli cabinet meeting and a statement by the US, representatives of the Madrid Quartet – Russia, the EU, US and UN are meeting in Paris today and are set to agree the terms for monitoring the so-called 'road map' to peace.

Remarks with UN Secretary General Kofi Annan, Foreign Minister Igor Ivanov of the Russian Federation, Foreign Minister Josep Pique of Spain in the capacity of EU Presidency and Javier Solana, High Representative for Common Foreign and Security Policy of the EU

Secretary Colin L. Powell
Benjamin Franklin Room
Washington, DC
May 2, 2002
[audio]

SECRETARY POWELL: *Good afternoon, ladies and gentlemen. I am pleased to welcome to the State Department today Secretary General Annan, Foreign Minister Ivanov, Foreign Minister Pique, and High Representative Solana of the European Union to the Department to continue the discussion that we began in Madrid on April 10th on ways to end the violence and move towards peace in the Middle East.*

Son's approach towards Europe misunderstood, says Bush Sr

MADRID: Former U.S. President George Bush said on Friday that some people had misunderstood his son's attitude towards Europe.
"I know there is a perception in some quarters here in Europe that this administration of his hasn't reached out to our friends and allies as much as some would like. I know that this is a misperception," the father of current President George W.Bush told a business conference in Madrid.
The elder Bush, 79, cited his son's close work with Spanish Prime Minister Jose Maria Aznar as an example of how the president had reached out to Europe in the run-up to the war in Iraq.

May. 12, 2003
Spanish foreign minister to tour Middle East
By THE ASSOCIATED PRESS
MADRID, Spain

Foreign Minister Ana Palacio said Monday she plans to visit governments in the Middle East to encourage peace efforts in the region.
Palacio said she intended to include Cairo, Egypt, in her tour but provided no further information. Her office said details of

her trip were not yet confirmed. The support of the region's leaders for the so-called road map to peace proposed by the United States, United Nations, European Union and Russia is "very important" in securing its success, Palacio told reporters.

It is time to move "from statements to action," she added.

Enacting the Middle East blueprint for peace has become one of Spain's main foreign policy goals. *It was one of the main arguments used by Prime Minister Jose Maria Aznar to justify to Spaniards his government's support for the US-led war in Iraq.*

http://story.news.yahoo.com/news?tmpl=story&u=/afp/20030
527/wl mideast afp/mideast spain 030527123711

Spanish FM to meet Arafat in Ramallah

MADRID (AFP) - Spanish Foreign Minister Ana Palacio will meet with Palestinian leader Yasser Arafat (news - web sites) and prime minister Mahmud Abbas in the West Bank town of Ramallah, diplomatic sources said Tuesday. Palacio was due to head for Jerusalem later Tuesday after a meeting of EU and Arab ministers on the Mediterranean island of Crete.

She will meet in Ramallah with Abbas and her Palestinian counterpart Nabil Shaath on Wednesday before a "short visit" to see Arafat the same day, the sources here said, adding there were no plans to meet with Israeli officials.

*** Now surely, even the most stubborn adherents of their own understanding of reality, saw the pattern. Powell and Bush run to Spain and Rome before planning their moves in the Middle East. That they are pulling the strings is an illusion. That they intend to bring peace to Israel is an illusion. That they are doing the Vatican's dirty work is the only truth that can be discerned from their actions.***

ALM 2 -THE SHIMON PERES WETBACK THEORY OF AMERICAN HISTORY

Shimon Peres hates brown people and in 1984, it cost him an election victory. With Prime Minister Begin bogged down in Lebanon, it looked like he was going to coast to victory. Then came the Tel Aviv rally hosted by comedian Dudu Topaz. The popular funnyman looked at the white faces in the crowd and noted, "At least there are no chakhchahakhim here." Meaning, in the most derogatory way, at least there are no dark Sephardim here. Shimon smiled at the comment. By so doing, instead of expressing his indignation, he lost the Sephardic vote then and forever.

In a documentary called Kadim Winds, Peres' bigotry is caught on film, as a reader notes:

I told you that in Kadim Winds a younger Peres made a campaign speech in Beit Shean and the audience was not too thrilled with him ... Peres did say (parapharase) "ATEM IN HA TNUOT HA MIZRACHIT SELACHEM. MA ATEM ROTZIM.
ATEM SHATYANIM? TITBAYSHU ... "WHY DON'T YOU GO BACK TO MOROCCO ..." The film ought to be checked for actual transcript. It may be good if you incorporate that and a few other episodes in a talk and into videos/CD-s.

Translated, Peres told the gathered, "You and your Sephardic movement. What do you want? You're a bunch of drunks and should be ashamed of yourselves. Why don't you go back to Morocco."

Not content with despising brown Jews, this week Peres went after brown Americans:

Peres: Browning of America serious problem
Aaron Lerner Date: 5 August 2003

Labor MK Shimon Peres explained his statement yesterday

that America had a problem because it started white and is now going brown. He explained in a live interview today on Israel Radio's "It's All Talk" program that in America it is recognized that the United States has a "problem" that there are so many Hispanics in the U.S. today.

Peres explained that he had nothing to apologize for saying that the changing in the racial composition of America is a problem since Americans themselves write that they see a problem in the change and there is even a book titled "The Browning of America."

Here is Peres' thinking. If there isn't a Palestinian state, Israel will be flooded with brown Arabs and things will become as bad as in America, where the wetbacks are wrecking the country. It's hard to say if his statement is more insulting to Arabs or Latinos but that's how he really thinks. The "peacemaker" is an ethnocentric racist. And this bigot is going to become prime minister because his Vatican pals are arranging it. Once in power, as noted in the previous article, he is going to make Jerusalem a UN-controlled "world capital" with the Vatican gaining sovereignty over the Temple Mount.

Perhaps, a reminder is appropriate:

http://story.news.yahoo.com/news?tmpl=story&cid=586&ncid=586&e=3&u=/nm/20030722/wl_nm/mideast_jerusalem_dc
Peres Raises 'World Capital' Solution for Jerusalem

JERUSALEM (Reuters) - **Shimon Peres, the head of Israel's opposition Labor Party, has suggested resolving Israeli-Palestinian conflict over Jerusalem by putting its holy sites under U.N. stewardship, a spokesman said Tuesday.**

*His plan calls for declaring a holy area of sites sacred to Jews, Christians and Muslims in Jerusalem's old walled city as a **"world capital,"** with the **U.N. Secretary-General*** *serving as mayor*, Peres' spokesman Yoram Dori told Reuters.

Israel claims Jerusalem as its capital, including the Arab eastern part captured in the 1967 Middle East War and annexed in a move that is not recognized internationally. Palestinians want to make East Jerusalem capital of the state they hope to establish in the West Bank and Gaza Strip under a U.S.-backed peace plan.

Peres raised the idea in a meeting with visiting Russian diplomats-in-training when they asked how he envisaged a solution to conflicting Israeli-Palestinian claims to the city, Dori said.

Israel has previously rejected proposals raised by the Vatican to internationalize Jerusalem.

Peres, a former prime minister and an architect of interim peace deals with the Palestinians, has not raised the proposal with Israeli or Palestinian leaders, Dori said.

So here is how the Jews will lose Jerusalem. In late May, '03, Peres was in Rome plotting with the Vatican. He would return to Israel and take over the leadership of the Labor Party. To do so, he had to blackmail the party frontrunner, Binyamin Ben Eliezer, out of the race. Once this was accomplished, he won the party leadership, though, with a minority of votes.

Sharon was proving recalcitrant and would have to be removed. That process will begin in earnest this week when he and his sons are investigated for some serious financial scandals. The attorney general Elyakim Rubinstein was cajoled into bringing Sharon down and he announced his retirement at the same time as he recommended prosecuting the Sharon clan. He doesn't want to stick around for what's coming.

Needless to say, Sharon's predecessor, Ehud Barak and his gang, committed even worse electioneering crimes in 1999 which have gone unprosecuted to this day. It's not fair but Rubinstein understands the game of selective justice.

145

Barak was cooperative with the international scheme to bring down Israel, Sharon is proving too reluctant. So out he will go and quickly.

With Sharon forced to quit in disgrace, opposition leader Peres will be in the right place to take over the helms of state.

It's coming. The bigot Peres is on his way back to the prime minister's office. The last time, he had to remove Rabin violently. This time, he will merely subject his nation to a painful scandal ending with the resignation of the sitting prime minister.

And then, Jerusalem will be lost and Israel will soonafter cease to exist. Recall, the current intifada broke out immediately after the pope's visit to Israel in 1999. When they plot, Jews die.

ALM 3 - NAZI JESUITS

In late May, 2003, The Voice Of Israel radio broadcast a report from Rome. After visiting his papal pals, Shimon Peres decided to run for chairman of the Israeli Labor Party. The eighty year old Peres promised to keep Israel on the Roadmap and fulfil the promises of Oslo.

Peres, educated in his youth at a Jesuit school in Poland, is the highest ranking operative run by the Jesuits in Israel and his task is spreading chaos ending with national destruction. The destruction of the Jews is a primary goal of the Jesuits and I am presenting proof of this assertion through a book that collected the facts brilliantly but missed the most obvious conclusions. I speak of Unholy Trinity by Mark Aarons and John Loftus.

This is not the first time Aarons and Loftus collected evidence with flair but missed the whole picture. In their far better known, the Secret War Against The Jews, the authors exposed the likes of the Dulles brothers and the Harriman clan and their machinations against the Jews without understanding their direct connections to the Council On Foreign Relations and ultimately, the Jesuits.

I pointed this out to John Loftus several years ago and he replied that he didn't miss the connection, he didn't believe it. However, since then, he has grudgingly budged a bit, twice writing that my own evidence gathering was, at least, "interesting."

So let's help the boys again, shall we? I am citing the St. Martin's Griffin edition of Unholy Trinity. I have no intention of describing the gruesome acts of the diabolical characters portrayed in the book, nor will I even identify their roles. For that, get the book. My intention is to expose the Jesuit connection to the Holocaust, and the escape of the perpetrators to the four corners of the planet by way of the Jesuit's Ratlines to safety.

Before we examine Unholy Trinity, it would be helpful to supply some historical background. John Daniel does so admirably in his book, The Grand Design, (CHJ Publishing, 1999).

pp 151: The most important factor in the recatholizing of Germany was the educational activity of the Jesuits. They succeeded in rapid succession the founding of colleges in all the important towns of the German Empire.

pp 159: When Rome launched her counter-offensive to halt the progress of Protestantism, she began in Germany; one of the areas she felt sedition was most deeply rooted. When Rome had finished, Germany was depopulated. Its people had either been killed by the Thirty Years War or had fled the area. Germany itself had been reduced to a virtual wilderness area.

pp 162: When backtracking to the origin of this complexity of deception, it brings us straight to the real heart of the matter, the intense hatred of the Roman Catholic Church for anyone or anything that opposes her goals. It positively isn't a Jewish conspiracy, but strictly Roman Catholic, who have strategically used certain Jews for their cause's advantage.

Now on to Unholy Trinity. The subject of the book is the smuggling out of Europe of tens of thousands of Nazis after World War 2 via the Vatican ratlines. Included also are clear pictures of the Jesuits' activities against the Jews preceding and during the war.

***

pp 22: American intelligence had been taking an active interest in the Vatican's response to the 'Red Menace' for some time. Indeed 'high-ranking Allied intelligence officers' were reportedly in 'close relations with high Vatican dignitaries' well before the Nazi collapse. In October 1945 the Americans noted the 'preponderant influence which the Jesuit fathers, who always present concrete and well-reasoned projects, tend to exercize at the Curia. According to their source, the Jesuits were leading the Holy See's struggle with Moscow, and the, 'one positive step so far taken by the Vatican has been the organization of a penetration program; especially resourceful that is being sent into the area to lead the catholic elements and through their zeal and example to keep these elements from wavering. Most of these agents are Jesuits.'

pp 31: Father Burkhart Schneider, a German Jesuit, is also certain that, 'Bishop Hudal was not at all close to the Vatican.' Schneider, who prepared the Holy See's defence of Pius XII's wartime role, was adamant that Hudal was 'very much on the fringes.'

pp 57: In 1932, Draganovic went to Rome to study at the Papal Oriental Institute and the Jesuit Gregorian University...Draganovic had returned to Rome in August 1943, representing the Ustachi and the Croatian Red Cross.

148

This allowed him to build his escape routes for Nazi war criminals.

pp 58: One of Draganovic's most important lay colleagues was Miha Krek. Leader of the Catholic Slovene People's Party, Krek worked for British Intelligence. Draganovich's own contacts reached to the very top of the Italian Interior Ministry. The two men had another thing in common: high level Vatican contacts.

pp 59: In October 1945 the OSS had identified the Jesuits as key Vatican agents in a 'penetration program' inside Communist-occupied areas.

pps 61, 68: Vajta worked for the Hungarian secret service before the war. He had also been a senior Nazi propagandist for German-sponsored newspapers...that poisoned Hungarian public opinion... Vajta arrived in New York on 16 December 1947...The Embassy had passed the details of Vajta's trip together with a list of people he wished to meet in America. These included Cardinal Spellman, Jesuit leader Father La Farge and a host of emigre political leaders.

pp 79: Father Draganovic was the man who could lead to Pavelic's arrest and extradition...The Jesuits were among his closest Church helpers at this time, assisting his plans to leave Italy by arranging for his passage to Spain.

pp 162: For security reasons, Pius XII stated that he would not meet with Muller directly, but would receive his communications through a Jesuit priest, Father Leiber, a Vatican archivist, whom the pope trusted absolutely...On October 27 Muller was summoned to meet Father Leiber at the Jesuit Gregorian University.

pp 165: This may have been Turkul's first espionage work for the Jesuits... It is perhaps only a coincidence that Turkul was running his own Japanese Ratline into the Soviet Union for the Abwehr at the same time as the Jesuits. Even if Turkul had no direct Jesuit connection in 1938, his Abwehr boss certainly did...Turkul's NTS network had longstanding relations with British intelligence. Several of Turkul's close associates were Uniate and Orthodox clergymen who were well known to the Jesuits. Indeed, the Jesuits had built an entire college in Rome to train Uniate seminarians.

pp 175: A united Eastern Church had been the Vatican's dream since the great Orthodox schism tore Christianity apart in 1024 A.D. The hybrid Uniate Church was a compromise devised in the sixteenth century by the Jesuits and encouraged by the Habsburg dynasty.
pp 181: The centrepiece of Wachter's strategy was the five million Catholic Uniates. Their religious leader Archbishop Szepticky pointed the way by blessing the Galician SS Division. The Galician SS, complete with Uniate chaplains, would soon be a Catholic army in crusade against the 'Godless Bolsheviks.'

***

Aarons and Loftus, whether they intended to or not, provide evidence of Jesuit manipulations in the rise of nazism and the near total disappearance of European Jewry. To make certain their goal of the complete extermination of the Jews was reached, they saved their carefully cultivated exterminators. With that understood, see if you find a pattern in the Roadmap of recent events:

http://famulus.msnbc.com/FamulusIntl/reuters07-02-162744.asp?reg=MIDEAST

Spain offers to host Middle East peace conference

MADRID, July 2 — Spain offered on Wednesday to host a Middle East peace conference and a top Palestinian official said he would be glad to see the conference held in Madrid.

Madrid hosted a 1991 conference that launched a series of Arab-Israeli peace moves. Spanish Foreign Minister Ana Palacio took advantage of a meeting with Palestinian Foreign Minister Nabil Shaath to push Madrid's claims to hold a second conference now Middle East peace efforts have resumed.

"For Spain, it would be a very great honour to host a conference...If such a decision is taken, we would facilitate it, by providing a venue for a conference," Palacio told a news conference held jointly with Shaath.

Shaath said the Palestinian administration would be "very happy and proud if the next peace conference were here in Madrid."

He said the Spanish government had tried to host a peace conference last year but the time had not been right. "According to the (Middle East peace) road map, this conference will be necessary at the end of 2003 or at the beginning of 2004," he said.

Palacio and Shaath were in an upbeat mood with both saying it was a "moment of hope" in the Middle East.

Palestinians and Israelis have this week taken the first tentative steps to implement the "road map," which envisages a Palestinian state by 2005 in the West Bank and Gaza alongside a secure Israel

Shaath said he believed an agreement on Jerusalem, which both Israelis and Palestinians claim as their capital and is seen as one of the toughest obstacles to overcome, was possible.

"I really don't see anything as impossible. On the contrary, I see that we can reach an agreement," he said.

East Jerusalem would be the capital of Palestine and the other part of the city the capital of Israel, he said.

Both Palacio and Shaath said they believed that three Palestinians given refuge in Spain last year should at some point return to Bethlehem.

The three were among 13 Palestinians flown to European countries in May 2002 under a deal which ended a siege by Israeli forces of Bethlehem's Church of the Nativity.

"There is a European agreement for all of the Palestinians (who left last year) to return to Bethlehem," Shaath said.

Palacio and Shaath signed an agreement under which Spain will provide 10 million euros ($11.54 million) in aid to the Palestinians this year to fund health, education and job creation. Some 80 vehicles were expected to be shipped from Spain soon for the use of the Palestinian police.

**

RUSSIAN SENATOR DISCUSSES STATUS OF JERUSALEM HOLY PLACES WITH ISRAELI MINISTER

TEL AVIV, June 16, 2003. /From RIA Novosti correspondent Andrei Pravov/--Head of the Russian Federation Council's international committee Mikhail Margelov, who is on a visit in Israel, on Monday met Israeli Minister for Jerusalem and Diaspora Affairs Nathan Sharansky. They discussed the proposal of the Russian parliament's upper chamber to hold an international conference "Holy Places of the Holy Land" in Geneva early next year. The idea has already been endorsed by the Vatican and the Russian Orthodox Church.

**

UN and America say multinational force is only way to end violence
By Rupert Cornwell in Washington

15 June 2003

As violence threatens to engulf the barely launched roadmap

152

plan for peace in the Middle East, calls are growing for a large-scale international force to be sent in, as the only hope of imposing some sort of a ceasefire between Israelis and Palestinians.

The demands came as a team of US monitors arrived in the region, and - after intense pressure from Washington and Arab countries - Palestinian and Israeli security officials agreed to resume contacts. This follows a week of bloodshed during which at least 50 people died.

The dispatch of a multinational force is increasingly seen as the only means of securing a breathing space, allowing meaningful negotiations to begin.

http://news.bbc.co.uk/1/hi/world/middle_east/2186922.stm
Aug/2002

Pope backs Mid-East peace force

Pope John Paul II has lent his support to the creation of an international peacekeeping force to try to bring an end to the Israeli-Palestinian conflict.

*In one of his strongest denunciations of the continuing violence, **the Pope said the international community should take "a more determined role on the ground" to help bring about peace.***

Jordan's King Sends a Message to Pope
http://www.zenit.org/english/visualizza.phtml?sid=37112

VATICAN CITY, JUNE 12, 2003 (Zenit.org).- John Paul II received a message from King Abdullah of Jordan, which was handed to the Pope personally by Jordanian Foreign Affairs Minister Marwan Muasher.

153

The Vatican press office gave no details on today's papal audience with the Jordanian envoy. The audience was held at a critical time in the relaunching of Mideast peace talks.

The king's message addresses "the situation in the region," according to the Jordanian news agency Petra.

Muasher also met with Archbishop Jean-Louis Tauran, Vatican secretary for relations with states, to discuss "means of stepping up efforts to find a just and lasting solution to crises facing the region," Petra said.

On Tuesday, Muasher was in Bahrain, where he attended a meeting of Arab Foreign Ministers entrusted with following up on Arab summit resolutions, including efforts to resolve the Palestinian-Israeli crisis, Agence France-Presse reported.

Last week, Jordan was host for a summit between U.S. President George W. Bush and the Israeli and Palestinian Prime Ministers, who both pledged to implement the peace blueprint.

***

June 2, 2003

http://www.catholicnews.com/data/stories/cns/20030602.htm
POPE-POWELL Jun-2-2003 (970 words) With photos. Xxxi

Pope, Vatican officials meet with Powell, discuss Mideast peace
By John Norton
Catholic News Service

VATICAN CITY (CNS) -- As a U.S.-backed peace plan began taking shape in the Middle East, **Pope John Paul II and top Vatican officials met U.S. Secretary of State Colin Powell for talks on ending the Israeli-Palestinian conflict.**

June 12, 2003
http://www.haaretzdaily.com/hasen/spages/303037.html

Annan : Armed peace force should be sent to territories

New YORK - United Nations Secretary-General Kofi Annan, in a joint interview with Haaretz and Channel Two News, said that the Israelis and Palestinians are apparently unable to reach an agreement on their own, and that in the present circumstances he supports sending an "armed peace force as a buffer zone between the Israelis and the Palestinians."

http://www.agi.it/english/news.pl?doc=200306092155-0218-RT1-EST-0-NF82&page=0&id=agionline-eng.italyonline
Sicily offered as peace conference venu.e
http://www.agi.it/english/news.pl?doc=200306111208-0043-RT1-EST-0-NF82&page=0&id=agionline-eng.italyonline
Mazen's going to Rome.

***

Note:

Aarons and Loftus and Daniel crossed paths on a certain key to understanding the real war against the Jews.

Daniel, pps 166-7: In less than forty five years, which brings us to the time of the French Revolution, France is said to have counted over two thousand lodges affiliated to the Grand Orient...The Grand Orient de la France being instituted in 1773 was a plan being orchestrated precisely when the Jesuit Order was supposedly being dissolved. Actually, nothing could have served the Jesuit purpose greater, working in dark secret as those at the apex of power in Freemasonry did.

Aarons, Loftus, pps 52-53: According to Vajta, the historical convergence of French and Vatican interests in Central Europe played a crucial role in de Gaulle's schemes 'to employ the factor of Catholicism.' Vajta told French intelligence of his pre-war role in their clandestine operations in Central Europe. While studying at the Sorbonne in the early 1930s, he joined the secretive Grand Orient, an organization specializing in Central and Eastern European affairs which linked Francophiles from these regions to French activities.

ALM 4 - YOU THOUGHT IT WAS TOO FANTASTIC TO BE TRUE

LET US RECALL a few of the things I wrote in my new book Save Israel that almost all of you thought were too fantastic to be real. Shall we begin with the latest Peres scheme?

http://story.news.yahoo.com/news?tmpl=story&cid=586&ncid =586&e=3&u=/nm/20030722/wl_nm/mideast_jerusalem_dc
Peres Raises 'World Capital' Solution for Jerusalem
JERUSALEM (Reuters) - **Shimon Peres, the head of Israel's opposition Labor Party, has suggested resolving Israeli-Palestinian conflict over Jerusalem by putting its holy sites under U.N. stewardship, a spokesman said Tuesday.**
His plan calls for declaring a holy area of sites sacred to Jews, Christians and Muslims in Jerusalem's old walled city as a **"world capital,"** with the **U.N. Secretary-General serving as mayor**, Peres' spokesman Yoram Dori told Reuters.
Israel claims Jerusalem as its capital, including the Arab eastern part captured in the 1967 Middle East War and annexed in a move that is not recognized internationally.

Palestinians want to make East Jerusalem capital of the state they hope to establish in the West Bank and Gaza Strip (<u>news</u> - <u>web sites</u>) under a U.S.-backed peace plan.

Peres raised the idea in a meeting with visiting Russian diplomats-in-training when they asked how he envisaged a solution to conflicting Israeli-Palestinian claims to the city, Dori said.

Israel has previously rejected proposals raised by the Vatican (<u>news</u> - <u>web sites</u>) to internationalize Jerusalem.

Peres, a former prime minister and an architect of interim peace deals with the Palestinians, has not raised the proposal with Israeli or Palestinian leaders, Dori said.

THE JERUSALEM POST added that under the Peres plan, the sovereignty of the holy places would revert to their owners. And since the Vatican has the lion's share of real estate claims, guess who gets to own the most holy land in Jerusalem?

AFTER PERES let the cat out of the bag, I was deluged with letters asking how ten years ago I knew this was his real objective. The explanation is found in Save Israel, pp. 131:

In March 1994, the newspaper Chadashot revealed a most remarkable secret of the Middle East "peace" process. A friend of Shimon Peres, the French intellectual Marek Halter, claimed in an interview that in May 1993, he delivered a letter from Peres to the pope. Within, Peres promised to internationalize Jerusalem, granting the UN political control of the Old City of Jerusalem, and the Vatican hegemony of the holy sites within. The UN would give the PLO a capital within its new territory and East Jerusalem would become a kind of free trade zone of world diplomacy.

Halter's claim was backed by the Italian newspaper La Stampa which added that Arafat was apprised of the agreement and it was included in the secret clauses of the Declaration Of Principles signed in Washington in September 1993.

In March 1995, the Israeli radio station Arutz Sheva was leaked a cable from the Israeli Embassy in Rome to Peres's Foreign Ministry in Jerusalem confirming the handover of Jerusalem to the Vatican. This cable was printed on the front page of the radical leftwing Israeli newspaper, Haaretz two days later. A scandal erupted and numerous rabbis who had invited Peres for Passover services cancelled their invitations in protest of his treachery. Peres reacted by claiming that the cable was real but that someone had whited out the word, "not;" the cable really said that Israel would "not" hand Jerusalem over to the holy pontiff.

Illustrating the sorry political state of Israel's rabbis, they accepted this cockamamie excuse and re-invited Peres to their tables. However, in the widely distributed minutes of a meeting with Clinton in 1997, Peres reiterated his diplomacy, ending with the words, "as I had previously promised the Holy See."

**

Save Israel pp. 82-86

THREE MORE DEAD IN RABIN RAMPAGE

The latest Rabin hushup murders were Dr. Dalia Eyal, her husband Nimrod Eyal and son Assaf. Dalia Eyal had been employed at Ichilov Hospital since the early 1980s. Currently, she was director of a health fund located there but shift-worked in the trauma department throughout her career at Ichilov. So far, she has not been positively located in the trauma center on the night Yitzhak Rabin died there but let's not rule out the possibility. What is certain is that she knew the doctors and nurses who attended Rabin and was privy to the truth.

Let us repeat the murder motive: Dr. Eyal undoubtedly knew how Rabin was really murdered.

Who conducted the autopsy on the Eyal family? Dr. Death himself, Yehuda Hiss, the head of the police pathological institute, which was raided last week for hoarding the internal organs of 81 corpses without informing the families of the dead. And as we all know, it was Dr. Death Hiss who changed Rabin's wounds in his infamous pathologist's report.

Let us repeat the motive for the coverup: Dr. Eyal knew Hiss lied about Rabin's real wounds.

Now let's look at another really sloppy mass murder.

The Chronology Of A Slaughter

Thursday night, Jan. 10 - Dalia and Nimrod Eyal die embracing in their bed. Friday morning - Jan. 11 - Assaf, 22, dies sitting upright in a salon chair. According to the Jerusalem Post (15/1/2002): "Police theorize that Assaf came home and found his family dead. Failing to detect the presence of the odorless, colorless gas, he too, passed out and died."

Saturday, Jan. 12 - Yona Eliad, Nimrod's brother-in-law, discovers the bodies, as well as the family cats, very much alive.. Police announce that it was an apparent family suicide. Friends and relatives of the Eyals vigorously deny the   possibility.
Sunday, Jan. 13 - Police reinvestigate and come up with the answer within a day. From the Jerusalem Post: "They died as a result of inhaling carbon monoxide fumes leaked from the water heater in their closed luxury apartment, after a bird's nest blocked the exhaust pipe." The Post reports that about 100 victims a winter, "are overcome by gas from home heaters," though only one hospital in the country is equipped to revive carbon monoxide poisoning victims.

Now let's start thinking clearly:

The Bird's Nest - Birds do not nest in Israel in January. They do not put up a nest overnight anywhere in any season. They do not put up a nest on a pipe venting carbon monoxide. If they tried, they would not finish the nest.

159

The weather - It has been cold and rainy for most of the winter. The water heater was not turned on for the first time that night. If a summer nest had blocked the exhaust vent, the Eyals would have discovered it or suffocated by the cold November past.

The cats - The bodies were discovered 48 hours after they had succumbed. The apartment was sealed. The cats should have died as well by then.

The son - Assaf comes home, discovers his dead parents and instead of immediately calling an ambulance, sits down on a comfy chair and dies.

Ichilov Hospital - Every doctor and nurse who tended Rabin on Nov. 4/1995 has received written and verbal death threats. Two of the doctors, Kluger and Gutman, suffered unexplainable and almost fatal disorders. They learned to be silent afterward. Dr. Eyal, it seems, had not properly learned the lesson...

By murdering Dr. Dalia Eyal, one ticking bomb was neutralized but there are many more. So, expect many more murders. The Eyal family was poisoned, maybe with CO, maybe with another asphyxiating substance. And it wasn't a little birdie that did it.

NOW LET us look at the following item, reported by all the major Israeli media. Hebrew readers, please visit:
http://rotter.net/forum/scoop/6775.shtml

FOR everyone else, here is the translation:

Sunday, June 15, 2003 - Paz Gaz-
The Eyal Family Died Of Cyanide Poisoning

Paz Gaz presented the findings of its investigation of the deaths of the three members of the Eyal family and concluded they died of cyanide poisoning, possibly caused by a fire in the clothes dryer...

160

OR, JUST as likely, by being force-fed cyanide.

***

Self-explanatory. Save Israel pp.216
"Israeli biological and nuclear scientists are being knocked off one by one and this covert war is going unnoticed. A plane carrying scientists to Russia's biological warfare center at Novosibirsk was blown up over the Black Sea and no one questions that the Ukrainian missile that supposedly did the job was a hundred miles out of range. Then a Swissair Corsair crashes killing the head of Ichilov Hospital's Hematology department, as well as directors of the Hebrew University School Of Medicine and the Tel Aviv Public Health Department and not a word of suspicion is raised. "

http://www.rense.com/general21/micromarconi.htm
http://www.cooperativeresearch.org/timeline/main/AAanthrax.html

***

SO FAR, about no one believed me when I wrote that Peres wants to hand Jerusalem over to the Vatican and UN; now they have to believe me. Not many believed me when I wrote that a plane exploding over the Black Sea was, in fact, the murder of Israel's top microbiologists. Today, this serial removal of micobiologists is acknowledged worldwide. And just about everyone thought a bird's nest suffocated the Eyal family until I pointed out that in Israel and all northern countries, birds don't nest in January.

AND NOW onto the biggest claim of Save Israel, which is that the Council On Foreign Relations (CFR) runs American diplomacy and that its intentions towards Jews are deadly, no matter how many Jewish pawns are members of the think tank.

A READER provides more verification, as if any more

were really needed. However, since Jews are notoriously slow to catch on, add this to the pile of evidence:

A while back I wrote an article titled "The Council on Foreign Relations & Mein Kampf" http://www.geocities.com/CapitolHill/2807/emhitler.html.

It fits in well with the material in your e-mail. It reveals that at least two editors of the American Version of Mein Kampf were Council on Foreign Relations members. They were also OSS operatives. One of the Editors, George N. Shuster, was closely connected with the Church. The article doesn't go into the connection. Among other things he was editor of a Catholic publication called Commonweal.

Many CFR members are connected to Georgetown University. It is a Jesuit University in Washington DC. Clinton graduated from Georgetown. One of his Georgetown University professors was Carroll Quigley, author of Tragedy and
Hope.

***

THE POINT BEING, nothing is fantastic. Not even the background of the Madrid bombings.

ALM 5 - WHY THE MADRID BOMBINGS

(Many of the following concepts will be unfamiliar to those who have not been following my research steadily. It is the author's contention that Spain is playing a central, though covert, role in Middle East diplomacy, believing it has a God-given, if Medieval, right to rule Israel and especially Jerusalem. Its Jesuit King, Juan Carlos, owns the title, Protector Of The Holy Places Of Jerusalem, and he takes the responsibility seriously, as do his superiors in Rome.)

The Spanish people are clamoring to know who was responsible for the March '04
bombings which killed over 200 of their people. They will not receive a true answer. They will be told Al Qaida did the deed in retaliation for Spain's support of the Iraq invasion and will display some Moslem bombers as proof.

The more conspiratorial analyses places the blame on the Bush/Blair New World Order gang who fomented another atrocity to justify their war on terror and give a boost to its flagging popularity. All such proponents point to the conveniently found van with the Koranic audiotape beside the unignited bombs as a set-up, like the 9-11 van with the Koran and 767 flight manual found in Boston.

The Spanish government initially lied to its people, claiming ETA, the Basque separatists, were the main suspects and were thrown out of power in national elections a few days later, which seemed to be a motive for the outrage in the first place.

The lie was formulated to keep the public off the real trail of the bombings, which leads to Spain's secret role in the Middle East, as well as its goal of eliminating Israel by shoving a suicidal "peace" process down its throat. The leaders of the Middle East know Spain controls their fate, and that all diplomatic roads pass through Madrid.

But the rest of humanity remains ignorant of Spain's covert power. Let us try and clear the fog with the events that led to the slaughter in Madrid as seen through the media. My commentary will begin and end with three stars ** *.

We begin the journey that led to the bombings on Aug. 18 '03. On that day, the PA prime minister Abbas, and his foreign minister Shaat, announced they would be visiting Damascus on September 8. The announcement was made as Spain's Foreign Minister is in Damascus announcing that his king will be visiting Syria that autumn.

So, the story begins as the PA, Syria and King Juan Carlos plot to coordinate diplomacy.

Abbas to meet with al-Assad in Syria in September
Syria-Palestine, Politics, 8/18/2003
Palestinian foreign affairs minister Nabil Shaath said that the
Palestinian prime minister Mahmoud Abbas will visit
Damascus in September.

Shaath explained following his talks with the Syrian foreign
minister Farouk al-Shara in Damascus that the Palestinian
leadership wants to deepen consultation and coordination
with each of Syria and Lebanon concerning the peace
process in the region.

The Palestinian minister said that Abbas will meet during the
forthcoming visit with President Bashar al-Assad.
http://www.middle-east-online.com/english/syria/?id=6468
Spain's King to visit Syria

Spain's economy minister announces King Juan Carlos,
Queen Sofia are to visit Syria in autumn.

DAMASCUS - King Juan Carlos and Queen Sofia of Spain
are to visit Syria in the autumn, Spanish Economy Minister
Rodrigo Rato said here Monday.
Rato told a news conference that he had informed Syrian
President Bashar al-Assad of the visit.
Assad and his wife Asma paid an official visit to Spain in May
2001 - the couple's first to a Western country after Assad
took power in July 2000.
Rato, who arrived in Damascus Sunday night, said his own
visit also aimed to "strengthen economic relations" between
the two countries, particularly in the tourism, transport and
industry sectors.

*He said Spain supports Syria "economically and politically",
adding that Damascus is important in the quest for peace in
the Middle East.*
*Spain also supports talks to broker a partnership agreement
between Syria and the European Union, the minister said.*
*A Syrian-Spanish accord giving Damascus five million dollars
was signed Monday, Rato added.*

*** Now why would Spain commit itself to pushing for a
Syrian partnership   agreement with the EU? What could
Syria offer the EU but some canned dates and its fine human
rights record? Note the $5 million bribe to Assad and ask
what was behind it. The PA's prime minister lands in
Damascus on September 8 and look at the reaction on
September 9. ***

Article....
http://www.scoop.co.nz/mason/stories/WO0309/S00113.htm
Powell, Palacio Discuss Middle East, Iraq, UN

Tuesday, 9 September 2003, 9:34 pm
Press Release: US State Department

http://english.daralhayat.com/world_news/09-
2003/20030913-20030913-9a701d2b-c0a8-01ed-0036-
3068473ecbbf/story.html

*Spanish Foreign Minister Says Israeli Threat To Expel Arafat
Is A Big Mistake*
*....."We (the Spanish government) have always said that
Arafat has been part of the solution and the decision by the
Israeli government (to expel him) is a big mistake," she told
reporters.*
*...Palacio spoke at a joint press conference with Syrian
counterpart Farouk al-Sharaa after arriving in Damascus on
the first leg of a three-nation tour, which includes Iraq and
Kuwait.*

...Palacio said her talks with al-Sharaa focused on Israel's threat to expel Arafat, plus Iraq.

...She said Syria and Spain shared some basic principles, including the role some regional players could have in Iraq's reconstruction and returning that country to its rightful place in the international community.

Al-Sharaa said Syria and Spain have identical views on Iraq, including the maintenance of its integrity and "getting rid of the foreign occupation as soon as possible."

He said both states also believed in the formation of a legitimate Iraqi government elected by Iraqi people.

*** The PA prime minister has just left and a day later Spain's Foreign Minister announced that he will be meeting with Colin Powell of the Council On Foreign Relations (CFR). And where was the announcement made but in Damascus? But look what else is in the Spanish FM's repartee. First comes the defence of Arafat against Israeli threats to expel him for his direction of terror against their country. Then come what have to be huge lies. Do Spain and Syria really hold "identical views" on Iraq? Is Spain really in favor of "getting rid of the foreign occupation" or its American and British partners, in Iraq?

Or was Spain threatened by Syria with terrifying violence?

When Palacio met Powell did she pass on the message that if American troops don't get out of Iraq, Syria would pulverize us at home? She most certainly did, but since the troops are still there, Powell obviously didn't pay heed, or care.

However, Powell and his CFR backers must have given Spain still another assignment...Libya. ***

http://famulus.msnbc.com/FamulusIntl/reuters09-17-131342.asp?reg=MIDEAST
Spanish PM makes historic Libya visit

166

A Spanish government source said Aznar's ground-breaking trip was aimed at helping bring Libya back into the international fold.

Spain would like to see Libya play a bigger role in the partnership between the 15-nation European Union and 12 Mediterranean countries. Libya has observer status in the grouping at present.

*** And now we know who was behind Libya renouncing its weapons of mass destruction. Little old Spain must have carried one nasty message to persuade Libya to return to the fold. And in the process, Spain must have angered not a few of Libya's terrorist allies.

Now we step forward to October 4 when Maxim's Restaurant was bombed in Haifa, killing 22, including members of one of Israel's most prestigious military families. Israel reacts by bombing empty warehouses in Syria.

But note Syria's reaction to the futile attack on its soil. It threatens to re-open the MADRID conference of 1991, a very peculiar threat indeed and one which must have meant something to those in the know in Israel.

Spain, apparently got the message, condemned Israel's attack and stepped up Juan Carlos' visit to Damascus. ***

http://www.haaretzdaily.com/hasen/spages/347908.html

Syria vows military response if Israeli attacks continue.

Last paragraph:

Asked if that meant militarily, he said: "By all means. If Israel continues to attack us and continues its aggression of course we shall react to the attacks in spite of the fact that we are fighting for peace and wish to reopen the (1991) Madrid (peace) conference."

http://www.middle-east-online.com/english/?id=7460
Spanish king meets Syrian leader in Damascus

...Madrid condemned Israel's raid on a suspected militant Palestinian training camp near Damascus on October 5 - the first such attack in 30 years and one which Washington regarded as self-defence.

The English-language government daily, Syria Times, hailed the royal visit as "an important event" that will "rectify the holes in the relations between the Arabs and the West" and "play a significant role in the dialogue between Islam and Christianity".

Talks will redress the "many misunderstanding in the West about Syria's attitudes towards Iraq and Palestinian resistance," the paper added.

Spanish diplomats say the trip is intended to foster "intensified political dialogue" between Damascus, Madrid and the European Union.

For the past six years, Syria has been negotiating a partnership accord with Brussels due to be signed at the end of 2003, after Assad ordered discussions to be stepped up a gear.

http://www.europedaily.com/p/0f/553df16bb687.html?id=16bc11b

http://www.arabicnews.com/ansub/Daily/Day/031017/2003101701.html

king of Spain to visit Syria
Syria-Spain, Politics, 10/17/2003

At the invitation of President Bashar al-Assad and his Wife, King Juan Carlos and Queen Sofia of Spain pay an official visit to Syria during the period from 19 to 23 of the current month.

*** And now Juan Carlos is in Damascus and the fun begins. We have already observed that the Syrians are doing their best to drive a wedge between Spain and America, or more precisely, the CFR.

Now observe the machinations. While Juan Carlos is in Damascus, Yossi Beilin is in Geneva formulating an alternative diplomacy which gives the Arabs all they want. Once the ink is on the paper, Beilin flies to Washington to meet with Powell. A concerted effort is being made to appease the Arabs at the cost of Israel's basic security.

However,,Spain offers Syria the ultimate appeasement; a renewed Syrian empire if it behaves itself. ***

.....al-Assad visits Spain to inaugurate the role of the Umayyads with KJC and other officials.....two days later PJP visits Syria to visit the Umayyad Temple and call for inter-faith dialogue. Interesting the way visits go.......KJC visits Spain Oct. 19 just after the Geneva Accord is announced but just before it is signed in Geneva on Nov. 4th.
http://www.arabicnews.com/ansub/Daily/Day/010504/200105 0413.html

Damascus 18-10 (SANA)-

President Bashar al-Assad, in a speech opening the Fair of "From Damascus to Cordova" during a visit he paid with the First lady to Spain, said " the Arab civilization in Andalusia was an important era marked with accord, tolerance, social and intellectual richness among different peoples. That era transferred the civilization from Shami-Andalusia to Arab-Andalusia, creating a sort of civilization merger that it was impossible to attain without the dialogue among civilizations".

Syria has always sought as a strategic aim for dialogue, not conflict, among civilizations, and has always called for fostering meeting points among cultures of different peoples, for the creation of a civilized, harmonious mixture that takes humanity to higher levels.

From this point of view, Syria looks for the forthcoming visit of His Majesty King of Spain Juan Carlos and Her Majesty Queen Sofia, and warmly welcomes their Majesties The Royal Couple in Damascus, capital of the Omayads who were the first to establish and deepen the dialogue of civilizations when they set for Europe and the world through Andalusia to spread their message of tolerance. They also carried with them the latest digest of human thinking in various fields of knowledge, assisted by the fertile land in Andalusia, for long the settling point for different ancient civilizations. That climate led to a unique state of interaction and communication among civilizations in the Omayad-Andalusia epoch, and became an example for the whole world. Cordova at that time attracted Europe as a source of new knowledge in philosophy, arts, architecture, poetry and literatures.

We also pin great hopes on this visit for strengthening existing relations of cooperation between Syria and Spain, and through her with the European countries to further deepen a constructive dialogue and the establishment of a real partnership based on reciprocal respect, equity and mutual benefit. We hope that the European countries would take a more active role in building world peace, establishing security and stability in the Middle East region by bringing about a just and comprehensive peace and the return of rights to their owners so that this would be positively reflected on the region's prosperity and for the sake of dialogue, not conflict, among civilizations.

Welcome to His Majesty King of Spain, to Her Majesty Queen of Spain, to Damascus the land civilizations and cradle of divine faiths which call for amity and peace.

http://www.library.cornell.edu/colldev/mideast/popsyr.htm
http://www.cbc.ca/stories/2003/10/13/genevaaccord031013

The 'Geneva Accord' will be released with great ceremony in Switzerland on Nov. 4.
Nov. 27, 2003

Accusations mar London talks; Israeli-PA forum in Madrid
By JPOST.COM STAFF

Madrid: International forum seeking a solution to the Israel-Palestinian problem
Meanwhile, Israeli Knesset members and Palestinian administration officials are meeting in Madrid as guests of an international forum seeking a solution to the Israel-Palestinian problem, Israel Radio reported Friday.
Among the guests are also ex-US ambassador to Israel Martin Indyk, ex-EU special envoy Miguel Morratinos, ex-Jordanian foreign minister Abdullah Hativ and Spanish government officials.
Israeli delegates include MK Gideon Sa'ar (Likud, MKs Dalia Itzik and Danny Yatom (Labor) and MK Ahmed Tibi (Balad). Mohammed Dahlan and Nabil Sha'at are representing the Palestinian side.

*** Now how do you like that? Look who's meeting in MADRID just a month after Juan Carlos' sojourn in Damascus? Why its the creme de la creme of the Israeli government and parliamentary opposition, the head tyrants of the PA, the one and only Martin Indyk of Oslo fame, all meeting Spanish officials. Now what makes MADRID such a magnet for these NWO bigshots?

Whatever came of these meetings, the world public is not privileged to know. But immediately after, Pres. Bush made us all privy to the consensus. Whatever the BARCELONA process may be, it was central to his State Of The Union address: ***

http://www.reuters.com/newsArticle.jhtml?type=reutersEdge&storyID=4159384

BRUSSELS (Reuters) - *The United States is seeking to engage European allies in President Bush's drive for democracy in the greater Middle East, partly to heal the rifts of the Iraq war.*

U.S. officials say involving Europeans through both NATO and the European Union in the initiative launched by Bush late last year is one of the administration's top priorities for 2004.

Bush is expected to give more pointers to his approach in his State of the Union message to Congress Tuesday.

"We are looking at ways to work better together with the EU on the greater Middle East, in security, economically and in promoting democracy and human rights, as we did in the Cold War toward Eastern Europe," a U.S. official in Brussels said.

He said Washington wanted to build on the EU's existing Euro-Mediterranean dialogue -- known as the Barcelona process -- which offers North African and East Mediterranean partner states trade and aid benefits in return for economic and political cooperation and reform.

*** Now compare his father's State Of The Union Address. ***

State of the Union address Jan. 29/91 George Bush Sr.
http://www.geocities.com/americanpresidencynet/1991.htm
"What is at stake is more than one small country; it is a big idea: a new world order, where diverse nations are drawn together in common cause to achieve the universal aspirations of mankind -- peace and security, freedom, and the rule of law. Such is a world worthy of our struggle and worthy of our children's future.

"We have within our reach the promise of a renewed America. We can find meaning and reward by serving some

higher purpose than ourselves, a shining purpose, the illumination of a Thousand Points of Light. And it is expressed by all who know the irresistible force of a child's hand, of a friend who stands by you and stays there, a volunteer's generous gesture, an idea that is simply right."

*** This was a State Of The Union address that no one apparently understood. Whatever this BARCELONA process is, it inspired the President to announce a "New World Order," illuminated by "a thousand points of light." The Spanish diplomacy was more than part and parcel of the world order we are entering, it was central to it.

So what is this Barcelona Process that Bush is certain will usher in a new order on the planet? Let us go back four years before the Madrid bombing to get well more than a hint ***

http://www.arabicnews.com/ansub/Daily/Day/000522/200005 2252.html

Mubarak's Madrid visit to focus on Euro-Mediterranean cooperation
Egypt-Spain, Politics, 5/22/2000

"President Hosni Mubarak's itinerary of the visit to begin on May 29 includes three separate meetings with King Juan Carlos, in addition to expanded session of talks with Prime Minister Jose Maria Aznar and the speakers of the Congress of Deputies and the Senate," he said.

"The issue of Euro-Mediterranean partnership is expected to top the agenda of talks with Spanish officials, specifically on the activation of the Barcelona process, and the Middle East peace process started in Madrid and bilateral relations," he said.

Ambassador Haridi stressed the importance of activating the Barcelona process during President Mubarak's visit to Spain.

173

"The EU will expand in the near future and European states will be busy trying to acclimatize themselves with this expansion," he said.

"It is this pre-occupation with how to correspond to and face these new changes that raise fears among south-of-the Mediterranean states," he added.

Will Europe's interest in Euro-Mediterranean partnership and the Barcelona process subside?, he questioned.

"Spain is the European country to activate the Barcelona process and to set aside fears arising in this respect, given its geographic proximity to the Arab world and its exceptional relationship with Egypt in particular and Arab countries in general," Ambassador Haridi told MENA.

"Spain presented the Mediterranean initiative to the European union to unite all European policies in one that all states must follow," he said.

*** So Spain has chosen itself, or has been chosen, to unite the warring factions of this simmering World War III. It plays the role of the Jesuit mediator between all the factions: Islam versus the EU, Vatican, Bilderberg, CFR, or to simplify matters, Europe and America. However it may try to fool Islam, its sympathies lie with what is known as the West. And Islam is getting madder and madder. All the bones thrown at it are not calming the wolf.

And the Islamic wolf is clearly catching on to the deeper game. Now we reach one of the most significant acts which preceded the Madrid bombing, that somehow was   left unconnected to the upcoming carnage.

Two days before the Madrid mass murder, a Masonic Lodge was bombed to rubble in Istanbul. This was not a coincidence, it was a message. And one can be certain, the real power brokers got it.

One of the points of the so-called illumination that Pres. Bush referred to was the Sabbataian movement. Founded by followers of the false Jewish messiah, Shabtai Tzvi in the

1660s by the Donmeh cult of Turkey, this anti-Jewish cult determined to upend humanity's morality, and found a home in the lodges of Turkish Freemasonry. From Turkey, the movement spread through Europe in the 18th century through Jacob Frank and his followers, the Frankists. However, others have reached the conclusion that this is one of the main addresses of the NWO Bush referred to as coming out of the Barcelona process: The Turkish bombing preceding Madrid was no coincidence. And Turkey was all set to play its role in the creation of the new planetary order.***

Fritz Springmeier, who is currently in Federal prison, has written several books on Illuminati blood lines. In Illuminati Formula for Undetectable Total Mind Control we read: "There is a connection between Marxism and a group of Satanists called Frankists. One of the strongest satanic cults to take control over the Jewish population was called Sabbatianism. Jacob Frank assumed the role of leader of this group, and afterward this brand of satanism was called Frankism. (Freud's sexually-obsessed theories came from Frankism.) Frank taught his followers to convert to another religion and hide behind that religion to practice their satanism. (One of several books on the subject of Frankism is The Contemporary Faces of Satan by Ratibor-Ray M. Jurjevich.)

*** The Islamic rulers want no part of the New World Order. All the bribes and attractions to Syria are falling on deaf ears. So in comes Vatican agent Shimon Peres to sweeten the deal.
Though the leader of merely the Israeli opposition, Peres will back an Israel mortally weakened, joining a coalition of Arab states in a united World Order led by Europe, led by Spain. And where does this wacky proposal to unite Islam and Europe get its public airing but in MADRID? And where will the agreement be signed, but in Istanbul? ***

175

NATO to upgrade relations with Israel
By ASSOCIATED PRESS

NATO is seeking to deepen political and military contacts with Israel and a number of Arab states and may invite their representatives to a summit of alliance leaders in June, officials said Thursday.

According to The Associated Press, it was not yet clear at what level these nations would be represented at the June 28 - 29 summit in Istanbul, Turkey.

http://www.haaretzdaily.com/hasen/spages/391957.html

Spain offers EU ties as incentive for peace talks

Spain will help Israel and the Palestinians achieve closer ties to the European Union as an incentive to advance the Middle East peace process, Spanish Foreign Minister Ana Palacio said Sunday.
Peres brought the proposal up the day before in Madrid at a meeting of the Socialist International.

On Sunday, the co-winner of the 1994 Nobel Peace Prize said, "Once the two parties reach an agreement for peace, each will be admitted to the European Union, and the European Union will serve as a common ground for economic and social life."

http://story.news.yahoo.com/news?tmpl=story&u=/040208/481/xpw11102081747

Spain offers EU ties as incentive for peace talks

Spain will help Israel and the Palestinians achieve closer ties to the European Union as an incentive to advance the

176

Middle East peace process, Spanish Foreign Minister Ana Palacio said Sunday.

Her remarks came on the same day that Jordanian King Abdullah called for a "heavy-handed" international alliance to force a negotiated settlement on Israel and the Palestinians, who he said had shown they were incapable of making peace alone.

Speaking at a brief news conference in Toledo with Labor Party Chairman Shimon Peres and Palestinian negotiations minister Saeb Erekat, Palacio said that, "an association of Palestine and Israel" with the EU at "the conclusion of this peace process... is an idea" worth consideration.

"We need to discuss it in the European Union and see how we can integrate it into the peace process," she added. "So, my commitment is to discuss it, to put it before European" institutions.

Peres brought the proposal up the day before in Madrid at a meeting of the Socialist International.

On Sunday, the co-winner of the 1994 Nobel Peace Prize said, "Once the two parties reach an agreement for peace, each will be admitted to the European Union, and the European Union will serve as a common ground for economic and social life."

Asked whether the proposal really was membership in the European Union, he replied, "There are variations how to do it. And anyway, the European Union already put their legs in the Mediterranean by admitting Cyprus and Malta. So they're no longer innocent. They're Mediterranean."

*** And who is the ultimate source behind the Peres sellout of Israel; who lo and behold but the Vatican? Without an ounce of understanding of who is manipulating their nations and cultures, both Israelis and Moslems have rejected the plots of the New World Order. The difference is in style. Israel tries to limit civilian mortality while Islam attempts to increase it for effect.

The inciters of world violence know this difference and exploit it. But subtract the style for now, and reach a common cause: Judaism and Islam are being tricked into slaughtering each other by precisely the same forces. Israel has paid deeply for the hidden war between planetary fascism and now Madrid got a taste of the same medicine Jerusalem has been forced to swallow since Oslo was foisted on it in 1993.

Now trace the common address for both of our pain: ***

http://www.haaretzdaily.com/hasen/spages/391957.html

Qorei, who has yet to meet with his Israeli counterpart Ariel Sharon since taking office last autumn, confirmed he hopes the meeting could take place by "the end of this month if the preparation succeed."

Palestinian foreign minister Nabil Shaath said the meeting could take place as early as next week.

"We are determined to pursue the peace process and that is why the meeting will take place around February 20," he said at a joint news conference in Madrid with Spanish Foreign Minister Ana Palacio.

The EU advocates Israel and the Palestinians taking a series of small steps to move the peace process forward, and said such measures should be discussed by the prime ministers at their meeting, said Ahern.

Qorei heads next to Italy, where he will meet late Tuesday with Prime Minister Silvio Berlusconi, and on Wednesday with President Carlo Azeglio Ciampi and lawmakers.

On Thursday Qorei is due to meet with Pope John Paul II at the Vatican.

*** The same forces are at work: the CFR, Jesuit Vatican, and Sabbataians. Spain has chosen itself as the uniter of all these factions with Islam. Islam rejected the offer in Madrid with its own form of heartless evil. And this battle between two evils will continue to engulf the world. Israel is at the forefront of the war, but Madrid offered a foul taste of what's in store for all of us. ***

ALM 6 - HERE COME THE TROOPS

For the past ten years I've been repeating the same message: The Oslo "Peace" process was a planned war process whose final goal was the occupation of Israel and, especially, Jerusalem, by the troops of the architects of the global takeover known commonly as the New World Order. Soon we will witness the fulfillment of still another logical prediction as Israel turns into another Bosnia, Afghanistan or Iraq and patrons of Jerusalem's outdoor cafes will see UN/US tanks rolling past their tables.

The following pattern is self-evident, yet Israelis continue to miss its significance, and don't ask me how. I'll let the items speak for themselves. As always, when I intrude with an observation, it will begin and end with ***.

http://www.menewsline.com/stories/2003/august/08_27_1.html

U.S. considers international force to stop Israeli-PA war

WASHINGTON [MENL] -- The United States has been examining the prospect of organizing an international force to stop the Israeli-Palestinian war. "We're not talking about another U.S. military deployment," an official said. "Instead, we're discussing a NATO-type heavily-armed combat force that would be based mostly on troop contributions from Europe. There has been some discussions and positive feedback from some of our European friends."

Thursday, August 28, 2003
[10,000 Human Shields?] U.S. MULLS INTERNATIONAL FORCE FOR PA

[IMRA: What exactly could a heavily armed combat force sent by countries whose top priority is to keep on the good side of the Arabs do? Protect terrorists from Israeli security forces.]

WASHINGTON [MENL] -- The United States has been examining the prospect of organizing an international force to stop the Israeli-Palestinian war. Officials said both the Bush administration and Congress have quietly discussed an effort to recruit at least one division of combat troops that would patrol the West Bank and Gaza Strip and enforce a Palestinian ceasefire with Israel. They said many in the administration and Congress have concluded that a Palestinian state can not be established without an international force that will impose a ceasefire in the region.

"We're not talking about another U.S. military deployment," an official said. "Instead, we're discussing a NATO-type heavily-armed combat force that would be based mostly on troop contributions from Europe. There has been some discussions and positive feedback from some of our European friends." Officials said congressional leaders, both Democrats and Republicans, have supported the deployment of U.S. troops in the Palestinian areas as part of an international force. They said NATO and the international community would require at least a pool of 30,000 troops, aircraft and armored platforms to form a credible deterrent against Palestinian insurgency groups that operate in the West Bank and Gaza Strip. At any one time, about 10,000 troops would patrol the West Bank and Gaza Strip in cooperation with Israel and the Palestinian Authority.

The troops are coming. get ready. Feinstein is big CFR mouthpiece as is Lugar. Get ready. http://www.sfgate.com/cgi-bin/article.cgi?f=/news/archive/2003/08/24/national1457EDT0489.DTL

E.U. - RAPID DEPLOYMENT FORCE AIMED AT ISRAEL (NOTE THE DATE 12/22/02) by Emanuel A. Winston, a Middle East analyst & commentator

For some time I have detected and written about the stench of European collaboration with Jewish Leftists and various Arabists in the U.S. State Department. It was hard to put together because such groups are not anxious to announce their intentions nor show collaboration.

However, more is surfacing. For example: The E.U., (European Union) wishes to assemble a RDF (Rapid Deployment Force). Such a Force needs a 'raison d'etre' (reason for being) or at least an excuse. One reason will be to deploy European and, possibly, Canadian forces in the Middle East to forcibly 'separate' Israel and the Arab Palestinians. (Read this article and plan carefully.) That translates into sending forces into Israel, against that nation's will to ostensibly force into existence another Arab Palestinian State. This requires 'protecting' the 'unwarlike' Arab Palestinians after they conduct Terrorist operations, from Israeli counter-Terrorism assaults. Seemingly unconnected, it is in fact a direct extension of the Bush "Road Map" plan which will start its implementation at the end of January 2003 - in one month?!?

Since the E.U. does not have any troops of its own, it wishes to borrow from existing NATO's standing military, including men, equipment, tanks, planes, ammunition, planning, computer technology, etc. Much of this armament has been supplied by America (at U.S. tax-payer's expense). Any decisions by NATO to allow this transfer must have approval of the American Administration.

Since this may seem contrary to the Bush/Cheney/Rice/Rumsfeld mind-set, is it possible that such approval has been given by the U.S. State Department as the main operator of the Quartet, which includes the E.U., United Nations and Russia. Perhaps the State Department even orchestrated this concept.

Saudi FM Hails Idea of International Forces in [Arab-Israeli]Mideast Conflict

CEP20030903000130 Moscow ITAR-TASS in English 1302 GMT 3 Sep 03

[FBIS Transcribed Text] [By Olga Levitskaya, Maria Pshenichnikova]

[With thanks to www.mideastweb.org/mewnews1.htm]

MOSCOW, September 3 (Itar-Tass) - Deployment of international forces in the zone of the Palestinian-Israeli conflict might be the best way of stopping bloodshed there, Saudi Arabia's Foreign Minister Prince Saud al-Faisal told reporters Wednesday after a meeting with the Russian Foreign Minister, Igor Ivanov.

While the Israeli government is sticking to the use-of-force tactics against the Palestinian people, introduction of international disengagement forces into the area seems to be the only way of settling the problem, Prince Saud said. The best of putting an end to the bloodshed would be to exert effective international pressure on Israel, he indicated.

Discussions of the Palestinian problem have revealed the closeness of Russian and Saudi positions, Prince Saud said.

-0-kle 031600 SEP 03

[Description of Source: Moscow ITAR-TASS in English -- main government
   information agency]

http://news.bbc.co.uk/1/hi/world/middle_east/1470680.stm
Thursday, 2 August, 2001, 17:54 GMT 18:54 UK

As tensions continued to escalate on Thursday, Palestinian leader Yasser Arafat met Italian Prime Minister Silvio Berlusconi and Pope John Paul II as part of a drive to win support for a team of international observers to monitor clashes between Israel and the Palestinians.

Interesting day in ME diplomacy........Saudi Prince meets with King Mohammed VI,
http://www.riyadhdaily.com.sa/display_assay.php?id=35234
Wed. Aug. 27, 2003
Saudi Crown Prince visits Egypt, Syria, Morocco......and Spanish King all in a day's news........and KJC visits Syria soon.

Casabanca [Agencies].................................

Crown Prince Abdullah bin Abdulaziz, deputy premier and commander of the National Guard of the Kingdom of Saudi Arabia, arrived in Casablanca Monday for a state visit to Morocco, his third leg of a four-nation tour which already took him to Syria and Egypt. He is scheduled to visit Russia at the end of the tour.

Crown Prince Abdullah's official delegation comprises Prince Nawaf bin Abdulaziz, chief of General Intelligence, Prince Faisal bin Abdullah bin Mohammed Al-Saud, assistant chief of General Intelligence, Prince Mohammed bin Nawaf bin Abdulaziz, ambassador of the Kingdom to Italy and senior protocol officials.

August 27, 2003 -
Spanish King receives Saudi Governor for talks

Spain's King Juan Carlos received in Mallorca on Wednesday Prince Salman bin Abdulaziz, the Governor of Riyadh region, SPA reported.

In the course of the reception, the Spanish Monarch and Saudi official exchanged cordial talks and discussed bilateral relations between both countries.

(Albawaba.com)

http://www.middle-east-online.com/english/syria/?id=6468
Spain's King to visit Syria

Spain's economy minister announces King Juan Carlos, Queen Sofia are to visit Syria in autumn.

DAMASCUS - King Juan Carlos and Queen Sofia of Spain are to visit Syria in the autumn, Spanish Economy Minister Rodrigo Rato said here Monday. Rato told a news conference that he had informed Syrian President Bashar al-Assad of the visit. Assad and his wife Asma paid an official visit to Spain in May 2001 - the couple's first to a Western country after Assad took power in July 2000. Rato, who arrived in Damascus Sunday night, said his own visit also aimed to "strengthen economic relations" between the two countries, particularly in the tourism, transport and industry sectors. **He said Spain supports Syria "economically and politically", adding that Damascus is important in the quest for peace in the Middle East.** *Spain also supports talks to broker a partnership agreement between Syria and the European Union, the minister said.*

Jerusalem Post
Jul. 12, 2003
Italy's Berlusconi wants Israel in EU

..Italian Prime Minister Silvio Berlusconi wants to see Israel join the European Union, and discussed this recently with the 25 ambassadors of the EU countries both in the "club" or scheduled to join in 2004, Berlusconi told visiting Foreign Minister Silvan Shalom.
..Berlusconi said that even though Israel is geographically on the other side of the Mediterranean, culturally and economically it is a Western European and democratic country. The Italian Prime Minister further said that not one of the ambassadors at the meeting was opposed to the idea.
..According to Israeli officials, Berlusconi again raised two issues that he discussed with Prime Minister Ariel Sharon during his recent visit in Jerusalem the idea of a massive economic Marshall-type plan to help the

economies in the region, especially the Palestinian economy; and the convening of an international Mideast peace conference in Sicily.

http://www.guardian.co.uk/italy/story/0,12576,824146,00.html
Saturday September 28, 2002

UK Guardian
First among Billionaires
*The Berlusconi legend is projected in a 128-page booklet, An Italian Story, that he first put out in 1994, then mailed, updated, to 12 million people in Italy at the last election. **It's a fable of self-improvement but also of Biblical destiny - he has claimed to be "the Lord's anointed".***

http://www.arabicnews.com/ansub/Daily/Day/030715/200 3071512.html
Pope's stances are appreciated in the Arab states
Regional-Vatican, Politics, 7/15/2003

The Vatican announced yesterday that the denouncement pronounced by Pope John Paul II of the American military interference in Iraq and his call for a just and comprehensive peace in the Middle East were appreciated in the Arab states.

The message was conveyed to the chairman of the Papal council for dialogue among religions, Michael Fitzgerald, during a meeting with heads of other churches from the Middle East held on July 7 and 9 in Sednaya (in the outskirts of Damascus, where one of the oldest churches in the world is situated), in Syria.

The statement explained that the participants expressed their appreciation for the Pope's position and the Catholic officials on the Middle East, especially their condemnation of the war

185

against Iraq and their demand of a just and comprehensive peace in the Middle East especially in Palestine."

VATICAN CITY, JULY 11, 2003 (Zenit.org).- **John Paul II wants to see the Israeli-Palestinian peace process accelerated.**
That desire was transmitted on Thursday by Cardinal Angelo Sodano, Vatican secretary of state, to Israeli Foreign Affairs Minister Silvan Shalom.
A statement issued by Father Ciro Benedettini, assistant director of the Vatican press office, said the meeting between the Israeli Minister and the cardinal focused on "the current process of reconciliation and peace between Israelis and Palestinians."
"Cardinal Sodano expressed on behalf of the Holy Father the fervent desire that the process will intensify and conclude rapidly," the Vatican spokesman said.

Father Benedettini said that during the meeting "some bilateral questions were also analyzed, relating to the life of the Catholic Church in the Holy Land, which will have to be urgently resolved on the basis of the commitments of the Fundamental Agreement of 1993."

*** Thus concludes the ugly portait of real global Middle East diplomacy. In 2001, the Vatican dictated foreign troops in Jerusalem; Italy and Spain, under the Jesuit-trained King Juan Carlos go to work, and by 2003, the US, EU and UN all agree. The only way to get those troops in is to aggravate the conflict into an unsolvable bloodbath under the guise of what is now called a roadmap, which was initially known as the Oslo Peace Accord.***

CHAPTER FIVE –
INTERNAL DISEASE

ALM 1 - THE PILOT HANGS

Sept. 25, '03 - I'm walking towards the supermarket and a reporter from The Modiin News stops me. She is writing the people's opinion column and would like mne to answer two questions. I agree.

One - Who will I ask forgiveness from this Yom Kippur?: "From no one. Until our leadership begs forgiveness for their murderous crimes against us, we have no reason for anyone to forgive our petty personal indiscretions."

Two - How do you feel about the pilots who refuse to participate in military operations against the 'palestinians?' : "I'm asking who got to them? This was a another psy-op ploy to weaken Israel's resolve to fight for her survival."

For the first time since the paper started this particular column, it didn't appear the following week. But something well beyond coincidence did appear in the Haaretz literary supplement, just five days later. It was a review by Dr. Reuven Podhatsur of a study published by the Defence Ministry of why Israeli pilots refuse to obey orders, written by one Shmuel Gordon.

Six days after the Israeli public was disgusted to learn that 25 reserve pilots, spearheaded by a brigadier-general, signed a petition refusing to fight the PLO and its allies, Haaretz reviewed a book justifying their moral choice. How truly uncanny and how likely we are looking at a planned demoralization operation.

Within days of this announcement, it was exposed that at least five of the refusing pilots were employed by El Al. In an instant, the web server Rotter had a boycott of El Al going with a lot more signees than on the pilots' petition. The newspaper B'sheva asked the El Al spokesman why any passenger should feel safe when his pilot sympathises with potential highjackers. The company replied that it's an internal matter, or simply, no comment. B'sheva concluded by advocating the boycott of El Al until it fires the pilots.

Too late for me. My boycott began after my last flight with this rude, ignorant airline. But there is still time for you to catch up. Stay away from this airline. You don't know who your pilot could be.

But you do know who he will not be. Because on September 30, El Al First Pilot for its fleet of 757s, Oded Tsur, was found hanging from a tree in Canada Park, a few miles from Modiin. As usual, the death was quickly declared a suicide. Modiin News noted that Tsur was depressed because he failed an upgrade test. Meaning El Al flies depressed suicidal pilots.

His family, including his three young children saw no suicidal signs, nor did his fellow El Al employees.

All we know publicly, is that Tsur received a cellphone call while he was travelling on the Modiin-Jerusalem Highway, then drove his car seven miles west to a grove in Canada Park and he was found hanging from a tree there a day later.

We don't know if he was one of the El Al pilots who signed the petition or knew who the ringleaders really were and what they were up to.

**

As we count the dead and mutilated in Haifa, we can be assured that our government will do as much to fight the slaughter as it did after September 9, in Jerusalem. Of course we all know what the solution is: we go to war and smash the enemy so completely that it begs for surrender on our terms.

But that's not what will happen. After a few useless symbolic acts of "revenge," it'll be back to talks with the PLO. Here's who our leadership mafia chooses to protect:

The KGB's Man *Moscow turned Arafat into a terrorist.*

BY ION MIHAI PACEPA - Saturday, September 27, 2003 12:01 a.m. EDT

The Israeli government has vowed to expel Yasser Arafat, calling him an "obstacle" to peace. But the 72-year-old Palestinian leader is much more than that; he is a career terrorist, trained, armed and bankrolled by the Soviet Union and its satellites for decades.

Before I defected to America from Romania, leaving my post as chief of Romanian intelligence, I was responsible for giving Arafat about $200,000 in laundered cash every month throughout the 1970s. I also sent two cargo planes to Beirut a week, stuffed with uniforms and supplies. Other Soviet bloc states did much the same. Terrorism has been extremely profitable for Arafat. According to Forbes magazine, he is today the sixth wealthiest among the world's "kings, queens & despots," with more than $300 million stashed in Swiss bank accounts.

*** What this Wall Street Journal piece forgot to include is that in Pacepa's book he claims that Arafat was given little boys as playthings. Thereafter he was filmed with his boy toys and further blackmailed. The same system was used to turn Yossi Beilin into an enemy agent. Arafat is not only a paedophile, the author underestimated his larceny by two thirds. If you think we should be seeking revenge, think of his own people who were pickpocketed to the tune of $900 million. ***

Arafat diverted $1.35bn: IMF
From correspondents in Dubai, United Arab Emirates
21Sep03

AN audit of the Palestinian Authority revealed that President Yasser Arafat had diverted $US900 million ($A1.35 billion) in public funds to a special bank account he controlled and most of the money was later invested in Palestinian assets, an International Monetary Fund *official said today.* **Now what sane people would permit strangers to turn its holiest site into rubble?*

Temple Mount Wall Collapses

Temple Mount Wall Collapses
http://www.israelnationalnews.com/news.php3?id=50321

One side of a wall in the Temple Mount compound - completely visible to worshippers at the Western Wall - collapsed on Tuesday, uncovering an area of some 40 square meters of dirt and fill. The wall belongs to the Islamic Museum on the Temple Mount, a building to the right and above the worshipers at the Western Wall.

http://www.arabicnews.com/ansub/**Daily/Day/03**0924/20030 92415.html   (24.9.2003)
The Islamic al-Awqaf department in Jerusalem have accused the Israeli authorities of being behind the collapse of an internal wall in al-Aqsa mosqueThe director of the Islamic Awqaf in Jerusalem Adnan al-Husseini said that the wall collapsed as a result of "the Israeli intervention in our work and preventing us from maintaining it after we stated it was in an urgent need for a rapid action to prevent its collapse."

___*** And do the trespassers accept responsibility for the damage they caused? Of course not. They just do the usual Middle Eastern lying. And does our leadership try to stop the destruction of the center of its nation's soul? No, that would require winning, which is forbidden._And while a notorious liar, one Edward Said, discovers the subtle glories of Hell, the world kicks in, celebrating him as, now get this, a "peacemaker." ***

http://www.commentarymagazine.com/9909/weiner.html

*** And if $900 million isn't larceny enough, the PLO continues to collect the suckers' dough, through, what else, the banking arm of the Labor peacemakers, Bank Hapoalim. Here is the account number of the Jews who finance the murder of Jews.

INTERNATIONAL SOLIDARITY MOVEMENT

Bank Account G&G&H&N (ISM)
Bank Hapoalim Main Branch Tel Aviv 600
Account No. 360883

Once the bodies of Haifa are buried, and Israel's non-hearted response is done, in will come the CFR to push the Roadmap peace process. It should be recalled that 9-11 in Hebrew is Tisha B'Av, the fast day commemorating the loss of Jerusalem and the First and Second Temples. Av is the 11th month and Tisha is the number 9. While Pres. Bush expresses his pre-written condemnation of the Haifa bombing, consider who he really is and what he really intends   on   behalf   of   his   controllers: ***

http://www.informationclearinghouse.info/article4582.htm

*** But why rely on published reports, when my own witnesses are so much closer to the battlefield? ***

Hi Barry,

I was wondering if you ever heard of a guy named Chris Feld? He works for the American Embassy here and I'm told is one of the main liasions between President Bush and Bibi. A friend a mind lived next door to him in Jerusalem and talked to him and his wife on many occassions. His wife is apparently Jewish but obviously we'd have some doubts about him. In any case he revealed that the intent of the US is to turn Israel into an American colony, actually far more than it already is and what's more is he said (I don't know how he knew this) that the violence was going to get much worse here.

*** Now how did Chris Feld know the violence would get worse? Because that's been the plan all along. All you have to do is appoint the mafia of your choice to destroy the targetted country. It's just a matter of keeping Arabs incredibly stupid and Jews, resigned to a painful suicide.

This Yom Kippur our mafia has to finally beg our forgiveness and starting telling the whole truth of Oslo and sundry related crimes. If we don't hear their atonement, we will have to atone for them...our way. We can either abandon the country, as any person would escape a nation that refuses to protect the lives of its people.

Or we can remove the criminals and try to save the place.***

ALM 2 - OLMERT AND THE FINE ART OF MANIPULATION

The globalists are united in arranging Israel's demise and are busy reducing the country to undefendable borders. Are they ever busy! Most Israelis see the Beilin Geneva Accord as basically harmless, when it should be viewed as basically treasonous. Admittedly, the thought did cross a few minds that since the money behind it was European, they were being manipulated by foreigners. But no one uttered a peep when the front man for this funding was announced as one Alexis Keller, who funneled his father Pierre's fortune at Beilin. Papa Keller is VP of the International Red Cross of Holocaust ignoral fame and which singles out Israel for membership refusal. Nor did many understand the significance of Colin Powell of the Council On Foreign Relations inviting Beilin to his office to discuss his "useful" initiative.

The Geneva signing was a publicity stunt coordinated with the highest ranks of the Israeli government and media to fool the Jews out of their homes in Judea, Samaria and Gaza. Just previous to it was the murder of three disarmed soldiers, two of them young girls, in Netzarim, preparing the ground for the withdrawal from the village, but what interests us now are the days following the Geneva performance. Here are a number of incidents, seemingly unrelated, but they are not:

- A 90 year old former hack Jerusalem Post TV writer named Philip Gillon dies and Haaretz devotes a page to his removal from our midst. To give you an idea of what a despicable character he was; when the soldiers' vote of 1984 prevented a Labor victory, he wrote that his fondest wish was to see them all die in battle. The page consisted of two eulogies. One was written by Jerrold Kessel, CNN's Israel correspondent, yes the selfsame CNN founded by Ted Turner of the CFR, and other was written by P. Gillon's nephew Carmi Gillon; yes the selfsame former head of the Shabak and it's Jewish department, responsible for innumerable crimes including the Hebron massacre of 1994 and the Rabin assassination, which he planned with Shimon Peres. In his self-serving little piece of mind-twisting, he wrote that he had some personal problems with uncle Philip, who was just too left-wing for his tastes.
- If the irony of Gillon's parting words to his uncle were lost on the readers of Haaretz, the events surrounding another character in the Rabin assassination shouldn't have been. Dr. Yehuda Hiss was the pathologist who changed Rabin's wounds for the public. He

also steals body parts from fallen soldiers, hapless tourists, and whoever goes near his scalpel. But these crimes didn't bother attorney general Elyakim Rubinstein who ruled that the Hiss crimes weren't worthy of prosecution. And not one editorial in the Israeli mainstream media condemned this ugly aberration of basic justice. The globalists know if the Rabin murder truth ever gets out, their primary agents in the Israeli government, those who brought us the joys of Oslo, will fall like kingpins and take their Oslos and roadmaps down with them. Media and court manipulation are the primary defences, but co-opting those who once fought to have the facts exposed is useful as well, as we shall soon see.

- After shutting down the popular radio voice of the Resistance, Arutz Sheva, the Shabak started rounding up those pesky local leaders who were likely to organize the fight against withdrawal. Fourteen innocent men have been arrested without charge, and placed in intolerable prison conditions under an obscure but highly exploited procedure known as administrative detention. The most highly publicized case is that of Noam Federman, who is now a cause celebre in certain rightist circles. However, more than a few clear thinkers smell a rat here. The well publicized appalling state of Federman's incarceration is just too obvious. It serves the timely purpose of scaring away other protesters from public activity opposing the upcoming withdrawal.

- The climax of the manipulation was the announcements of the leaders of the Right that they favored withdrawal. Within two days of each other, Chief of Staff Mofaz ordered the removal of three outposts to begin with, and PM Sharon declared his unilateral withdrawal plan. But the greatest impact belongs to former Jerusalem mayor and Likud stalwart, the Trade Minister Ehud Olmert. In Stage One of his role, he agreed to specially label all products from beyond the Green Line, so importers worldwide can have an easier time of boycotting them. He may as well just have put a yellow Star Of David on the labels. Then, four days after the Geneva ceremony, he declared his advocacy of a near complete withdrawal from those places cited on the labels. AND the timing was not coincidental. By the weekend, Yediot Achronot's poll now showed that over half of Israelis favor withdrawal, with 58% favoring Netzarim first. This shattering change of public perception proves how well coordinated manipulation succeeds in a "democracy."

HOW THEY GOT TO OLMERT

Last night (14/12/03) I set my book table down at a rally against Olmert at the Jerusalem Theatre. Olmert was was guest of honor at an awards ceremony sponsored by the Israel Media Watch, an act itself inconceivable enough to sow confusion. We now return once again to that Rabin assassination, which must be kept under wraps at all cost.

The gentleman who invited Olmert and refused to rescind the invitation was Yisrael Medad, not long ago a central figure in the battle to expose the events leading up to the murder of Rabin. In the months leading up to the assassination, the government-owned Channel One tv channel, its head Moti Kirschenbaum and a director Eitan

Oren, staged two reports of a dangerous hyper-radical organization called Eyal, whose most prominent and only leaders were Avishai Raviv and Yigal Amir, both Shabak agents provocateur. Medad led the battle to expose this piece of deadly media manipulation, going so far as to submit a (losing) petition to the Supreme Court to indict Kirschenbaum and Oren for fraud.

Medad lives in those very territories which Olmert decided warranted special labeling and had to be withdrawn from anyway. So why would he give his sworn enemy an invitation to watch an award given for for media honesty? And there is more. An astute activist at the rally, Gemma Blech informed me, "I attended Medad's lecture at the Ariel College media conference last month. He went over some examples of media bias and repression but didn't once mention the closure of Arutz Sheva. After his speech, I asked him why and he walked away from me without saying a word."

The last person I would have suspected of such easy co-option would have been Medad. That means that everyone is a candidate for it, including, certain members of the Yesha Council.

The speakers at this rally, just didn't get it. They actually accused Olmert of jumping ship for political advantage. Nothing more sinister than that. But Olmert was blackmailed, or bribed, probably a combination of both and ordered to play ball with disaster. Only one suspicious lady at the rally said so: "They got him the same way they got Sharon, through his son. His second son Ariel is a homosexual draft dodger who has more than enough scandalous behavior to hide."

A good try but with Olmert, there is no need to go for his son. Olmert is a crook and always has been. Allow me to present a few choice snippets from my book, The Fall Of Israel (Canongate Publishers, Edinburgh 1992).

pp. 44-45 - Olmert, one of the priciest lawyers in Israel, was accidentally discovered to be one of the most unscrupulous also. In 1987, police investigating the files of the North American Bank, which was involved in an embezzlement of at least $37 million, turned up some rather revealing information about Ehud. It seems Olmert had directed a client to the bank who deposited $1.6 million. The client, according to Olmert's own explanation, was a criminal fighting extradition charges and Olmert felt his money would be safe in this obscure bank. And the bank appeared to be grateful for his patronage. Olmert was rewarded with a $50,000 loan, not a penny of which was ever returned. Naturally, such a classic case of corruption would be the end of Olmert's career anywhere else. But in Israel he is considered a candidate for the leadership of the Likud sometime after the present generation burns out.

pp. 284 - The Likud was smart enough to know that flouting the funding law too openly would cause a backlash, so it created some straw companies and a slush fund so that corporations could bypass the legal system...The people in charge of Likud Party finances at the time were Ehud Olmert and his accountant Menachem Atzmon.

pp.285-287 - The Likud pulled another rabbit out of its hat. Israeli law prohibits individual party donations from exceeding $10,000, a sum most Israelis couldn't amass anyway. The answer to its financial woes could be found in sympathetic foreigners if a way around the restrictions could be found. The devious minds of the Likud fundraising team came up with a beauty of a plan. It involved getting foreign multi-millionaires to guarantee bank loans for the party. Now, let's say the Likud couldn't repay the loans, well then, the guarantors would have to pay the tab. And who better to put the plan in action than Ehud Olmert? In March 1991, Olmert flew to London and Zurich on "ministry business." The people he met symbolize all the shady and rancid connections between the Israeli government and money...In London Olmert met with Robert Maxwell and an American magnate named Alan E. Kasaden. While in Zurich, Olmert met with Edmond Safra...

Revelations of Olmert's secret life appeared in Haolam Hazeh on June 24, 1991, and this episode epitomises all the dubious dealings American Jews innocently support when they donate to the UJA. The Jewish Agency sold a losing real estate company, Hachsharat Hayishuv to the Nimrodi family, of Iran Contra fame, in 1988. Yaacov Nimrodi purchased the shares from Bank Leumi, which is owned by the Jewish Agency, which funnels most American charitable donations to Israel. By the mid-1980s, Agency chairman Arye Dulzin, had a tacit agreement with Leumi chairman Ernst Yaphet. Yaphet agreed to let Dulzin do what he wanted with Hachsharat Hayishuv if Dulzin gave Yaphet a free hand at Leumi. Yaphet's hand stole $7.5 million from the bank and ran away to America with it.

Now every crooked deal needs a great lawyer, and who negotiated this theft? None other than Ehud Olmert. He arranged the sale of Hachsharat Hayishuv, supposedly owned by the donors of the UJA, to Nimrodi, who dumped the company at great profit to the Bernard Moss Group in Australia. After mediation, Nimrodi paid Olmert $400,000 for his role in the scam. Since Olmert was about to be sworn in as a government minister, he was forbidden to accept the money. So he resigned from his law firm and we assume the money got to him through other channels.

And these are just samples of Olmert's criminal activities. The same man who would feloniously arrange the sale of a company owned by charitable donors would have no moral problem selling his country the same way. If anyone bothered to actually investigate why Olmert had a political change of heart, they will surely find that he was given a choice: exposure for massive acts of felony, or take our bribe.

A few days before this rally, I attended a gathering of the Ariel College in Tel Aviv. An informed journalist took me aside and said, "Don't quote me. The last act before withdrawal is being planned. They're preparing to frame another Goldstein. Watch out for a massacre or an outrage along those lines."

A woman at the rally had just finished a radio interview. She said, "I was going to tell them there's another Rabin murder in the air. That's how they're going to remove us from our homes."

I asked why she didn't say so. She answered, "I was afraid if I did, they would let me talk anymore."

**

How long must we hammer in the same message: Sharon is totally compromised by the CFR and does its bidding?

**

Reports continue to surface that Prime Minister Ariel Sharon's diplomatic policies are being run more in tandem with American dictates than with Israeli Cabinet decisions. Middle East Newsline (MENL) reports today that Sharon pledged to the United States that he would help establish an interim Palestinian state in 2004, regardless of whether the Palestinian Authority ends terrorism and eliminates terrorist infrastructures.

Anonymous Israeli officials quoted by MENL said that Sharon relayed this commitment to President Bush in late 2003. Sharon agreed, the report states, to a U.S. demand that the Road Map be implemented over the next year - even if the PA does not fulfill its commitment to fight Hamas, Islamic Jihad and others.

*** It doesn't matter who you vote for in Israel, you get the CFR. As if it's different in America! The next election may offer a choice between Bush and Howard Dean (CFR) who has announced that, if elected, he will appoint Bill Clinton

199

(CFR) as his Middle East advisor. So here's a real tossup for you. Take a gander at the bio of Bush's new Middle East advisor, James Baker: ***

James Addison Baker III *(b. 1930) -- also known as James A. Baker III -- Born in Houston, Harris County, Tex., April 28, 1930. Republican. Candidate for Texas state attorney general, 1978; U.S. Secretary of the Treasury, 1985-88; delegate to Republican National Convention from Texas, 1988; U.S. Secretary of State, 1989-92. Member,* **Council on Foreign Relations.** *Received the Presidential Medal of Freedom in 1991.*

The die-hard Communist site "Anti-War.Com" says this about the "Great Man";
James Baker: The Last Hope for America
Antiwar.com, CA - 1 Jan 2004

"A former Secretary of State who should be restored to his former position forthwith, my choice for Man of the Year is none other than the old Bush hand, the Fixer, James Baker."

Who are we to question the motives or abilities of such a political superstar? Baker's "James Baker Institute" at Rice University is chock full of "Friends of Israel". ***(These are active links, all the better for you to "Connect the dots.")***

The James Baker Institute's "Board of Advisors" includes "His Excellency Shimon Peres"

While the "Peres Centre for Peace" includes Mr.Baker on it's International Board of Advisors along with a plethora of other "Peacemakers".

*** Remember Ehud Olmert's sudden advocacy of a pullback from Yesha? Well look who he's been hobnobbing with this week! None other than George Mitchell (CFR, Georgetown), author of the Mitchell Plan which is Oslo, which became the Roadmap, which became the Geneva Initiative: ***

U.S. Senator George Mitchell, *Israeli Vice Prime Minister Ehud Olmert, Israeli industrialists Stef and Eitan Wertheimer, and U.S. former Congressmen Robert Livingston and Toby Moffett invite you to join them and Turkish Minister of State Ali Babacan, Jordanian Minister of Planning and International Cooperation Bassem Awadallah, Palestinian Authority representative Abdul-Malik al-Jaber and other distinguished individuals at a regional conference at Tefen Industrial Park on Thursday, January 8. Transportation is provided.*

ALM 3 -THE PERES SELLOUT; THE ZEEVI MURDER

Why do people fall for such obvious scams? Bush is really mad at Sharon for his unilateral Gaza pullout because it could hurt his re-election chances. So Sharon has to fly to Washington to beg for his approval.

"Please George, let me withdraw from Gaza?"

"Well, I don't know, Ari."

"Please, please, please."

"Oh alright. But you owe me one."

And even Likud members buy this stunt. It doesn't take much thinking nowadays to sell snake oil.

So if weary Israelis will buy this superficial piece of bunco, what chance is there for them to understand that the Gaza pullout is another step in the road to defeating the rise of Judaism in Israel and revenge against the people's rejection of the Sabbataian ideal of Labor Zionism?

Still, we try against all odds to supply the information hoping there is a spark yet left of the mythical Jewish intelligence.

The following hidden history was supplied by two informants, one being a columnist for Makor Rishon.

The planned disintegration of Israel began in 1988 and Shimon Peres was the agent. The locomotive was the Washington Institute For Near East Policy, the Martin Indyk - run monstrosity.

Informant One - Peres was going to be the instrument of a withdrawal to the '48 lines and he was shuttling between the Washington Institute and the Vatican to sell the plan. It was basically what you've been reporting for years; Israel becomes indefensible, the foreign troops patrol the country, the Vatican gets Jerusalem. The whole package. Indyk was the American coordinator of the plan. The new name for it is the Roadmap.

Informant Two - You have to ask who Indyk really is. How does an Australian just show up in Washington one day, get hold of a think tank, and then run Middle East policy for the country?
I thought your Sabbataian claims were far-fetched when I read them, but they explain Indyk's rise from nowhere as well as anything else. Why was Peres running to him to push his plan? Or more likely, who assigned Indyk to Peres?

One - A key player in Nimrod Novick. He was Peres's liaison to Indyk and after the Oslo Accord, was given a position at the Washington Institute. He's been keeping quiet since then, but he's the point man between Peres and Washington. He negotiated the fine points of the withdrawals and pullouts and the paperwork is stored at the Washington Institute. The plan called for Israel to pull out of Judea, Samaria and Gaza, piece by piece, all the while Israelis would be told that this would be the last withdrawal. That's the same system they used to get the PLO back. First, just Gaza and Jericho and if they don't behave, no more. Israelis would have to be convinced that their country was being compromised in the name of security to fall for this. It's a strong-arm extortion tactic. You get what you want by promising this is the last payment. But of course, the payments never stop.

Two - In 1997, Rehavam Zeevi heard about the Peres-Indyk records stored at the Institute and tried to get copies. His contact within the Institute was a researcher there named Sheldon Stern. His son Jonathan works there as well today but we are told, was not part of the Zeevi operation. Stern explained that he had seen the records and told Zeevi what was in them. He told Zeevi he could get the records to him for $900,000. Zeevi agreed. But then Stern started getting cute. First he wanted $15,000 up front to bribe two guards at the Institute. Zeevi agreed. Then Stern upped the stakes again, asking for $35,000 in legal fees which the guards would need if questioned.

ONE - Zeevi then figured out he was being taken for a ride and returned to his original offer: $900,000 paid in full once he had the documents. He wouldn't budge and the deal fell through. We don't know if Stern was an honest broker or not, but there is reason to believe that he was. Either way, Zeevi never forgot what he said was in the Peres-Indyk files and began a campaign within the government to short-circuit Peres.

Within two years, both Zeevi and Peres sat in the same cabinet led by Ariel Sharon. There Zeevi became privy first hand to Peres' continuation of his Vatican/Indyk program. In early October, 2001, Zeevi threatened Sharon. If Peres did not stop his secret diplomacy, he would publicly reveal what it involved. Sharon acquiesced and had a letter drawn promising that he would order Peres to cancel a planned meeting with Arafat in Greece. A week before his murder, Zeevi displayed the letter at a party caucus meeting.

Sharon's appeasement did not succeed for long. On October 13, 2001 Zeevi handed Sharon his final ultimatum: Peres is removed from the cabinet or he will resign from the government and take two parties with him; Yisrael B'aliyah and the National Party. Sharon was given a choice between Peres and suicidal withdrawal, or his coalition. Sharon went with Peres and withdrawal.

On Oct. 17, 2001, four hours before Zeevi was to give his resignation speech to the Knesset, explaining who Peres was and why he couldn't sit in the same government as him, he was shot dead outside his hotel room in Jerusalem. Arabs may have been the triggermen, but the order came from within the Israeli government.

Or, put another way: Zeevi died so Sharon could one day evacuate Gaza.

ALM 4 - THE LONG SWIM HOME

I know Sharon accepted the roadmap to extinction and many of my readers are in shock. Well, I'm not going to react because I told you he would when you foolishly went to the polls and voted for him. Yes, Israel Police mysteriously could not find enough evidence to investigate Yossi Ginosar and the $300 million dollars plus of Arafat's stolen money he hid in Switzerland. The police didn't even bother with obvious tax evasions and similar felonies. We know why they are protecting him and I told you it was inevitable. The peace team is immune from prosecution. Period!

So Israel police is not going to investigate the following swiming accident either:

On the last night of April 2003, two terrorists tried to enter a popular Tel Aviv watering hole, Mike's Place. The security guard suspected them and blocked their entry. So one terrorist blew himself up, and three patrons. But the other terrorist, one Omar Sharif, failed in his massacre attempt because, we are told, his explosives' belt refused to ignite. Thus, he ran off into the night and was subject to an international manhunt.

By May 1, a holy day in the New World Order calendar, we learned that the terrorists were British citizens who had taken a long odyssey from London, to Damascus, back to London, on to Jordan, through the West Bank, then finally to Tel Aviv for their final act. Now why all the trouble? Is there a shortage of brainwashed suicide candidates in Gaza?

Then barely two weeks after he disappeared into the Tel Aviv humidity, Sharif's body was found washed up on a Tel Aviv beach. The police reported he drowned but so far, haven't said when. The Israel police spokesman admitted the circumstances of his demise were, "mysterious" and "barely explainable," and promised to get to the bottom of the case. They won't because they won't be allowed to.

So let us try to, using the few facts at hand. A suicide bomber flies from Britain, makes a few stops, fails in his mission and walks to a Tel Aviv beach and drowns because:

* After a long night of terror, he felt like a refreshing dip in the Mediterranean.

* Having failed to murder his quota of people, he went after fish.

* He was trying to dogpaddle to the Gaza Swimming Club.

* He was hoping to break the world breast-stroke record by swimming to England.

* He was testing if his explosives were waterproof.

* He mistook his belt for a life preserver, a common error among surfing Semtex
users.

* He was quickly apprehended, interrogated under duress, drowned after he spilled all he knew and thrown into the sea.

I would guess he was dumped at sea and his body wasn't

meant to roll into shore. And I have no problem with the elimination of terrorists. But this time around, you can bet your bottom shekel, he knew too much about a much broader plan to be kept alive for trial.

***

An observation: I am sitting with my daughter and her two identical twin friends at a restaurant/store at Latrun junction. A northern European UN soldier in civies passes and mutters so we all hear, "F...ing Jews. We should kill them all." Why are we allowing the UN into our country?

***

A comment: Somebody throws a pro-Israel show in Washington and invites airhead crooner Achinoam Nini. She refuses to sing the Israeli national anthem, Hatikvah because of the line: "For two thousand years, the Jewish heart has yearned to be a free people in its own land." It's a disgrace justified in the Jerusalem Post by one Greer Faye Cashman who explained that Israel is also home to Muslims, Christians and Druze.

Now using this boneheaded thinking, why sing God Save The Queen when atheists abound in the British Empire, or what's left of it? Why have a star of David on the flag when clearly a cross and crescent should be added? Why call the country Israel at all?

And it just this kind of profound peace thinking that Sharon, under partial duress, is hoping will prevail by not saying no to the Roadmap.

***

But those of us who see through the machinations will prevail because we caught the "peacemakers" in a clumsy murder of gargantuan proportions.

The following legal declaration was signed in Tel Aviv on May 21, witnessed by Yaacov Verker, chairman of the Public Committee For The Reinvestigation of the Rabin Murder:

I, Amos Ben Dov (identity number) do declare the following to be the truth;

1. On Saturday 4/11/95, I was the manager of the branch of the security company which guarded Ichilov Hospital.

2. After hearing of the prime minister's assassination, I arrived at the hospital to oversee the crew responsible for public order. Because of my duty, I was given free reign to work throughout the hospital compound.

3. During the course of the night. I approached the prime minister's Cadillac, parked opposite the entrance of the Trauma Center. The vehicle was locked and was parked in a haphazard way. I looked inside via the front windshield and saw two large bloodstains; The first was just beyond the middle of the backseat, the second was on the front passenger seat beside the driver's seat. At the time, I supposed that the backseat bloodstain was the prime minister's and that in the front seat was the bodyguard's. I was later surprised to learn the bodyguard's wounds were insignificant compared to the prime minister's, yet the bloodstains were of the same proportion. The prime minister succumbed to his wounds while the bodyguard easily survived. Yet the stains on the seats were about the same size. I called a security guard, Tsur, who was responsible for hospital security (and I believe still is), to look inside the vehicle. He looked within without a noticeable reaction.

4. At the time, I assumed the frontseat bloodstain was the bodyguard's, despite its unusual size. Later, I learned the bodyguard never sat in the front seat and I couldn't imagine any circumstance where he would move to the front seat. For this reason, I concluded that something else must have occurred.

5. I declare this to be the truth. Amos Ben Dov.

With courageous and honest Jews like Amos Ben Dov, we're going to get the "peacemaking" murderers before they get us. Beware Sharon, moral Jews are out there!

ALM 5 - RABIN YEAR END REVIEW

Two independent polls show that a vast majority of the religious and right wing communities of Israel believe that there was a conspiracy surrounding the assassination of Yitzhak Rabin.

In July, Arutz Sheva polled its listeners and 79% answered yes to the question, "Do you feel there are serious open questions about the Rabin assassination?" Then, on October 31, Makor Rishon's readers responded to the question, "Do you believe in the conspiracy theory of the Rabin murder?" with a resounding 73%, Yes, to 27%, No.

What is fueling this growing believe is a continuing stream of evidence. From the very night of the assassination, there were reports that one of Rabin's bodyguards was murdered and examined at Ichilov Hospital. Members of Jerusalem's Givat Shaul burial society told friends and family that they were called in the middle of the night of Nov. 5/95 to bury a secret service officer but no one would put his name on record as having participated in the ceremony.

Amos Ben Dov, who was manager of Ichilov Hospital's security company, on
duty the night of Rabin's murder, wrote that he saw something then that has haunted him to this day. He wrote:"I was called there on the night of the murder. Rabin's Cadillac was parked outside the entrance to the Trauma Center. I approached the car and looked inside. I identified a large

bloodstain in the middle of the backseat. I also saw a not very small bloodstain on the front passenger seat next to the driver's seat."

"That evening I thought it came from the wounded bodyguard, Rubin. But in time I learned Rubin entered the backseat with Rabin and never came into the front. On top of that, Rubin's wound was relatively mild and couldn't explain the very large bloodstain. So whose bloodstain was it?" Ben Dov asked, and signed testimony as to what he saw that night.

The issue of when the murder really took place was solved. The Shamgar Commission Of Inquiry ruled that Rabin was shot at 9:50. Yet Amir's arrest warrant has him in police custody at 9:30. Someone had to be lying. On a photo of Amir's arrest, a closeup of the arresting officer's watch is clear visible: it reads 9:30. Shamgar changed the time of Rabin's assassination by 20 minutes and now we have the proof.

All the cumulative evidence is having an impact on my standing in the country. It is not 8 years ago when I stood very much alone and ridiculed by the mainstream media. This year my new book Save Israel! was published in a handsome Hebrew edition and it received widespread media coverage, including cover stories in the conservative Makor Rishon and the far left wing Kol Ha'ir of the Haaretz chain of newsmagazines. The far left of Israel, as judged by media coverage, became almost as interested in my work as the Right. And their tone has mellowed to a state of grudging respect.

All this culminated in my first tv appearance in Israel since 1996. It was on a talk show highly regarded by the secular Left called Pini Hagadol. I explained the Rabin evidence rationally, even accusing Carmi Gillon and Shimon Peres of being prime suspects in the hatching of the crime. The news, after years of total blockade, was fast flowing into the thinking of all sectors of Israeli society.

ALM 6 - DING DONG, THE BELLS
ARE GONNA CHIME

Mazal Tov Ve Siman Tov! Yigal's Getting Married In The Morning! So get me to the cell on time.

Avigdor Eskin is a wealthy Russian businessman who spends most of the year in Moscow, where he is director of an intelligence front promoting Russian trade with Asia. When he is in Israel, he is either sitting in prison to cover his agenda or up to mischief. He was the matchmaker between Amir and his lovely bride-to-be Larisa Trimbobler. Eskin was also a lead player in the public incitements which were orchestrated to blame the Religious-Right for Rabin's murder and to keep that image in the public mind.

One month before the Rabin assassination, Eskin gathered a quorum outside Rabin's house to recite a medieval death curse called the pulsa dinara. The ceremony received an enormous amount of publicity and was used as proof that Rabin was killed because of the incitement led by such personalities as Eskin and Eyal leader, Avishai Raviv. Now since Raviv was exposed as a Shabak provocateur, why not Eskin as well? Just look at his record.

Can we ever forget Yigal Amir's 30th birthday when Eskin and company appeared at Beersheva Prison with a cake for Yigal? In the parking lot, Eskin beat up a cab driver, who opposed his revelry, in front of the media cameras, and once again, made national news.

And then there was the pig lady, Tatiana Suskin. Eskin matchmade her with an Israeli husband as well. Then came that unforgettable Shabbat when Tatiana handed out leaflets in Hebron caricaturizing Mohammed as a pig. When arrested, Tatiana confessed that she and Eskin had planned to toss a pig's head into the Al Aqsa mosque in Jerusalem.

There is much in common between Tatiana Suskind and Larisa Trimbobler. Both are Russian-born newly-orthodox ladies...Yet if that is true, why would Suskind have handed

210

out her ugly leaflets on the Sabbath? And both talk like they are orbiting Jupiter, looking and sounding like they are deeply medicated.

Trimbobler and her ex were both part of Eskin's merry pranksters for Yigal. Together they would boost Amir's morale with letters of undying support for his courageous act of patriotism against Rabin. The media reported that Yigal met Larisa in the Soviet Union when he was sent there. Nonsense; she was in Israel in 1989, he was in Latvia in 1992. Just a year ago, Amir's lawyer Shmuel Kaspar, the only lawyer on earth who repeats his client's guilt at every opportunity, submitted an appeal to allow the couple to visit Amir in prison. The court agreed to permit only Larisa visiting privileges. Once she actually met her hero in person, she was so smitten she divorced her husband so she could concentrate on her true love, Yigal the hero.

Then comes the announcement of betrothal and the country is up in arms. Rabin's daughter Dahlia, already hiding her serious cancer from the public, comes down with heart palpitations and has to be hospitalized. Kaspar "defends" his client's right to wed by comparing him with a series of serial killers who have taken their marital vows while incarcerated. According to the polls, 52% agree that Amir should be allowed his wedding provided he is never released and the image of him as Rabin's real murderer is enhanced in the public mind.

But he was the patsy and the Israeli media and government know it. However, this truth must be covered up, so in comes the Knesset cowards and hypocrites passing new laws to stop the ceremony and the hack journalists repeating at every opportunity the phrase, "Amir, the murderer of the prime minister."

Eskin's publicity stunt has done its job. The public debate has shifted from doubts about Amir's role in the assassination to certainty again. And by shifting the blame back to him, we are all the losers. But the biggest loser will be Larisa. From the information I have received about Amir's earlier life, if she is anticipating nuptial bliss, she's in for a permanent disappointment.

**

And defeat goes on. The Rabin/Shabak coverups continue with renewed vigor. Just this past fortnight two people who know too much were hushed. On Jan. 20, Dr. Vladimir Yikerivich, past head of cardiology at Ichilov Hospital, was convicted of manslaughter and corruption. Recall that he was the surgeon who operated on Rabin's heart on the murder night. Three years ago, when charges against him were first published, he threatened to open his mouth about what happened that night if the claims against him were pursued. He seems to have had a change of heart.

Then there was the untimely demise by cancer of former Shabak Deputy chief, Yossi Ginosar at age 58. As numerous correspondents noted, convenient cancer strikes again. Now who would want Ginosar hushed up permanently? This computer doesn't have enough memory to list them all, so let's concentrate on the most corrupt and dirty.

The decision to make Ginosar mortally ill may have been made in February 2001. That's when his partner Ozrad Lev revealed to Maariv that Ginosar had laundered over $300 million of money stolen from the Palestinian Authority by Yasir Arafat, in Swiss bank accounts. To cover the trail of theft, Ginosar opened straw companies for the money to pass through and who was appointed CEO of these phoney firms, Dr. Stephen Cohen, then executive partner with former Utah Congressman Wayne Owens in an influential Washington-based Middle East economic think tank.

Once the scandal got rolling and threatened to get out of hand, Cohen and Owens flew together to Tel Aviv to bring peace to the land. Owens wasn't in Israel half a day before his body was found dead on the beach opposite the Tel Aviv Hilton. The last person known to have met with him was Shimon Peres' personal aide, Avi Gil.

Now look what happened right after Ginosar was out of the picture. On the advice of Colin Powell's (CFR) personal Middle East advisor, Dr. Stephen Cohen (CFR), American ambassador to Israel, Daniel Kurtzer (CFR) held a tete-a-tete in his home with Geneva initiator frontman, Yossi Beilin. This was followed by a meeting between PA prime minister frontman Abu Ala at the Herzlia home of UN envoy and member of the Peres Peace Center board, Terye Roed-Larsen, and Shimon Peres, Oslo deceiver Uri Savir and Wayne Owens nemesis, Avi Gil.

Certain Shabak officers informed Sharon of the meetings and he was furious, as well he should be. The coup d'etat was working to plan. Peres was named the Labor Party head just in time for Sharon to be ousted on corruption charges. The takeover is well on the way.

And Yossi Ginosar won't be around to, accidentally or not, sabotage it again.

ALM 7 - PITCHING IN TO EDUCATE THE ISRAELIS

The climate of desperation in Israel right now is so palpable, that talented people have volunteered to educate Israel with the data I have spent years gathering. I can't begin to express my gratitude to the multi-talented web designer Michael Fridrich who produced my very own site in English and Hebrew:
http://www.barrychamish.com. It's still in construction but finally the latest Hebrew documents are on the web and English readers can put them in context.

And please admire the elegance of Judah Tzoref's translation of my article Deutsch Devils into Hebrew. The Hebrew translation of Deutsch Devils and its expose of the Shabbataian curse consuming Israel coincides precisely with the release of Rabbi Antelman's book, To Eliminate The

Opiate Volume One in Hebrew. Get it from me and give it to every Israeli you know. Rightfully, call it an act of educational charity.

And the surge of volunteerism does not stop there. The printer Israel Cohen visited me at home and proposed a way to further spread the message...while we still have time. He asked me if I have another book in me. I told him I have two years of research sitting idle in my computer that could be edited and turned into a book. He insisted that now was the time to get it out. I told him I couldn't come close to paying for it. He volunteered to publish it and only charge me for each book sold. On top of that, he'd cut the price to make sure it's within the range of everyone. I told him if I received enough response from my readers that I'd prepare a new book for him. You're reading it.

The desperation fueling this energy reached a new peak this week when our government handed 435 highly motivated terrorists to Hizbullah for the bodies of three soldiers murdered by the same Hizbullah and one live Mossad agent. Of the living Elhanan Tannenbaum, a lieutenant colonel in the IDF, we know from the Jerusalem Post that he, "worked as a consultant for a major arms firm which deals with the Defence Ministry's most sensitive technology...The firm's records were destroyed in a fire that gutted its basement in July, 2001...They have maintained that Elhanan served his country more than anyone imagines and more than they can publicly say."

Or in other words, he was not just the crooked businessman the public has been fed to believe. The government released 435 of the enemy, and has reportedly promised to release another 3000 or so for one of its own agents. In return, Israel received three bodies and conducted a vulgar and tasteless televised ceremony on their behalf, and not a few people wondered if they even were the real bodies. The doubts stem from the fact that body parts snatcher Dr. Yehuda Hiss, the same pathologist who changed Yitzhak Rabin's wounds in his tainted autopsy report, was the one chosen to verify the veracity of the corpses through DNA testing. And who trusts him to tell the truth?

"An IDF delegation has set off for Germany to confirm that the three bodies Hizbullah is sending to Germany are indeed those of the three soldiers killed by the terrorist organization 40 months ago. The delegation, headed by IDF Chief Rabbi Brig.-Gen. Yehuda Weiss and Abu Kabir Forensic Institute head Prof. Yehuda Hiss, is bringing DNA samples of the family members of the fallen soldiers Adi Avitan, Benny Avraham and Omar Souad."

___Then the never-ending German saga was recognized as the moving force behind the suicidal prisoner/body exchange. Of course the Germans were the negotiators, and that's why sending Deutsch Devils to the Israelis is so vital. The Germans are gloating at their "humanitarian" success, just as they gloated in 1992 when they were the first and only nation to recognize the new state of Croatia, which provided the impetus for a bloody Balkan war, the breakup of Yugoslavia and the creation of a Muslim Bosnian state. Along the way, the Muslims had to mass-murder their own and blame it on the Serbs, as in the infamous Sarajevo bread line massacre, but the Germans got their way. They're just repeating a winning pre-tested formula on Israel with their latest spirited "humanitarian" gesture.

And lost in the morass is the most obvious question of all: does the country of Lebanon exist? If it does, why wasn't the country of Israel negotiating the release with it and not Hizbullah?

Needless to say, the "humanitarian" exchange of living murdering bodies for the dead and corrupt was followed by a revolting bloodletting on a Jerusalem bus, which cost the lives of many, including my contemporary Yecheskiel Goldberg. But that's what happens when Frankist Germany conducts peace negotiations and our elected governors choose to let them.

**

What continues to rankle my readers more than anything else is the never-ending coverup of the Rabin assassination. Have a look at the kind of response to the last report, on Yigal Amir's betrothal to Lisa Trimbobler, elicited.

A Russian-language journalist met me and was visibly agitated that I implicated Avigdor Eskin in a plot to divert the public's attention from the real perpetrators of the murder by matchmaking Larisa with Amir. He refused to believe there could be any malice in Eskin's act.

Recall that in the summer of 2002, a gentleman whose first name was Amir, who was Rabin's special liaison to the PLO in 1994-95, met me and furnished us all with some vital inside intelligence. Although he comes from the far Left, he is an honest truthseeker who believes his boss was knocked off by a group within the Shabak, and he more than suspects that Shimon Peres guided this group.

Then recall that he considered Yaacov Kedmi, head of the intelligence agency Nativ, to be one of the top five or six most powerful men in the country. Then remember that Yigal Amir was sent to the Soviet Union in the spring and summer of 1992 on behalf of Nativ.

Now consider hard what the diplomat, Amir witnessed: Kedmi and his wife, met Eskin at a social event. Yes, Eskin, the slanderer of Rabin and admirer of Amir was directly connected to the man through Kedmi, who was directly employed by Rabin through Nativ, whose official name is The Prime Minister's Liaison Office.

We jump to the story told to me this week by Yaacov Verker, chairman of the Public Committee To Reinvestigate The Rabin Assassination. In late December, 2003, Eskin asked to meet him in Verker's office and here is what transpired according to Verker:

"He offered to trade information. I agreed and showed him what I have proving Amir shot blanks. In exchange, he promised to arrange a phone conversation with Hagai Amir from prison. A few days later he does it and not just between me and Hagai, the mother Geula Amir in on the line as well. All of them took turns trying to persuade me how wrong I was and that the best way to support Yigal was to join Eskin's movement on his behalf. I had no doubt then that Eskin had set me up. I'm just asking who sent him to me."

Another reader, a distinguished MD, is most upset at Amir's impending wedding:

I have a major moral dilemma and I don't know how to handle it. On the one hand, halacha (Pitchei Tshuva on Orach Chayim 156) requires me to warn a person if that person would be damaged financially if he/she didn't know a certain fact, especially if it has to do with a potential *shidduch*. To quote the Pitchei Tshuva: "v'chen b'inyanei shidduchin she'habachur ish ra u'bliyal v'nochel" (the potential husband is evil).

On the other hand, if I open my mouth, all hell will break loose. The ramifications are enormous, literally affecting many thousands of people, and in fact the entire country and the Orthodox community specifically. In the immortal words of Sgt. Joe Friday shlit"a [tm], here are the facts of the case. Former neighbors of ours (1987-1990) Larissa Trembobler (and her recently divorced husband) were friends. Her mother works with me at the medical school. Last night, Larissa stunned Israel by announcing her engagement to Yigal Amir who is sitting in jail for the murder of Ytzchak Rabin.

If I don't tell Larissa that Amir is a pedophile [the police here are furious that Dorit Beinish as Head of the DA's office in 1995 bordered police to release Amir although the police had substantial evidence and a confession that Amir was a pedophile rapist] Larissa will be hurt and the marriage may actually be termed a "mekach ta'ut" (marriage under false pretenses).

ALM 8 - LIGHT MY FIRES

How much lower can Israel sink without reaching the endless flames?

Just before the opening of the Rabin Week commemoration ceremonies, an Israeli court scared the willies out of the owners of Arutz Sheva, the hugely popular voice of the religious community. The government had had enough of this truth over the airwaves business and crushed the voice of half a million people in one swift blow.

And what a blow it must have been. Arutz Sheva's owners didn't waste a breath after conviction dumping their broadcast ship. Of course, final sentencing was postponed,awaiting the correct actions undertaken by the beaten ownership of Arutz Sheva.

A week later, Carmi Gillon, who plotted the Rabin assassination when he was head of the Shabak, and plotted the Hebron massacre when he was head of the Jewish department of the same Shabak, was elected new town council head, like a mayor, of the Jerusalem satellite city of Mevaseret Tzion. Half the vote went to a serial killer.

Then the attorney general drops all charges against Ehud Barak for blatant campaign fraud and ordered Ariel Sharon grilled for seven hours on similar charges. And no matter how you read all this, it isn't good. Just forget the subtleties and conclude that all our prime ministers are corrupt. Must be something in the system.

And something predictable took place in Israel on the day before Nov. 1/03, when the Rabin memorial rally was scheduled at the square now named after him. It seems some really bad people painted swastikas on the stone monument surrounding his eternal flame just a few feet from where the rally was to be held. Oh, the significance, the significance. And the bad people sprayed awful messages on the sacred stone like, "Kahane Lives." Why that must mean those radical religious setllers did this to Rabin's sacred memory!

And if that wasn't too much of an atrocity, another baddie tried to extinguish Rabin's eternal flame with his spit. But thank goodness, he was caught. Enough is enough. We all have to get to that rally and fight the religious, right wing settler fascists!

Do you believe there are still Israelis who know the Shabak wasn't behind this farce? But fewer every day. The day before the rally, the conservative newspaper Makor Rishon published the results of a poll of its readership, asking, "Do you believe in the conspiracy theory behind Rabin's murder?" 73% - yes, 27% - no. And don't think a whole lot of people didn't take note of those numbers.

Shimon Peres clearly didn't. At the rally, he incriminated himself, telling the assembled that, "three bullets pierced Yitzhak Rabin." Yes, they did, but the findings of the Shamgar Commission, which you accepted as Prime Minister in 1996, concluded that Rabin was shot twice. So go explain that one away, Shimon.

ALM 9 - UNHAPPY BIRTHDAY SHIMON

Even Shimon Peres wife, Sonia, refused to attend the monstrosity. Shimon Peres is having a birthday party and all of Israel will foot the bill, as if anyone asked us if we wanted to. So while 20% of Israel's children are malnourished, the country still found the time and money to feed Shimon's guests, who will include:

Guest list:

Bill Clinton
Polish PM Alexander Kosniski

Michael Gorbachev
Helmut Kohl

And if you don't think the public is paying for this atrocity, this party has been in the works for six months; and look at the list of organizers, all Likud, and ask who pays for their time?

Organizing committee:

Pres. Moshe Katsav
PM Ariel Sharon
Ehud Olmert - Invitations Organizer
Former Chief Rabbi Israel Lau

Location - Mann Auditorium, space donated by Tel Aviv mayor, followed by a cocktail party at the Cultural Ministry office in Herzlia Pituach, hosted by media magnate Yossi Maimon. There, singer Achinoam Nini will warble for the assembly.

Speakers - Peres, Sharon, Katzav, Clinton

No Shows:

Hosni Mubarak
All Arab "peace" partners
Sonia Peres

Also on the no show list is Yitzhak Rabin, missing because Peres had him murdered. One may assume Sonia knows this and much more, which is why she is staying away or being kept away.

Day Two:
9 AM - Tel Aviv University, symposium on Peres political "accomplishments" chaired by Itamar Rabinovitch. Featured

speaker, Bill Clinton. Three more panels follow, the last on Peres' environmental "accomplishments" chaired by "journalist" Ilana Dayan.

Afternoon - Luxurious meal at Green House restaurant for lucky 300 participants. Cost, 100 shekels a diner.

More public expense: the publicly supported President's House is being rented by us to host stage one of Peres' festivities. Other politicians had 70th and 80th birthdays including Rabin, Shamir, Sharon and Begin, far greater figures than Peres. Well who isn't? But they all had the dignity to celebrate modestly, and presumably felt it was unethical for the public to foot their bills.

Which is why a very angry public did what it could to give Peres a most unhappy birthday.

ISRAEL DIARY - BIRTHDAY WEEK

While Israel disintegrates, Shimon Peres threw a birthday bash for himself at much public expense. Little did he know that he provided an opportunity to awaken a nearly defeated people by wrecking his celebration. But would the people exploit their moment? The signs were hopeful on Sept.19/03 when the left wing newsmagazine Yerushalayim published a huge expose of the proceedings.

Not only was the public forced to pay the salaries of 1200 police officers assigned to secure the Peres' party, it was also made to pony up for the civil servants assigned by Likud cabinet ministers Ariel Sharon and Ehud Olmert who had been working for six months on the orgy; not to mention whatever it costs to feed and entertain the guests at the President's house. All pretty scandalous stuff but the really big scandal was the fraudulent rental of the Mann Auditorium in Tel Aviv by Peres staff for the 1100 guests.

Normally the hall rents for 31,000 shekels, a reasonable sum for the facility. But Tel Aviv mayor Ron Huldai pressed his city council to defer all costs, based on a request sent on the stationery of the Ministry Of Regional Affairs. That was Peres' last government office, but the problem is he hasn't been Minister Of Regional Affairs for over two years, and in fact, the ministry doesn't even exist anymore.

So how did Peres' spokesman Yoram Dori explain away this minor piece of buncoism? "We made a mistake." Well he fessed up, so all is forgiven...Unless someone actually submits a request to the State Comptroller to investigate the con, it looks like it will be.

But if someone does demand an investigation, Peres' staff will be there to save him. Asked about the irregularities, Dori explained, "This is a surprise party. Shimon doesn't even know what we're planning for him."

The challenge then was to trick Shimon into changing his plans for the evening and shocking him that all his friends would do such a nice thing without him suspecting a thing.

But crime has its own price and in Peres' case it was those hard to ignore no-shows. For weeks the birthday boy organizers had promised a glittering array of arriving Hollywood celebrants like Steven Spielberg, Barbara Streisand and Naomi Campbell. None of them showed up. The only star who did was the long faded Kathlyn Turner, and who noticed?

Shimon began his two day festivity by placing a wreath at Rabin Square to the man he murdered, Yitzhak Rabin. The irony was apparently not lost on the Rabin family, none of whom showed up for his celebration. And they were joined by nearly the full roster of the leadership of the far left including Yossi Sarid, Yael Dayan and Avraham Burg. They were furious that the organizers weren't from Peres' own party but were Olmert and Sharon from the enemy camp. To them, this signified that there was no political opposition in the country. Why they asked, would the birthday be not only sanctioned and paid for by Sharon but actually organized by him and his camp?

The answer is that the outside power elite ordered Sharon to boost Peres' standing and pay for it. The prestige of Peres and Oslo was at stake and while they would supply Clinton, Anan, Mandela and Gorbechev, Sharon had darn well better be prepared to make sure this con job worked.

But it didn't. The biggest embarassment of all was that Mrs. Shimon Peres, Sonia, refused to join the festivities. Here is Dori's amazing explanation for her refusal to return the RSVP; "Sonia is a feminist and does things her way. She hates crowds but will be there in spirit." Needless to say, Dori chose not mention Peres' well known womanizing or long affair with Collette Avital. Nope, 80 year old Sonia wasn't coming in order to take a feminist stand.

So far, a hopeful start, but it wasn't long before disappointment set in. The Women In Green had organized a protest outside Mann Auditorium and I was certain thousands would join in. The demonstration was too far from the auditorium to make a serious difference and only 200 showed up anyway. And the speakers were, with the exception of one reporter from Maariv, the usual spokespeople from the Right.

One of them was journalist Adir Zik, who is very ill. Everyone pray for him. He is irreplaceable. He sat beside me, looked at the small crowd and said, "I give this country thirty years."

"You're being optimistic," I replied.

That same night 10,000 people showed up for a "protest" in Jerusalem on behalf of Jonathan Pollard. By scheduling their get-together on the same night, Pollard's people had indeliberately sabotaged the Women In Green. There was a difference though. To fill their event, Pollard's people put on a free outdoor concert featuring well known religious musicians. Maybe some of the people who showed up actually cared about Pollard's fate, many wanted the free show, while every participant outside Mann auditorium cared profoundly that their nation was being buried alive. The Women In Green are the vanguard of Israel's resistance to

223

suicide and some of us are grateful to them. But 200 isn't some enough.

The rally ends and I walk to my car parked near the Mann Auditorium. I see the crowd is leaving so I take out my Who Murdered Yitzhak Rabin banner and stood there. I'm amazed that I'm not seeing the creme de la creme of the Left emerging from the event but one after another, from the Right and religious sectors. Here is Netanyahu's aide, there is Likud politico Avi Pazner, here comes Rabbi Meshi-Zahav, the government's agent in the Haredi camp. And then Shas Party spokesman Yitzhak Sudri passes me. I say to him, "Sudri what were you doing in there? You know who murdered Rabin." He answers, "You did."

In April 1997, I sat with Sudri in the office of Welfare Minister Eli Suissa. The minister had requested that Sudri inform me that the 1996 general elections were rigged. Peres was blackmailed over his leading role in the Rabin murder to lose the elections. That is what Sudri told me then and now he was spending his evening celebrating Peres.

My, my, how the religious political sector has been corrupted!

There were a half dozen protesters shaming the party-goers and one was Iris Cohen. I had received reports that she was instigating provocations among various anti-government movements and that she was considered an obvious Shabak agent-provocateur. But there she was, almost alone, doing the work that all of Israel should have been doing. I said to her, "Then you're for real after all?"

I recant my previous claim. The Shabak has planted so many instigators among the resistance movements that you don't know who to trust anymore. She is so aggressive that she appeared to be one of them. Now I think she is actually real after all.

The last person out of the hall is Greer Faye Cashman, the Jerusalem Post gossip columnist who has been grinding out pro-Peres puffery for years. I say to her, "Greer, I've been getting reports that you are being paid by Peres' PR agency to plant nice things about him in your column. Do you get money from them?"

Highly flustered, she denied it. "Then," I queried, "Why are you always going to bat for him?"

She ran away from me. The next day her report on the party had a different tone. Half the front-page article concentrated on the protests against the celebrations.

One more tiny, pin-prick victory.

***

When I go out and meet the public, I get information. One informant told me, "Get the tv films of the Rabin assassination night. I saw something important. The camera was aimed at Ibn Gvirol street and one of the crowd picked up a bullet clip wrapped in black tape. He gave it to a policeman. Whose clip was that? It wasn't Amir's."

Another concerned Israeli took me aside and whispered, "This is inside information and it's accurate. There is a new policy in the Shabak. They think the settlers only suspect religious-looking Ashkenazim as agents, so they've switched to Sephardim mostly."

Then attorney Menachem Koren-Weitz had a long conversation with me. "I knew there was a conspiracy before you did and here's why. I've been an attorney in criminal trials at the Tel Aviv Court building often enough to know the procedure. The building is designed to prevent the accused from having any verbal contact with anyone. When Amir was brought in for his hearing two days after the murder, all the regulations were lifted and he was allowed to say whatever he wanted to the media. All his public confessions then were a deliberate part of the coverup."

Attorney Koren-Weitz also gave me career advice. He suggested I don't publicize my Hebrew edition of Save Israel! anymore. "Everyone is saying the Shabak gave you something to make you crazy. Stick with Rabin and forget the new book. It's too much for our people."

I replied, "When I put out Who Murdered Yitzhak Rabin the same people thought I was crazy then. Nine years later, half the country know I was right from the beginning. It'll take nine years, if we have them, but Save Israel! will be vindicated."

A few days before, the influential newsmagazine Makor Rishon published a long cover story on my new book. The photographer was highly talented, the reporter not too bright. The result was precisely the sort of disbelief that Who Murdered Yitzhak Rabin engendered. Selling New World Order conspiracy to a tired and unthinking Israeli public has its down sides but the truth will out this time, just as last.

The birthday bash ends and I go home. At the protest rally, I'm told to turn on Channel One television at 12:15 for an unexpected surprise. Here, on government-owned tv is a one hour discussion of conspiracy with a well-respected host and three political scientists. They talk about the illuminati, the Jesuits, 9-11 and Rabin. They talk about me and show a clip of me lecturing. And the tone isn't angry or embarassing. The discussion includes admissions that some conspiracies are real.

Without Save Israel published in Hebrew, and all the attention it has received, would this program have aired? Would Israelis have been given a new perspective on political reality?

ALM 10 - IT'S SHOWTIME

I received an e-mail of great interest. The man explained that though we are from different political worlds, he had a very sensitive role in the Rabin government and has some information for me. I wrote back explaining that I support no political movement and I view all the available choices as criminal. He replied that he shared the view but I didn't really know how bad the situation was.

We met for two hours at a restaurant near my home. It turns out he was the emissary between Rabin and Arafat in 1994-5. He was highly sympathetic to the PLO's leadership at the time and still partly is though, "I found out that they are all crooks, totally corrupt."

He wasted no time getting to the point.

"I knew the night Rabin was murdered that the Shabak did it."

Did he have proof?

"No. But I saw things before."

He then told some pretty hair-raising stories, like the time he received death threats which he reported to the police. He was soonafter kidnapped in a police car and taken to a facility in Petakh Tikve where he saw Hamas spiritual leader Yassin locked up. He was told who made the threats, decided to drop the charges for close personal reasons and was released.

He took out a list of names. He said, "You have the right idea and you're getting close. But you're missing some key players. The top of the pyramid is Peres and higher and I'm not sure who is really controlling him. But I saw who is running the show below him. I would suggest you follow their trails and watch where they lead."

I took out a napkin, borrowed his pen and took notes.

"You got Ginosar and Carmi Gillon right. They've got the goods on everyone and can keep the lid on what they choose. But I don't know why you're not looking closely at Danny Yatom. Netanyahu appointed him Mossad chief out of fear. And he knows all about Rabin's murder.

"Next, the IDF Chief of Security Yechiel Khorev. You should have figured out how powerful this guy is by what happened to Yaacov Yitzhak."

I had been holding onto this story for months, not knowing what it meant. The former IDF chief scientist, Yaacov Yitzhak wrote a memoir and found a publisher abroad. To stop publication, Yitzhak was jailed for months, and his family was threatened with fatality if he didn't change his mind about publishing his book. The main problem was that Yitzhak named Khorev and Maariv probably saved Yitzhak's life by publishing his identity.

"If they went to all this trouble over Khorev, he was involved with the most sensitive secret army operations. You're right about how Goldstein was framed in Hebron. Eli Barak wasn't on top of that operation, army intelligence was.

"Next someone you've missed completely, as far as I've read you. Yaacov Kedmi, head of Nativ. He has his finger in everything."

Nativ is the Prime Minister's Liaison Office. It sends spies to the former Soviet Union under cover of arranging immigration to Israel. Yigal Amir spent the spring and summer of 1992 in Latvia on a Nativ program. Rabin was planning to shut down Nativ when he was murdered and many consider this a strong motive for murder.

"Kedmi was at a meeting I attended and guess who was with him? Avigdor Eskin."

Eskin is a show radical now doing prison time for his alleged far right wing activities.

"Eskin was all tied up with Kedmi and that means he was an intelligence operative of some kind. As for Kedmi, he has enormous power and influence and I would advise you to find out why.

"Finally, you have Meir Shamgar backwards."

Shamgar was the former Chief Justice of the Israeli Supreme Court and he headed commissions of inquiry which whitewashed the Rabin murder and Hebron massacre.

"The way you have him is he is basically a good guy being blackmailed somehow into doing the wrong things. Not so, he knows exactly what he's doing. He's running things, not the other way around."

RETURN OF THE ROCKY MEIR HORROR SHOW

The third Shamgar Commission of Inquiry released its conclusions and they were precisely what I told you they would be. Just check my past writings if you doubt me. Then again, why should you?

The Kishon River which dumps its effluents into Haifa port was used primarily by two groups of people; fishermen and Navy traineee frogmen. In the past few years, dozens of frog and fishermen developed agonizing cancers and the attrition rate was high and rising. If they were to sue, and several tried, the IDF would have to pay compensation to the families of the frogmen, while the chemical industries which did the dumping would be liable for similar payments to both groups of victims. This had the potential of bankrupting the IDF and most of Israel's petrochemical corporations.

So Shamgar chaired a coverup commission which concluded that there was no connection between the river and the cancers. This was such as ridiculous lie that even Shamgar rebelled. He got to be the dissenting judge, disagreeing with his two fellow commision panel members.

Showboat:

This show stunk but Shamgar didn't get panned. Two others got all the bad reviews. Shamgar's career survived the fiasco.

Which is more than Yitzhak Sharvit can say. He was a fisherman who, reportedly, knew all about the poisons of the Kishon River. The sick fishermen had organized into a noisy group demanding compensation for their mortal ills. A few days before Shamgar's conclusions were released, Sharvit was crossing Haifa Harbor when a Port Authority patrol boat gunned its engines and rammed Sharvit's boat, aiming perfectly for his cabin. Two crewmen died with Sharvit, whose body somehow remained undiscovered for over a week.

ALM 11 - THE BIGGEST GAMBLE YET

There is a wonderful new opportunity awaiting and I'll need your help to make it work. On Friday, Aug. 22, I moved the stakes up as high as I have yet. A feature article on me appeared in the far-left wing newsmagazine Kol Ha'ir and all signs are that it could be the opening we have all been waiting for, at a minimum to get the Rabin assassination reinvestigated in a court, or ideally, all of the lies within the Oslo "peace" process.

I am putting myself at great risk but my eyes are wide open. Please be there for me if this dangerous strategy works. I have long known that the only way to put Israel on a survival track, is to convince the Left that they have been fooled. And the most direct route is the Rabin assassination.

So when Kol Ha'ir reporter Assaf Carmel informed me last Sunday that he wanted to write an article about the Hebrew edition of my new book, Save Israel!, I accepted and prepared myself. I knew I was heading into a minefield and that a positive report from this Haaretz subsidiary was utterly impossible. But there WERE ways to get my points across to a broad leftwing audience. The tactics I decided upon were to goad the establishment into action despite the potential price to myself. And don't bother asking why I need this in my life. I don't even understand why anymore.

My plan was to build a major image transformation, one the Left, especially the young Left would come closer to relating to. And I didn't lie or deceive the reporter. I simply made a point of stressing my hippie youth, my growing up in a socialist home, my complete lack of association with any mainstream, especially, Right wing political movements. The picture I created was of an outsider in Israeli Bohemia, which really is not far off the mark to begin with.

Nothing tolls the death knell for any political interest group than to be pigeon-holed as Right Wing or Far Right. The mainstream media will ignore or mock it to ignomy or insignificance. If my work is to avoid the fate of ALL such movements for justice, I have to seek either the sympathy or visceral anger of the elites, and specifically, their children.

When Carmel first met me at my apartment, I showed him some of the documentation I had assembled. He was uninterested. However, I challenged him to examine the lot the week after the article appeared and he agreed. We'll see. Meanwhile, I knew by his questions that he was looking for salacious scoops and I carefully planted what he sought, while balancing personal details with the hard facts surrounding the Rabin murder and the sorry, mortal state our nation has fallen into.

The final result was what I expected, in fact, even better. First, there was a likelihood that the article would be the cover story for the week. A horrible act of terrorism in Jerusalem pre-empted that. However, I was given the secondary cover story, below the images of the death bus, with my photo within the text. Someone at this magazine has decided, for better or worse, to take me seriously. If nothing else, the phenomenon or so many Israelis believing me was recognized.

Next, and this is more important than perhaps many recognize, the newsmagazine printed a full page color photo of my by Rafi Kotz. It was respectful and friendly. Best of all, I looked quite handsome. I can thank the late Dr. Atkins for that. I have been on his diet for three months and most of my belly disappeared. The visual image was of a fit 51 year old, barefoot and casual. Kol Ha'ir, chose not to publish a photo that captured me at my worst. In fact, to their credit, they did me proud.

And the report was precisely as I anticipated. The reporter went for the weakest points in my book to prove that the rest is just as lying and wrong. BUT, and this is essential, Carmel also included some of my strongest evidence, ie. Rabin's 22 minute ride to the hospital, no gunpowder found on Amir's hands after police testing etc. and did not refute it, well could not, but it's the same. This is what I was after, and I got it, despite what preceded this victory.

However, it is what preceded it that has all the potential of blowing the Rabin murder and sundry scandals into full-blown national issues. No government official was available to or would comment on my claims. BUT, and here is our opening, the spokesman for Shimon Peres more than hinted that he would seek ways to shut me up. More to the point, he expressed confusion as to why I wasn't hushed up.

I think this time, there's a chance they'll try it. The game field has switched from the religious and right wing media, can successfully ignored, to Kol Ha'ir, in the heartland of the Left. The portrait was hardly sympathetic but it dispelled the false image of me being in the Kach camp of Israeli politics and replaced it with that of someone very close to the thinking of the Left. Which is not far off the mark anyway. While on security issues, I identify with the Right in real life, on all kinds of moral issues, I'm much closer to the Left. In short, I'm an anti-New World Order writer, something which has no place in either the mainstream Israeli Left or Right.

Which could leave me unprotected without you. If the establishment comes down hard on me through whatever dirty means, let's be prepared. May I suggest the following immediate courses of action:

* I have been holding something in escrow for the day I have to fight for my life and that of my country. I have in my possession over 2500 pages of documentation not just on the Rabin murder, but proving incredible illegalities committed by the government and Shabak before the murder, when illegal incitement was the order of the day, and after, when panicked coverup took over. If they are confiscated, they have been copied. My plan is two-fold:

* I have some 20 Israeli attorneys on my e-mail list. In the past, a few have offered to work pro bono to sort out the evidence in court. Please make the offer again. If I am to defend myself in a libel suit, I have the weapons to win with your help.

* It would be very nice if police stations across the country were bombarded with complaints. Let the police finally investigate the crimes which have taken over our democracyWhile, I will be attacked on my soft spots, fight back with our strong points. A few practical proven crimes:

- We charge Rabin's bodyguard Yoram Rubin with perjury in his testimonies to the Shamgar Commission and at Yigal Amir's trial. He testified that Amir's bullet entered and penetrated his arm at the elbow, exiting at the shoulder. I will supply 20 pages of Rubin's hospital reports. He "suffered" a superficial graze, treated with iodine.

- We charge the pathologist Dr. Yehuda Hiss with medical malpractise and evidence tampering. While all other doctors including Gutman, Sneh and Barabash reported that Rabin's spine was shattered causing death, Hiss removed the wound from Rabin's autopsy. I will supply all medical reports, as well as tapes of Sneh and Barabash reporting Rabin's real wounds. If I'm not around to do so, Hiss' report and those of the other doctors are easily printed out from the website.

- We charge Avishai Raviv with perjury at his recent trial. Raviv testified that Amir never informed him of his murderous intent. Please visit the previously named web site and download Raviv's signed police statements of Nov. 5, 1995, within which, he testifies to hearing Amir's threats on numerous occasions. While Raviv cannot be re-tried on his previous charge of not preventing the assassination of a prime minister, we can get him back in court for perjury.

- We charge Shimon Peres with gross misconduct and dereliction of public service. As prime minister, Peres approved the Shamgar Commission's conclusions that Rabin was shot twice in the back. I will supply a videotape of him describing Rabin shot three times and once from the front.

- We charge former Chief Justice of the Supreme Court, Meir Shamgar with gross judicial misconduct for changing the time of Rabin's murder from 9:30 PM to 9:50. I will supply Amir's 9:30 arrest warrant, as well as a photo of his arrest at 9:30, proven by the watch worn by one the policemen. Please download Shamgar's conclusion and the arrest warrant from the site, print them out and submit to your closest police investigator.

- We charge Eitan Haber of evidence destruction based on his own testimony to the Shamgar Commission that he absconded with Rabin's possessions at Ichilov Hospital, while later admitting to Kol Ha'ir that on the same night he cleaned out Rabin's filing cabinets at the Prime Minister's office. In this complaint, we demand, finally, that Haber account for what he took and return it all to the police. I will supply Haber's testimony.

- We charge the Shabak's bodyguard unit with massive dereliction of duty by abandoning Rehavam Zeevi at the Hyatt Hotel in Jerusalem, leading to his murder. I request that some wise attorney seek the 1997 Knesset Law, legislating a bodyguard to all cabinet ministers whether they choose such protection or not. Submit a copy of the law to the police investigator. He'll understand the significance.

- We charge Rabin's driver, Menachem Damti with perjury for testifying to the Shamgar Commission and at Amir's trial, that he drove to Ichilov Hospital in less than two minutes. I will supply his testimony as well as the just-mentioned proofs that the ride actually took 22 minutes.

- We charge Yoram Rubin with perjury for testifying to the Shamgar Commission that Rabin was shot at 9:50, using the same evidence. I will fax you Rubin's testimony as to the time of the murder.

- We charge Rubin, Damti and Shamgar with conspiracy to alter evidence, by coordinating a new, later time of murder, using the same evidence.

- We charge Meir Shamgar with unlawfully dismissing evidence at the Commision Of Inquiry into the Hebron massacre. Please request a copy of the protocols of this commission from the Justice Ministry and you will find that three of the soldiers on duty that night testified that Goldstein entered the Cave Of The Patriarchs at 4:45 AM, carrying an M-16. Shamgar concluded that Goldstein entered at 5:20 carrying a Glilon rifle, without explaining how the soldiers could be mistaken. Once again, we charge Shamgar of changing the time of a crime.

- We charge Rubin and Damti of being accessories to the murder of Yitzhak Rabin by deliberately denying him medical treatment. Go back to the site and download the pictures of the two ambulances beside Rabin's limousine and issue a complaint demanding to know why Rabin wasn't offered the services of trained medical professional waiting ten feet away from him.

If you wish further documentation on all issues, call Yaacov Verker 050 205 591 when he returns from abroad in early September. He is chairman of The Public Committee To Reinvestigate The Rabin Assassination and possesses all the necessary filmed and written evidence.

- We charge Yoram Rubin with perjury for testifying to the Shamgar Commission and Amir's judges that Rabin helped him get up after he was shot and then jumped head-first into the limousine. I, or Verker if necessary, will supply the murder film to prove no such thing happened.

I will also supply the testimonies of other bodyguards such as Adi Azoulai, that Rabin was forcefully pushed into the vehicle.

- We charge Menachem Damti with perjury for testifying to the Shamgar Commission that he was opening the door for Leah Rabin when he heard the first shot, and that he reacted by immediately jumping into the driver's seat, as he was trained to do. If I am not available, this and all previous testimonies are found in my book, Who Murdered Yitzhak Rabin. The Hebrew edition is available from Gefen Publishing 02 - 538 0247. It will guide you through the evidence. Leah Rabin was standing on the steps nowhere near her husband when Amir shot the blanks and Damti stayed outside after the shot. I will supply the murder film to prove Damti's perjury. Other evidence is found in the Hebrew edition of Save Israel!. Call 03 5569991, including the police tests of Amir's hands at 10:15 PM, revealing no metal particles or gunpowder was on them, an impossibility if he shot real bullets.

- We charge the chief judge at Yigal Amir's trial, Edmund Levy, with gross judicial misconduct for dismissing the testimony of police forensics expert, Inspector Baruch

Gladstein, who proved scientifically that Rabin was shot at 0 range, about half a meter closer than Amir ever got to Rabin. We charge that Levy acted with full knowledge and intent in this dismissal of evidence. Inspector Gladstein's testimony is found on the website, as is the defence summation of attorney Jonathan Goldberg. Within the latter is more than enough proof that Judge Levy deliberately ignored and dismissed relevant evidence throughout the trial. Submit it all not just to the police, but also to the Israel Bar Association, demanding that both Levy and Shamgar be dismissed for blatant trial rigging and gross abuse of the Israeli judicial system.

The timing of the Kol Ha'ir article was uncannily awful. The slaughter on Jerusalem's streets will convince some from the Left that their leaders invited the bloodshed, and a few might even, finally, understand that Israelis are entitled to an official inquiry into the Oslo "peace" process. The most direct route will have to be the Rabin assassination because we've got the goods on the criminals.

That makes this article doubly dangerous for these self-same leaders. I have left myself wide open for retaliation and I've made the decision to suffer any consequences. But with your help, the price can be very high for those who brought our country and people so low.

I realize how the system is protecting its felons. Shamgar is being set up to legally establish casinos in Israel. He will be well rewarded for his advocasy of gambling. Yoram Rubin has just been appointed to organize security at the Israeli embassy in Washington, another fine reward for crime. Needless to say, Peres has been rewarded with his renewed leadership of the Labor Party.

The only protection I have is the evidence, and you. We are not without resources. If the Kol Ha'ir article does what it should and leads to calls for a crackdown on me, spread that evidence through every media and use the authorities to investigate what should have been honestly investigated years ago.

Then there is the other possibility: that I waited nine years to achieve a cover story in the country's leading left wing newsmagazine and it's ignored. In that case, consider all this a guide to breaking the Rabin and other truths someday when Israelis are prepared to give a damn.

ALM 12 - COVERING UP FOR PEACE - THE MURDER OF JUDGE ADI AZAR

There is nothing complicated about the July 19 murder of Israeli judge Adi Azar. The murderers have already confessed but the Israeli government is rejecting the confession. Accepting it could ruin the "peace" process. So, the Israeli media is spreading salacious gossip about the judge"s personal life, including "a love triangle."

The key to the cover-up is convincing the public that Yasir Arafat never tells the truth. Let"s have a look at the events leading up to the murder:

July 10 - World Court In Hague orders Israel to remove its security fence.
July 11 - Tel Aviv bomb kills 19 year old soldier, wounds 34
July 12 - American court orders PLO to pay the family of American terror victim Yaron Ungar, $116 million in damages.
July 12 - Arafat: Israel Staged Tel Aviv Bombing by Abu Khaled Toameh, Jerusalem Post:

"Palestinian Authority Chairman Yasser Arafat condemned Sunday"s Tel Aviv bomb explosion that was claimed by his Aksa Martyrs Brigade, accusing Israel of masterminding the attack...This is not the first time Arafat has accused Israel of carrying out attacks against Israelis. In the past, he accused the Israeli security services of assassinating tourism minister Rehavam Zeevi."

237

The Tel Aviv bombing was out of character. It was not a suicide attack, rather a bomb hidden in bushes near a bus stop. It was designed to do the least possible damage while appearing to be a major incident. As for Zeevi, my research has Arafat dead-on right about him. (Please read Save Israel! for details).

Now we look at the American court decision, also from the Jerusalem Post.

July 13 - US Court, PA Must Pay Terror Victims Family

"In what may be a landmark blow to global terrorist financing, a federal judge in the US ordered the Palestinian Liberation Organization to pay $116 million to the family of a US citizen murdered in Israel eight years ago."

There are thousands of terror victims, dead or mutilated, and at $116 million a pop, the PLO and its murder state would be bankrupted if this ruling sets a precedent. Now, on to Judge Azar. He was adjudicating terror compensation cases in Tel Aviv and the PLO could not have liked his rulings. Nor could their supporters in the Israeli "peace" camp.

Let us look at how Judge Azar handled the issue of the suit of the Egged bus company against Arafat and his "Authority."

Arutz Sheva IsraelNationalNews.com

"Arafat Goes To Court A bill for 52 million shekels did what nothing else was able to do: get PLO chieftain Yasser Arafat to recognize Israelis courts. He turned yesterday to the Tel Aviv District Court, asking it to overturn a decision of seven weeks ago obligating him personally to pay that sum. The court, ruling on a suit by Egged, Israel"s main bus company,

stated that Arafat must compensate the company for terrorism-related damages caused during the first year of the ongoing Oslo War.

"Egged had claimed in the suit that Arafat himself, as the one who drafted and sent terrorists to carry out terrorist attacks, must be made to know that the costs will come out of his own pocket. "This is just another way to wage the war against terrorism," Egged claimed. In the first year of the Oslo War, Egged suffered more than 50 attacks, in which 113 people were killed, including a bus driver, and 594 were wounded, including 19 drivers. Financial damage added up to over 164 million shekels.

"The court ruled in early February, after Arafat did not even bother to respond to the papers served against him, that he must pay the sum - plus court costs of 100,000 shekels.

"Atty. Yosef Arnon, representing Arafat, claimed in court yesterday that the lawyers representing the PA/PLO in the case were not his client"s, and that Arafat therefore cannot be judged to have received the court papers. Arafat"s lawyer also asked that the judge, Hon. Adi Azar, be disqualified from the case."

For more details of the Egged case, visit:
http://www.haaretzdaily.com/hasen/pages/ShArt.jhtml?itemNo=259128

As for Judge Azar"s treatment of the PLO lawyer Yosef Arnon:

http://www.haaretz.com/hasen/pages/ShArt.jhtml?itemNo=275214&contrassID=2&subContrassID=14&sbSubContrassID=0&listSrc=Y

"Attorney Jamal Abu Toameh, an Arab citizen of Israel, has been replaced by Yossi Arnon, a Jewish lawyer. "We realized that in an Israeli court you have to be a Jew to

accomplish anything," says Farih Abu Madin. Last week, Arnon made his debut as the PA"s lawyer in the Tel Aviv District Court, in a hearing on the Egged suit.

"'This is not a terrorist case, but a civil case involving a damage suit," he said. Cross-examining the director of the bus company"s financial division, Arnon focused on the question of whether Egged"s profits had shrunk not because of the terrorist attacks but because it lost its monopoly status as an intercity carrier.

""However, the judge, Dr. Adi Azar, refused to accept Arnon"s approach. "Even though this is a civil suit," he wrote in an interim decision, "it deals in its entirety with a lengthy chain of acts of terrorism and atrocity that are exceptional even by international criteria, which unfortunately occurred in the recent past in Israel ... It cannot be treated as a routine, regular breach of contract suit, as though we were dealing with a cupboard that someone ordered but was not delivered, or a check not honored by a bank.""

In another suit against the PLO, Judge Azar upheld his position, and his integrity:

"In a decision of January 2003 to place a lien on NIS 4 million in favor of Yosef Azouz, who was wounded in the March 2002 terrorist attack at the Sea Food Market restaurant, the registrar of the Tel Aviv District Court, Adi Azar, wrote, "Immunity accrues to those who follow accepted and civilized modes of behavior, and not to those who take hold of an instrument of war and embark on a path of indiscriminate murders.""

Judge Azar"s precedents threatened the PLO with more than an endless payout to its victims. He also forced the Palestinian Authority to reveal its assets in court.

Cause of losses

"A different reality is revealed in the courts. In an attempt to annul the temporary liens, the PA stated that it possessed considerable assets and would not have a problem meeting the payments required by the courts if the courts ruled that the PA had to compensate the plaintiffs. In an affidavit to the Tel Aviv District Court in the Egged suit, Muhand Aljaouni, an aide to Palestinian Finance Minister Salam Fayyad, stated that the PA owns assets "whose value is dozens of times greater than the amount of the suit ... The Palestinian Authority has investments worth about $600 million in various companies."

"A document attached to the affidavit provides details of the PA"s investments. The PA is said to have $74 million in cash and to be a partner in 64 companies, including communications firms in Jordan, Algeria and Tunisia, a Palestinian cement company, a gas and aviation project, real estate transactions worth $15 million, hotels, a flour mill, a convention center in Bethlehem and the companies that market Pepsi-Cola and Coca-Cola in the territories."

Judge Azar was forcing the PA to prove it could not pay the compensation his court was demanding. Does anyone believe that the PA only has $74 million in cash? Arafat has more than that in his piggy bank. Nonetheless, the revelation of the PA"s corrupt business interests was bound to scare the recipients of Arafat"s largesse.

So he had to go to save the "peace." The murderer dressed as a security officer and cased the judge"s home for three days before making his move. He placed a silencer on his pistol, shot the judge five times and managed to escape on a motorcycle. This was no mean trick in late afternoon Tel Aviv traffic. Odds are he drove to a nearby safe house. Which means, the killer was getting help inside Israel. Which means, the "peace process" hit squad of the Shabak was helping out Arafat.

Arafat"s Al Aksa Brigade took responsibility for the hit and the Israeli government took enormous pains to scoff at the claim. Most likely they were just accessories to the crime, but their boss derived all the benefits from the removal of Judge Azar. The next judge adjudicating compensation cases against the PLO, whether in Israel or abroad, will think twice before ruling in favor of the plaintiffs.

Watch out for a patsy to take the blame because if the Israeli public were to discover that Arafat ordered the hit, and turned to his allies in the Israeli "peace" camp to carry it out, the whole Oslo process would likely collapse. Which is why the lurid gossip about Judge Azar"s private life is being spread like the fertilizer it is.

ALM 13 - WIRM - What It Really Means

What an eye my readers have for News Speak! They keep sending me items from the mainstream media that were totally misunderstood by the intended audience, requesting that I put them in perspective. I've been collecting them in a brown envelope for long enough. Let us look at the items, followed by WIRM - What It Really Means.

ITEM - Haaretz (undated) - On Memorial Eve, Rabin Family Lashes Out,
by Jonathan Lis

"Avi Pelesoff, husband of Rabin's daughter Dalia, yesterday criticized the Shin Bet, the various commissions of inquiry, as well as the state...Pelosoff, who spoke on behalf of the family, blasted the Shin Bet for failing to protect Rabin, and for the state's failure to deal with the assassination. He said, the state, 'failed in dealing with the murder of the prime minister. Today, eight years on, another attempt must be made to understand what happened then.'

He said that the public deserved to see the real report on the murder. 'The musings of the legal commissions did not solve anything,' he said."

WIRM - We ask, why wasn't this a front page, banner headline, nationally discussed, article? On the 8th anniversary of his murder, Rabin's family announced that there was a coverup of the truth. And no one paid attention because the media chose not to.

ITEM - Haaretz, March 12, '04. This item presents a wealth of knowledge about the connections between the Israeli government, organized crime and Shimon Peres. It seems someone put a bomb in the car of the father of Likud MK Inbal Gavrielli. He was visiting convicted Russian mafia chieftain Grigori Lerner at the time. (Yigal Amir is incarcerated in Lerner's former cell). Try your best to follow all this:

"Gavriella's car was discovered after he went to Grigori Lerner's office where he met with Sofa Landver, formerly a Labor Party member of the Knesset. Lerner was convicted on three attempts to bribe elected officials...His arrest in 1997 dragged a parade of politicians to the National Unit For Serious And International Crime Investigations including Natan Sharansky, who received a $100,000 contribution from Lerner, and Labour MK Shimon Peres, who had promoted the career of Sofa Landver from being his Russian teacher to being a Knesset member..."

WIRM - Yuri Nudleman wrote a book claiming Sharansky was a former KGB agent, and today is on the payroll of the Russian mafia. Many who had dismissed his claims thought twice about them after an Israeli court ordered the impoverished Nudleman to pay Sharansky 900,000 shekels in libel compensation. This item more than implies that Sharansky is, in fact, on the take.

But it is the information on Peres which is even more compelling. It is well known that Peres rewards his dalliances, with the likes of Collette Avital and Dahlia Itzik, with political careers. But he even hands one out to his

Russian teacher? Of course we know she really wasn't teaching him Russian. But why was Ezra Gavriella visiting Sofa Landver as the bomb was being placed in his car? Or, offering a scenario, what did he do to get Shimon so mad?

ITEM - International Herald Tribune, July 16, 2004

"Elias Khoury went on to win landmark legal cases against Israeli settlements. He sent his children to a Jerusalem school with blended Muslim, Jewish and Christian children. His son George was studying at Hebrew University and was friends with both Arabs and Jews. One evening last March, George went for a jog in Jerusalem's French Hill neighborhood and was shot dead by members of the Al Aksa Martyrs Brigade, the Fatah militant group. The group put out a statement boasting that it had killed a settler."

WIRM - Now who did George Khoury (or his father) cheese off so much to get himself assassinated? Fatah is in the dirty business of mass murder. Their modus operandi is not to risk exposure by shooting lone joggers in suburban Jerusalem. Khoury was another victim of the Killers For Peace, hit squad.

ITEM - Jerusalem Post, July 14, 04 –
Moses And Herzl, Striking Parallels
by David Golinkin

"Herzl had a similar plan. He wrote in his, 'Address To The Rothschilds' in 1895: 'This simple old idea is the Exodus from Egypt.' He said to Baron Maurice de Hirsch in 1895, 'I will say to the German Kaiser: Let us go forth...'

"Herzl travelled to Constantinople in June of 1896. The sultan at the time owed Turkey's creditors the incredible sum of 106 million pounds. Herzl let it be known that if the Jews were given Palestine as an independent state, they would

undertake the regulation and normalization of Turkish finances and liberate the country from foreign control.

"There was only one hitch - Herzl did not have a penny in his pocket."

WIRM - Herzl may have had an empty pocket but he clearly represented people who did not, the Rothschilds and the Hirsches. The Post writer suffers from a common affliction in local journalism; he just can't make obvious connections. Herzl would never have made the offer if he couldn't back it up. The 1896 version of the IMF had the Sultan by his pantaloons but he still wouldn't budge. He and his country soon paid for his refusal.

ITEM - (undated); Sharon: Peace With Syria Requires Return Of Golan,
by Josef Federman (AP)

"Prime Minister Ariel Sharon told lawmakers yesterday that peace with Syria would require a full withdrawal from the Golan Heights. Sharon's comments, made to parliament's Defence And Foreign Affairs Committee, were an unprecedented admission by the career hard-liner."

WIRM - More longterm public preparation from Israel's greatest actor.. The hard-liner image is being pushed by AP and apparently its readers still buy it. However, most Israelis now sense or know that Sharon is a mole in the Right and when he makes any announcement, sooner or later, it becomes policy.

ITEM - From Makor Rishon, July 31, 04 an interview with Meir Palevsky, a private detective who was hired by a Shinui MK to set up the current Interior Minister for blackmail, forcing Shinui Party Chief Tommy Lapid to fire his errant colleague.

"I didn't think it was such a big deal. I've been involved in incidents ten times more serious. Like when Peres tried to kill Rabin and sent his rivals equally to their deaths or pensions. Do you know what was going on there?

"As we continue Palevsky describes his continuing break with the Labor Party:' After Rabin was murdered I abandoned them because Peres was the shit who created Satan. I'm a member of the Labor Central Committee but I voted Sharon.'"

WIRM - Did you catch this? Palevsky accused Peres of murdering Rabin in not so many words. Now, a little background on Shunui and Lapid: Yosef "Tommy" Lapid survived the Hungarian Holocaust, arrived in Israel and became a journalist. With these credentials, the late Robert Maxwell appointed Lapid to oversee his Israel investments, including Scitex and Maariv. Lapid owes all his current power to Maxwell, which means to Peres. Back in 1947-48, Peres was in charge of breaking a worldwide boycott and acquiring arms for the fledgling Jewish state. The bulk of his acquisitions came from what is now known as the Czech Republic, through Robert Maxwell. Thus when Palevsky talks, someone should pay attention. To contact him and ask him what he meant, or to listen to him try to get out of what he said, here's how to contact him:

Palevsky's office is at 191 Rechov Ben Yehuda, Tel Aviv (tel: 03-546-3442).

ITEM - Michael Moore's Fahrenheit 9 -11. A group of us trudged down to the Jerusalem Theatre to see the movie that is terrifying the American political establishment.

WIRM - The film is not about 9 -11 at all. It's an anti-war, anti-Bush movie which totally misses the big picture. Moore is just a Democrat who believes Kerry would fix the mess. He just doesn't get it. Look at three of Kerry's Middle East Advisors: Footlick, Berger, and Indyk. All are members of the board of the Peres Institute For Peace. Indyk was investigated for absconding with top secret information on his laptop, while Berger, former head of Americans For Peace Now, committed the same illegal espionage, literally, through the seat of his pants.

And these crooks are going to do an improved job of bringing peace to the Middle East? Moore just doesn't have the hang of the shared Skull and Bones occultism of both candidates, which made the film useful but superficial.

ITEM - Aug. 6, '04, Fox News interview with General Tommy Franks. We learn that four days before 9 -11, Franks gave a tv interview within which he said his greatest fear was that the World Trade Center would be attacked with hijacked planes. The WTC was hit while he was on his way to Pakistan. His first thought was, 'It's El - Qaida.':

WIRM - Carmi Gillon was head of the Shin Bet during Rabin's assassination. A few months before, he told a press gathering that his greatest fear was Rabin being assassinated and it didn't have to be by a settler. The murderer could be a curly haired, dark skinned Bar Ilan student who lives in Herzlia. Gillon was in Paris when Rabin was shot. His first thought was, 'It's a Jew.'"

Franks was on his way to Pakistan to coordinate the Afghanistan invasion. Like Gillon, he pre-established a few flimsy alibis. Franks was in on the real 9 - 11 plot. Now Gillon is back in the news and the world had better worry. His newest greatest fear is an attack by "Jewish extremists" on the Temple Mount.

http://web.israelinsider.com/bin/en.jsp?enPage=ArticlePage&enDisplay=view&enDispWhat=object&enDispWho=Article%5EI3890&enZone=Security&enVersion=0&

ITEM - Every Israeli news source; Avraham Burg and Dov Weisglass quit politics to go into "private business."

WIRM - We still don't know why Burg hit the road or who made him, but Weisglass' motives are clear enough to anyone who has trained himself to cut through the baloney and just read the news. It's this simple: All Of Weisglass' criminal activities on behalf of Sharon and Arafat are being exposed, and he's heading for the hills.

http://www.haaretzdaily.com/hasen/pages/ShArt.jhtml?itemN o=252528&contrassID=2&subContrassID=5&sbSubContrass ID=0&listSrc=Y

ALM 14 - NOT SEASICK IN MIAMI

I am in Toronto and I open my e-mails. Five people have sent me Yediot Ahronot's report on the Sharon giveaway. He had cut a deal with German Foreign Minister Fischer of the Bilderbergs and American National Security Advisor Rice of the Council On Foreign Relations. The Jews would be removed forcibly from Gaza. The Gaza Strip would be extended into the Sinai. Israel would hand Egypt most of the Western Negev to replace the land it "donated" to the "palestinian" state.

The forces of the New World Order had united against the Jews of Gaza and Sharon was leading their charge. This time everyone meant business and would stop at nothing to get their way.

The next day the Likud would hold a referendum on Sharon's Gaza giveaway. A rally was organized in Tel Aviv to defeat Sharon's nefarious plans. A pregnant mother and her four young daughters were slaughtered on their way from Gaza to the rally.

I knew it was DELIBERATE. Our secret secret services had provided the intelligence to our Arab "enemies" enabling

248

them to perform the most ghastly of atrocities to wreck the anti-pullout movement.

But the referendum passes anyway and everyone I meet in Toronto is delighted. They actually believe that Israeli democracy has triumphed. About 130 people gather for my lecture at the Toronto Zionist Center. I tell all that they just don't get it yet. Nothing will stop the pullout and revenge against the referendum defeat will be swift, ugly and deadly. Young Jews will die starting today and then Arabs too.

I fly to Miami to help film producer Peter Goldman put together a Rabin documentary. He was satisfied that Sharon was defeated by his own party. I say the same thing to him. If the New World Order wants something done, they could give a hoot about silly democratic referendums. The atrocities will begin and the Israeli public will be mind-controlled into demanding the uprooting of Jews from Gaza.

Then the blood starts flowing, but not just in Gaza. Thirteen young soldiers are blown apart when their WWII-vintage armored vehicles roll over powerful mines. You can be certain our secret secret services of the "peace" camp gave the "enemy" the precise details needed to murder these young men.

Now, 75% of Israelis want a Gaza pullout and 100,000 gather in Tel Aviv demanding it. We're on our way, but one more little push is needed.

So an Israeli tank shoots into a crowd of Gaza teenagers with the cameras rolling. This was NO ACCIDENT. Now world pressure for a Gaza pullout will turn the tide.

Odd, I think, that an American missile blows up an Iraqi wedding just a few hours later with even more fatal results.

Coincidence? I'll stick with coordination. A lot of blood will be spilled until the Gaza surrender. But nothing will stop it. The Jews will leave, the religious nationalists will be totally demoralized. The only people who believe in preserving a Jewish state will stop so believing. And a Sabbataian revival will replace love of Zion.

If not? Israel will face a new Holocaust as the CFR troops heat up the Arab world to the boiling point. How do you humiliate the Islamic sense of macho? You just go through your recruitment files and make prison guards of the most perverse sadists on the list. And no one will figure out how you arranged all the fun.

The Tour

We began in Sacramento with a cancelled conference and Ruel Jones saving the day. He hosted me and organized a successful last minute home meeting. I don't deserve to know so many wonderful people. So many, in fact, that I can't name them all without boring you. So here are a few highlights.

San Francisco is highly under-promoted and the crowd small. But Ari Goldberg and Bob Savage shelter me and provide much consolation. However, the ultimate compliment was the appearance of Gillian from my newsgroup who flew all the way from Chicago to hear me. She was the first of many to so flatter me. I think of the distinguished attorney who flew 2000 miles to hear me in Toronto, the rock star Paul of Poker Face who drove three hours to see me in Miami, not much further than the lovely Annie Tread who honored me in the same way in the same city. Wherever I appeared, people took great pains to see me and I will never forget anyone of them.

Reno was a nice improvement. Patty Lee did a nice job of organization, which included a major talk show interview a few hours before the lecture. The wise "Country Rebbe," Menashe Bovits invited me to lecture at the Temple Emmanuel, a very mainstream synagogue. It was a revelation. Mouths were agape for two straight hours. No one had ever heard even a rumor about the Rabin assassination. In mid-speech I asked the crowd, "Who here has heard of Avishai Raviv? No one, not a soul knew who he was. How great is the American Jewish media coverup!

Off to Fort Collins, Colorado. There I speak at a synagogue on Friday night. There are about 100 in the congregation including children. They perform a spirited kabalat shabbat service. Their faces are Oriental, black, American Indian, Nordic.These are Christians who returned to their Hebrew roots to be closer to their God. It's a wonderful idea. I know the suspicions in the Jewish world and I believe Jews were meant to be Jews. What I saw was Christians showing deep respect for Jewish ceremonies and I liked it.

The next day was the triumph in Denver. Don Weideman of the American Freedom Network had really made my visit unforgettable. About 500 people heard my Save Israel-Sabbataian lecture and when I concluded two hours later, I received a long standing ovation. In fact, this was a highlight of my life. The lecture was filmed and I will try to distribute it as soon as I can.

Of note. Rabbi Marvin Antelman provided me a carton of his book, To Eliminate The Opiate Volume II to sell at my Sabbataian lectures in Colorado and Toronto. It was no easy task hauling it from airport to airport. But Toronto never saw a copy. Denver purchased the whole heavy box. Rabbi Antelman's reputation is far more widespread than either of us realized.

Evidence In Toronto

Toronto was less hurried. I had a beautiful suite provided to me by the marvelous KC Black. And I had time to listen to people with information. Steve of middleeastfacts.com called to inform me that he had interviewed a very important witness who I should meet. And very important he was. His name was Eli and he was the IDF officer responsible for military security at the rally where Rabin was murdered. He had escaped his suspicions in Toronto. We drove to a restaurant to talk but he would not leave the car until he had told his story. Chain-smoking, the young and athletic Israeli related the following:

"I was the IDF officer in charge of security for the Tel Aviv area. Two days before the rally, all the security officers of the police and Shabak met in north Tel Aviv. I felt something was wrong right away. There was going to be a gathering of 150,000 people at a most sensitive moment and the meeting was open. Anyone could have come in. And the attitude of the meeting was all wrong. It was jovial. The police displayed an aerial photo of the City Hall square and instead of pinpointing problem areas, the meeting just discussed what a great photo it was.

"The Shabak controlled the security for the rally and barely gave the police any duties. But more shocking, they gave me nothing to do. They made it plain by ignoring me, that they just didn't want the army there. I left the meeting and decided I'd send a jeep and crew backstage anyway.

"I ordered the jeep to park near the stairs where Rabin was supposed to descend and then had a look around. It was at about 8:00 PM, just before the rally was to begin that I saw a reserve officer from my unit coming down the stairs from the stage. He had a security pin on his shirt but I didn't issue it to him. I asked him, 'What are you doing here? I didn't call you here.' He answered that he came of his own volition. I asked him, 'Who issued you the security pass?' and he didn't answer me. Something wasn't right and I decided to inspect the stage myself.

"I walked up the stairs with my gun in its holster. No one stopped me and there was no metal detector anywhere. On the stage I saw Benny Lahav, he was the Shabak's personnel officer and he was busy shining a flashlight at apartment windows opposite the square. That wasn't his duty. He was supposed to be coordinating his forces, not playing with a flashlight. I walked up to him and pointed to my gun, saying, 'I could kill Rabin if I wanted to.' He answered, 'Why would you do that?' I replied, 'How did I get a gun on this stage without being stopped?' He ignored the question and went back to shining his flashlight off buildings.

"I stayed until the rally ended and decided I was no longer needed. I ordered my jeep crew to stay backstage until everyone had left and took a bus home. Not ten minutes later, the crew radioed me that something happened backstage and Rabin may have been hurt. But at that moment I saw Rabin's limousine led by a squad car on Dizengoff Street. I assumed he was headed to a party in Herzlia Pituach and that everything was alright.

"Later, when I heard he was murdered, nothing made sense. What was Rabin's car doing so far from Ichilov Hospital? If he was shot, why was only one squad car accompanying him?

"The next day, I went to my base and expected, at a minimum, to be dressed down, and more likely, to be stripped of my rank. Rabin was murdered on my watch and I knew I was going to be investigated for dereliction of duty. But my commander, Col.Shlomo Arad, didn't call me. In fact, he never asked what happened that night. And when the Shamgar Commission convened, I expected to be called to testify about military security at the rally. But I never was and I still don't know why.

"I knew I could have done better if I was a bit smarter and I left for Toronto to sort out my life. I was set up to fail and I strongly suspected it was by the real murderers. Your book woke me up and that's why I wanted to talk to you."

So did my lecture. After hearing it, Eli bought a ticket back to Israel, realizing he had a country to try and save.

Friday night Shabbat with Dr. Reuven Lexier and his lively family. He has evidence for me. It is an account of Sam Bronfman's relationship with Canada's Prime Minister in 1939, Mackenzie King, as related by Mordechai Richler in an aged copy of Saturday Night Magazine. Richler wrote that Bronfman conspired with King to make certain that no Jewish refugees from the Nazis found a home in Canada. The evil of the Bronfmans extends back further than many people know and does much to explain the behavior of the bootlegger Sam's children, Charles and Edgar (CFR), today.

Not all is so serious. After my lecture, beautifully organized by Atara Beck, as usual I offered an open invitation to anyone who so desired to meet me for drinks. Joining me were two academics, one a physics professor, both members of my newsgroup list.. The journalist Marshall Shapiro was accompanied by a strikingly pretty lady named Deanna. Her mother was Jewish, she learned just months before, and her father Norwegian. Her looks were all Scandinavian but her curiosity was now Jewish. She had taken to lighting candles on Shabbat and learning her prayers. Hers was a fascinating story and she had the charm to mesmerize any man who heard it.

Over time, I've grown comfortable in the presence of beautiful women but my academic guests were too intimidated by Deanna's beauty to even address her. This would not do for members of my list. After visiting hundreds of my advocates on my tours, I knew they all shared the same decency, intelligence and concern. It was just a question of overcoming a little awkwardness.

Deanna asked me, "Is it easier to be a Jewish man or woman?" I didn't really have a good answer so I turned to my professorial guests and said, "I can't answer this lady's question."

From then on the conversation flowed. I remember the little human triumphs as much as a successful speech. I'm delighted to bring the special people of my newsgroup together.

And Away We Go To Miami Beach

The Gaza pullout atrocities are building steam. I know the real bloodshed is coming. I am interviewed by such great radio hosts as Stan Monteith, Keith Vyzgoth, Nelson Thall, Tsachi Gadish and repeat the message: The Gazan Jews are on the chopping block. The violence will increase until they are chopped. Israelis are told that Gaza will be the last payment before peace. They can't see the Mafia extortion. The payments will never stop until Jerusalem. The American-British CFR forces are building their world war and a truncated Israel will be the biggest loser. It's 1938 all over. They are putting up walls again, not to keep Arabs out but to keep Jews in.

I ask, "Is it worth the life of one American to bring democracy to Iraq?"

Peter Goldman informs me that three of the backers for his Rabin film have pulled out, taking half the budget with them. I think, Australia again. Last year my Australian tour was marred when certain upstanding Jews decided that taking down posters of my lectures and censoring press coverage was the patriotic thing to do.

But Miami turns out to be different. All three local Jewish papers publish impressive reports of my work. The Bnai Isaac synagogue is filled for my speech. A second lecture is hastily arranged in order to find Peter replacement backers. The Miami Jews are willing to listen.

I have just one stop left, the surprisingly pretty city of Birmingham, Alabama where I recorded two tv shows for Marge and Marvin Randolph. It's now or never. I have to go fishing.

On my previous American tour I went deep-sea fishing in Hawaii in nine foot swells and caught nothing but the most disgusting seasickness ever suffered by man. Australia was an improvement. Gillian and Trevor Norman took me up the Murray River where Israeli techniques worked wonders. The Israeli miracle bait is chicken fat and it caught me about fifteen nice mullets. But the Murray River is not the open sea, so there was no danger of seasickness.

Miami was different. My one opportunity to try the ocean again came on the windiest day of the year. Beaches were closed because of the riptides, and the swells were again, nine feet. I was asking for it by getting on that boat. But my reckless nature won out and I stepped onto the deck. I received my rod, put a little chicken fat on the hook and let it sink into the waters of the marina. I brought in a pinfish within seconds.

My fellow fishermen, four Japanese tourists, were very impressed. "Chicken catch fish?" he asked.

We left the harbor and the rainstorm hit just as we reached the open sea. The swells were ridiculous. The bow of the boat was totally out of the water. We tilted 45 degrees starboard, then 45 degrees port. Not ten minutes into the sea, the first Japanese angler rushed to the head. "No," shouted a crewmate. "Over the side." Then came his buddies to join him. The first said to the skipper, "This is too much. We must go back." The skipper explained that he was stuck on board for the next four hours. That is how long the three Japanese unwilling sailors lay prone in the cabin. Their unsick buddy sat earnestly on his chair but not a fish bit his line all trip long. He told me, "We paid $125 to get sick and hold a rod for nothing."

An hour before, the crewmate baited the other anglers' hooks with baby swordfish. When he came up to me I turned down the bait. "I'm from Israel," I proudly stated. "And I'm using chicken fat."

"To catch fish?" he queried.

"That's why I'm here."

He grinned and walked to his own rod.

I noticed something. We were in a storm that could sink lesser boats. But I wasn't getting seasick in Miami. I threw my line in and was the first to hit a fish. I knew by its fight that it was strong and probably pretty big. After an invigorating battle I brought in a five pound ugly, inedible fish called a remora. I didn't care. This monster of the deep made me very happy.

The crewmate took it off the hook. He looked at me and said, "Chicken fat works."

"Yup," I answered. "Chicken fat works."

CHAPTER SIX –
OUTSIDE INTERVENTION

ALM 1 - REJOICE NOT, HOPEFUL ISRAELIS

When Labor deserted the Sharon government, joy reigned in many quarters of Israel. At last, Peres and his gang of treacherous defeatists were gone for good. And when Sharon announced that Binyamin Netanyahu would be his foreign minister, pure glee emanated from the same hopeful, deluded corners of the nation.

Nothing will convince these desperate but good-hearted souls that Netanyahu is a duplicitous cretin, part and parcel of the same New World Order deadly games that the previous Foreign Minister, Peres, plays. Nor will these people understand that this Likud-led temporary government is just as manipulated by the same outside forces as the Left.

But let's try and point out a pattern for them anyway. Those aware of my conclusions will know that Israel's (and the world's) primary enemies are the Council On Foreign Relations (CFR) of New York, whose permanent chairman is David Rockefeller and the Jesuit-Vatican axis of Italy, Spain, France and Germany, whose secret titular head is King Juan Carlos of Spain. While Netanyahu was funded and groomed by the CFR, he is not above jumping ship to the other enemy camp. Recall when he was prime minister that:

Thurs. March 26, 1998 –
Jerusalem Post Courting Europe
By JAY BUSHINSKY

(March 13) - Seldom has an Israeli premier made such a concerted effort to bring key European Union members into the Middle East peacemaking picture. In a flash prime

minister Netanyahu was away in his flag-bedecked motorcade to see King Juan Carlos at the royal palace, at the start of a meticulously planned trip.

Just before he was removed as Foreign Minister, Peres was busy making deals with the PLO's pathological liar, Saeb Erekat, in where else but Spain:

http://www.jpost.com/servlet/Satellite?pagename=JPost/A/JP Article/ShowFull&cid=1036122686525
Nov. 1, 2002
Peres meets Erekat in Spain, says will not stop working for peace

It took Netanyahu barely two days as Foreign Minister before he was off to Italy to continue Peres' diplomacy.

Ha'aretz newsflash: Sun. Nov. 10/02

16:Foreign Minister Netanyahu discusses possibility of Israel joining EU with Italian Prime Minister Berlusconi

So much for the difference Netanyahu will make. But he is far from the only member of this government who marches to the NWO beat. Just like former Defence Minister Ehud Barak, who had to spend several months in Washington receiving his marching orders before he could take up his post, Shlomo Mofaz was appointed the new Defence Minister only after his was indoctrinated for several months in Washington. He learned the NWO ropes at Martin Indyk's notorious "think" tank, The Washington Center For Near East Studies.

In Feb. 02, I was invited to address the Likud Central Cultural Commitee convention. Sitting on the dais alongside me was Deputy Internal Security Minister Gideon Ezra. He walked off the platform when I proved that members of the Shabak led by Carmi Gillon and Shimon Peres organized the

Rabin murder. When he returned to speak, several Likud members, led by a former football great Israel Ben Dror, left the auditorium in protest.

Lest anyone think otherwise, this government will cover up the Rabin assassination and the crimes of Oslo just like any other government we are allowed to elect.

ALM 2 - IMAGINE THERE'S NO BEILIN

Last night while surfing the tv, I reached a movie just starting called Mr. Holland's Opus. When I read that it starred Richard Dreyfuss, I reached for the clicker. Because Dreyfuss had hosted Yossi Beilin's Geneva atrocity, I had vowed to boycott Dreyfuss forever.

This wasn't a simple decision because he had made an important imnpact on me once. In 1979, I received my MA from the Hebrew University of Jerusalem. My thesis title was; Us Against Them: A Comparative Study Of Leonard Cohen's, The Favourite Game and Mordechai Richler's, The Apprenticeship Of Duddy Kravitz. Both were outstanding works of literature created by two Montreal Jews in the late 1950s and I felt this was something worth investigating. But what turned the tide for me was Richard Dreyfuss' brilliant portrayal of Duddy Kravitz in the film of the book's title. The depth of his understanding of Duddy Kravitz inspired me to dig deeper.

So, breaking my vow out of sentiment or curiosity I started watching Mr. Holland's Opus, a very moving film, and thought to myself, "What an intelligent actor Dreyfuss is, and what a stupid individual." How could he be hoodwinked into becoming master of ceremonies for the Geneva ceremony?

As the film progressed, I saw startling parallels between it and the Geneva fiasco. The climactic moment of the film occurs when John Lennon is murdered and Mr. Holland sings a Lennon song to his deaf son. The climax of Geneva was the signing of the non-accord followed by all participants and audience breaking into a rousing rendition of Lennon's Imagine.

Imagine is the evilest song ever written. Just look:

Imagine

Imagine there's no heaven,
It's easy if you try,
No hell below us,
Above us only sky,
Imagine all the people
living for today...

Imagine there's no countries,
It isn't hard to do,
Nothing to kill or die for,
No religion too,
Imagine all the people
living life in peace...

Imagine no possesions,
I wonder if you can,
No need for greed or hunger,
A brotherhood of man,
Imagine all the people
Sharing all the world...

You may say I'm a dreamer,
but I'm not the only one,
I hope some day you'll join us,
And the world will live as one.

Let us conduct a perfunctory examination of these lyrics.

"Imagine there's no heaven...no hell below us." In simpler terms, imagine there's no God, nor morality, no judgement. In such a world there's no fear of "living for today.

"Imagine there's no countries...no religions too." Skipping the sloppy grammar, Lennon is now spelling out the New World Order vision of what many refer to as the illuminati. But there's more"Imagine no possessions." Here you have some communism thrown into the pudding. If only there was a world without heaven and hell, good and evil, where mankind holds no property or sentimental goods, we can all live in peace in a "brotherhood of man." Now why would Lennon write such wicked, rotten, dangerous lyrics? Easy, he was exploited by the leaders of this globalist fascist world takeover they are in the midst of perpetrating on mankind. A few years ago, Yoko Ono decided to visit Israel and display her art. There was much fishy about the trip so I looked into the matter. I discovered a world of research painting a very different picture of her and Lennon. There are pretty good researchers out there claiming Lennon, far from being a man of peace, was violent and may have been responsible for the murder of Brian Epstein. Don't laugh this off until you see the evidence. One thing is for certain, immediately after Epstein's death, Yoko Ono came into the picture and it may not all be coincidence. A good starting point would be to read Fenton Bresler's book, Who Killed John Lennon. Here's what I wrote:

IMAGINE THERE'S NO LENNON
by Barry Chamish

" However Ono did it, Lennon began writing songs that fit the NWO agenda like a glove. In his first solo album, the most memorable song, called God, attempts to destroy religion as thoroughly as possible. The song begins with the line, "God is a concept by which we measure our pain," a patently false observation. As any religious person will explain, God is a concept by which we measure our joy. The song then lists Gods from Jesus to Elvis which Lennon rejects, in favor of, "I just believe in me, Yoko and me."

"Just previous to and after this, Lennon recorded a series of meaningless radical anthems like 'Give Peace A Chance' and 'Woman Is The Nigger Of The World', a song which one can argue whether it is more insulting to women or blacks. But the ultimate disgrace was a ditty called 'Imagine', which attempts to brainwash and inculcate his listeners in the full NWO agenda.

" 'Imagine' paints a world with no heaven or hell, that is with no morality, with no countries, possessions or religions. It is a thoroughly dreadful vision of a robotic state without devotion to any higher good; just what the NWO ordered.

"During this period, Paul McCartney attacked Lennon's behaviour and his irrational attachment to Ono. Lennon went on a vengeful rampage, posing for a photo of him holding a pig's ears, a mockery of McCartney's Ram album cover and attacked McCartney viciously in a song called 'How Do You Sleep'.

" But the ultimate revenge was rumored to have been Ono's. Just prior to McCartney's performance in Japan, he was busted at Tokyo Airport when the police found a small amount of grass in his equipment. McCartney was jailed and in ways he refuses to divulge, the cops forced him to sing 'Yesterday' for them. The humiliation of McCartney was complete and Lennon's vendetta against him stopped.

"That freed Lennon to ruin his career with the close cooperation of his Dragon Lady. He now released albums and appeared on stage with her cacaphonious contribution sabotaging his musical integrity. That was the state of affairs in 1979, when Lennon returned to the studios to record his final album. Once he was dead, the mediocre cuts became hits and even Ono had a number one bestseller. The exact motive for Lennon's death remains unclear but there is no doubt that his killer was mind-controlled and fulfilled a covert operation in the exact mode of most political assassinations since the 1960s. And now Yoko Ono is doing her unique *thing in Israel, and whatever the real reasons she is here, there is evil in her motives. That's her way of doing things."*

Right after the Oslo "peace" process went public, I interviewed Ron Pundak, one of the two academics Beilin shipped to Oslo to negotiate Israel's final war of destruction. Among the many things Pundak told me was, "Beilin doesn't believe in borders. He believes they are the cause of war. Israel can only live in peace if it eliminates its borders."

No wonder Pundak was also singing Imagine at Geneva. Peres should have been but he's been pushed out of the limelight and he gets very vindictive when that happens. Yitzhak Rabin, wherever he may be, learned this the hard way. But Peres' New Middle East was the same idea. Israel eliminates its borders and becomes the New Jersey Turnpike of the Middle East, a good place to stop for trucks going from Morocco to Iran. Out of this vision, Israel has built a toll road through the center of the country. It's mostly empty now, but the motels will be built when the Middle East becomes one big bloc of the world government.

Not just politicians, like the incredibly crooked Ehud Olmert, are used by the globalist powerbrokers. Popular artists are useful as well. Lennon was exploited by the NWO and I think he was waking up, which is why he had to be snuffed out by Mark David Chapman, the Yigal Amir of Hawaii, whose motive was that he wanted to prove that he was the real Catcher In The Rye; a natural enough reason to spend his dying days in prison.

Dreyfuss is being exploited by the same forces, but I'm certain he doesn't know it. However, the patent of using popular artists to forward the global agenda carries on. Later this month, a delegation led by Jason Alexander, Jennifer Aniston and Brad Pitt arrives in Israel to push the Geneva peace vision. The organization sending them is called Silent No Longer. Look them up at www.silentnolonger.com and you'll see who is sponsoring their journey. High on the list are the Rockefeller Brothers of CFR and NWO fame. Just below them you'll find Edgar Bronfman Jr., son of the notorious CFR namesake father, despite the Jewish ban on naming children after living relatives.

It is Junior who bought Universal Studios and is working hard to acquire Sony's film archive. What better way to control the entertainment industry and the stars within it.

Alexander, Aniston and company have no idea the suffering they are going to promote. They will be directly responsible for war and slaughter and they haven't a clue how they are being used. Still, before they arrive, perhaps they should consider the final fate of John Lennon.

ALM 3 - THE Q IS ON THE FLOOR: THE CHEATING OF ISRAEL

In light of the results of the last Israeli election, let us consider Sharon's withdrawal plan. If we recall, 67% of the voters chose to elect the Likud and it's leader, while a mere 18 seats out of 120 went to the Labor Party. The electorate chose overwhelmingly to throw out the scions of Oslo and get back on the survival track.

Yet Sharon on 18/12/03 publicly announced that he was going to cheat Israel on a massive scale by adopting the Oslo track of withdrawal from most of Judea, Samaria and Gaza and uproot tens of thousands of Jews by flattening their villages, and at least one full- fledged city. Sharon did not consult with the government cabinet before making the announcement, in fact, he didn't even inform his own ministers. But look who he did choose to consult with!

According to the weekly newsmagazine Makor Rishon 19/12/03, Sharon formulated his program by first consulting with Labor leader Shimon Peres. This meeting was followed by advisory sessions with Labor stalwarts Matan Vilnaii, Ephraim Sneh, Shalom Simchon and Ehud Barak. With them, he not only coordinated his withdrawal plan, but assured them that Labor would be invited into the government after his partners on the Right bolted in revolt.

And there's much more. Who are Sharon's two closest political advisors? One is Dov Weisglass, the attorney and business partner, along with Sharon's son Omri, of Jibril Rajoub, the PLO's chieftain of Jericho. The other is Eli Landau. Look at the masthead of the greatest deception of the year, The Geneva Initiative, and under the sullied moniker of Yossi Beilin, there is Landau's name. Sharon, for all his lying protestations, sponsored the Geneva stunt.

The electorate may have voted Likud but they're getting Labor and Oslo. This is the most flagrant display of cheating Sharon has ever pulled and my reading of the general media is that he's going to get away with it.

The question is, how? How can he cheat 2/3 of the Israeli people, and 80% of the country's Jews, without the vast majority understanding how they've been cheated? No amount of logic can explain it no matter how hard one seeks the reason.

I mulled the question for a long night, then a personal vignette hit me that did more to explain the cheating acceptance than any political analysis. Bear with me for a few paragraphs before we examine the upcoming consequences of Sharon's wool pulling.

Soily Is Good

There is a club in Jerusalem that meets to play Scrabble. For a decade I was a member and through arduous dictionary memorization, became a perennial champion. However, even in its earliest days, widespread cheating infected the club. Initially, the rule was that the tiles were reversed, placed face down on the top of the box lid and picked at random. But some players marked the good tiles subtly, so the rule changed that tiles had to be picked from a bag. That led to new forms of cheating. One involved feeling the tiles one by one until the telltale smoothness of the valuable blanks was detected. Another method was looking at the tiles in your hand and sneakily sliding the bad ones back in the bag.

No tile was more dreaded in the end game than the Q. It was hard to get rid of on a crowded board and if you got stuck with it at the end of the game, you had to deduct 10 points from your score. One remedy was to simply and quietly, drop the Q on the floor and claim it was there all along.

Early on, I got very good at finding the cheaters. My method was to appear to be concentrating on my own tiles while watching the opponent's hands and eyes very closely as he picked his. The most infuriating moment occurred at a national tournament when I clearly saw my opponent throw a tile back during a tight end game. There were only two tiles left in the bag, and wouldn't you know it, I picked the Q after my turn. What unsettled me more than the cheating was the supposed high character of the opponent, a respected scientist.

Sickened by the situation, I became agitated and quit the game for a year or so. But I was persuaded to return for a tournament with a big prize: a trip to the world scrabble championships. I played three games that evening.

Game one was with a woman I had known since the founding of the club. It was a close game ending with, you guessed it, the Q on the floor. And I sure didn't drop it there. Game two was fair. Game three was with an orthodox religious lady. Near the end she added an s to oily making soily. I knew it was wrong and challenged. She looked it up in the dictionary and declared, "Soily is good." I accepted the announcement, believing this upstanding woman would never cheat me to win. Only later, well after the game ended, did I look the word up myself, to discover that I had been cheated.

I appealed to the club president to overturn the game. He turned to the cheater and she lied through her teeth to him. He was fooled and the club supported the cheat.

In this case, justice was ultimately served. I stopped

wasting my life in a pointless pursuit and it blossomed. And the cheater continues with her pathetic existence. This was my first lesson in Israeli cheating. The most unexpected people are engaged in it and the people would rather believe there was no cheating in their world.

I quit the game for good in utter disgust and then Rabin was murdered. I had honed the skill of catching cheaters and this time I vowed I would not let them prosper. I caught Rabin's real murderers and though about half the country know it, they cannot be properly motivated to bring justice to their land. They would rather believe that their leaders are honest, the leaders know it, so the cheaters they elected can get away with anything. It is a national character flaw that is proving too costly in lives and integrity.

Nonetheless, Sharon is discovering a few major roadblocks to his latest cheat. Perhaps the most significant was the pronouncement earlier in the week by Rabbi Mordechai Eliahu that it is a sin to remove a Jew from his land. Rabbi Eliahu is the most influential Sephardic rabbi, and most of Israel's policemen are Sephardic. They will not defy him. If the police will not remove the Jews of Yesha from their homes, Sharon's scam won't work. And if the Yesha residents resist in number, the only way of securing their removal will be extreme violence or state-sanctioned murder.

We know the state is capable of this in secret. Recall the disarming and murder of the three soldiers in Netzarim last Oct. 26. Three young Jews were murdered to persuade the Israeli public that a withdrawal from Netzarim was in the best interests of our endangered youth. Makor Rishon added new details to the Netzarim campaign this week. Haaretz followed the murders with an article in which four officers of the reserve unit which served in Netzarim were quoted saying that the village had to be abandoned. The four officers gathered together to reveal that they said nothing of the kind and that Haaretz had simply, lied to them and to their readers. All for withdrawal.

The bloody Netzarim campaign has been dirty but surreptitious. A public slaughter of Yesha residents is another matter. This, most soldiers will refuse to engage in. So, according to a few of my sources, Sharon has brought in Turkish Moslems to the job. Let us begin with an article from the prince of defamation, Haaretz, and assume that this time they got it right:

11/04/2003

PM okays 800 Turkish workers here in return for tank deal

By Ruth Sinai, HAARETZ

Prime Minister Ariel Sharon has permitted 800 Turkish construction workers to work in Israel as part of a $687 million deal with Israel's military industries to upgrade Patton tanks for the Turkish armed forces. The workers are being employed by Israeli contractors to build private homes. The money they send home will be deducted from the sum that Israel is obliged to spend in Turkey, under the military agreement which includes mutual procurement.

The deal was worked out during long months of secret negotiations between Ta'as military industries and the administration of Turkey's military industries. It was not brought to the attention of the Employment Service which is supposed to distribute the permits for foreign workers.

The workers are sent to Israel by a private Turkish company, which is registered also in Israel, and offers them to the contractors. "Instead of the workers earning $200 a month, they will get $800 here.

Through his Israeli representative, Nissim Giyus, Arik said that Yilmazlar has succeeded in persuading the directors of the Turkish military industries in Ankara to agree to a year's trial. An Israel Miliary Industries spokesman said: "The permission to employ 800 Turkish workers was given to IMI as part of the agreement for mutual procurement.

The deal to upgrade 170 Patton tanks for the Turkish armored corps is worth some $687 million over a five-year period. It is the single largest military export deal ever carried out by the Defense Ministry. As part of the agreement, Israel agreed to acquire Turkish products or services to the tune of several tens of million shekels a year.

Israeli contractors are furious about the deal. They consider it a means of circumventing the arduous route they are forced to take to get a limited number of permits for foreign workers. One senior source described it in this way: "Suddenly some firm starts calling contractors who didn't get permits from the employment service, to offer them workers at the highest price possible."

"This is trading in humans - tanks for workers - a corrupt use of government channels to get private profits," says Hannah Zohar, who heads Kav Le'Oved, the hotline for protection of workers' rights. She believes it is a dangerous precedent. "China also has tremendous business and strategic potential for Israel but it would demand sending 10,000 workers, not 800. If this is such a good and kosher deal for Israel, why was it not done through the employment service, openly and according to accepted criteria?"

A senior government official is perplexed by the arrangement. "How is this possible? The prime minister has closed the skies, forbidden the entry of foreign workers and ordered 50,000 expelled. The government tells the unemployed they must go out and work and on the other hand, it is bringing in 800 foreign workers."

The first Turkish workers arrived over the past few weeks and got permits for a year from the interior ministry. Some of them are employed in the prestigious Mashtela project near Zehala, by contractor Yehuda Mizrahi, whose name is not on the list of those permitted to employ foreign workers. Despite numerous requests, Mizrahi was not available for comment.

The names of the workers must be sent to the defense ministry for approval. The reason for this is unclear since they are not involved in security work but rather in building villas. Other foreign workers do not have to undergo the scrutiny of security authorities.

Why are these "workers" under the scrutiny of the security authorities? Why are they earning 4 times the salary of other foreign laborers? Why are they authorized by the Turkish military? Why weren't they required to apply for work visas like everyone else? Here are two reports sent to me:

"About 800 Turkish fellows were "contracted" by the Misrad Ha'Bitachon to work as offset on the Turkish battle tank upgrade to be performed in Israel. Remarkably, most of those were still "idle" until a couple of weeks ago.

"No one really knew what "ultimate work" those fine people would do until then. About then, one of our field people received TWO phone calls to meet with the field guys, from mid-rank officers, permanent force. "Two of their sources informed that they just had many TURKISH "immigrants" being inducted into special units. The "immigrants" acted quite well trained already and stayed as a unit. As you know there are SECRET facilities closed to any scrutiny and our conclusion is that those are far from being just "prisons".

"Other folk informed that there are Ukrainian and Russian specialized people also dressed for the occasion.We reported a while back that US special units were also seen transporting the HEAVY equipments that may be used. There are no traces of where they are. That some of THOSE PEOPLE ARE NOT high "Q" specimens, is a foregone conclusion."

*

"Our info is that Turkish mercenaries are to be used to ethnically cleanse the Jewish village of Migron, with 40 families, situated in a strategically important point on the

highway from Jerusalem into the Shomron, tomorrow or the next day. Verification has been requested of the Defense Ministry, just so that they know we have heard about it."

*

Another informant spoke to me in person. He doubts that the Turks will be deployed so quickly and believes they will be called into action only in a few months and only if events turn critical for Sharon. He insists that the mercenaries are currently being taught Hebrew and are not ready to begin their operations. When they are, they will be outfitted with IDF uniforms and attack the resisting Jews with Islamic relish.

That Sharon is going ahead with the Geneva plan is now doubtless. That rebellion in the police and IDF is a real possibility is equally doubtless. That this ugly Turkish alternative to civil war is being prepared has to be examined quickly if we are to cheat Sharon's fate.

ALM 3 - REVENGE OF THE CFR

Here is a short list of CFR members who have shoved the Oslo/Roadmap processes down Israel's throat, resulting in thousands of dead Israelis and Arabs in barely ten years, not to mention the total demoralization of Israel and the mass insanity of its Islamic neighbors:

Clinton, Christopher, Baker, Albright, Zinni, Powell, Rice, Kurtzer, Seigman, Bronfman, Tenet, Haass, Friedman, Stephen Cohen, Carter, Armitage, Burns, Wolfowitz, Berger, etc. etc.

Oh yes, and Pipes, but he's pretending otherwise for the time being. That is why he spends much of his waking hours plotting to eliminate my voice. Imagine the nerve of me pointing out that he is a proud member of the little think tank that could wreck Israel and is leaving a trail of blood throughout the Middle East.

Now let us look at just how tied up he is to the CFR establishment:

**

http://rightweb.irc-online.org/org/mef.php
The Middle East Forum has existed since 1990, but in 1994 it became a nonprofit organization with <u>Daniel Pipes</u> *as its director.*
MEF is closely linked to the Washington Institute for Near East Policy, where Pipes is an adjunct scholar. Patrick Clawson of the Washington Institute for Near East Policy is senior editor of MEF's Middle East Quarterly, and the institute's Robert Satloff and Samuel Lewis sit on the Quarterly's editorial board, along with Fouad Ajami of Johns Hopkins, Anthony Cordesman of the Center for Strategic and International Studies, James Phillips of the Heritage Foundation, and Steven Plaut of the University of Haifa.

*** I have thoughtfully provided a list of CFR members. Visit the site and confirm the facts. Now we all know that the Washington Institute For Near East Policy is the Martin Indyk - run monstrosity that became the locomotive for Oslo, so considering his public stance on Israel, Pipes' chair there is suspicious enough, but let's look at his own board: ***

From the 2001, Membership Roster Of The Council On Foreign Relations <u>http://www.stanley2002.org/pfiles/a_f.htm</u>

Robert B. Satloff - CFR
Samuel W. Lewis - CFR
Anthony H. Cordesman - CFR

** Continuing... **

"Virtually all 31 signatories of the MEF report, which was used to persuade Congress to introduce and pass the Syria Accountability and Lebanese Sovereignty Restoration Act in 2003, were USCFL members, and several became high officials or advisers in the Bush foreign policy team, including Elliott Abrams, Paula Dobriansky, Richard Perle, Douglas Feith, and David Wurmser."

Elliot Abrams - CFR
Paula J. Dobriansky - CFR
Richard Perle - CFR
Douglas J. Feith - CFR

** Now look at the final name on Pipe's MEF board: why it's that pesky economics teacher from Haifa! Could that mean that the big fish and little minnow are coordinating their attacks against me? And what does the little minnow get for his effort?

You can be sure, there is a reward but it's not membership in the CFR. Searching his name I came across one other namesake: **

Peter Plaut, Managing Director and Head of European Credit Research, BANK OF AMERICA SECURITIES LTD.

He is not merely on the CFR members' list, he is also one of its biggest donors.

http://www.cfr.org/about/pdf/ar_2003/termmember.pdf.

I tried but couldn't prove a family tie to the minnow, But I'll bet you there is and it's close. But even if not, the story of Peter Plaut bears telling. Here's who he is: **

http://www.euromoney.com/?Page=792&P=/creditresearchp oll2004/hyOVERALL

In addition, he was responsible for helping the Korean and Malaysian governments re-establish capital markets access through their highly successful global debt offerings during this difficult time. He was also credited with anticipating the debt and currency crisis in Brazil and other Latin American sovereigns in late 1998.

Mr. Plaut worked at UBS Securities Inc. from 1992 to 1994, as a U.S. and international corporate and bank credit analyst and prior to that was an associate at JP Morgan Securities, Inc.

Mr. Plaut has been in Institutional Investor ranked analyst. In June 1998, he was elected as a term member to The Council on Foreign Relations and currently serves as an active participant in issues concerning U.S. and international economic and foreign policy.

** Lucky old Pete, he gets to bail out countries after the IMF has bankrupted them. And since JP Morgan was a founder of the CFR, naturally he gets to manipulate currencies for his bank while he's at it. But that's not all, look who was in Singapore, Malaysia's financial headquarters, when Pete was sorting out their World Bank debts. Why it was old Tom Plaut! And need we say that he also works for a JP Morgan affiliate?**

http://www.4-paragon.com/forex/key_executives.htm

Thomas F. Plaut
Mr. Plaut brings sixteen years of foreign exchange trading experience to F.X. Solutions. He is a former Member of Senior Management at Credit Suisse A.G. and Global Head of Proprietary Trading at Dresdner Bank A.G. While at Credit Suisse and stationed in Singapore, Mr. Plaut was in charge of all foreign exchange trading activities in the Asian region.

FX Solutions currently holds client funds at JP Morgan Chase bank.

** How the Plauts diddle with the tills of nations while their peoples starve. Yes, Peter must be a very important component of the CFR's global economics plan. But then, so is Pipes, diplomatically. Look how the CFR funnels him the money he needs to carry on. **

Funding
Between 1996 and 1998, the Middle East Forum received $130,000 from the Lynde and Harry Bradley Foundation, one of the top right wing foundations. (9)

Mark O'Keefe
Newhouse News Service
VALUES AND PHILANTHROPY
September 18, 2003
Foundation Excels at Fueling Conservative Agenda
Name a conservative idea -- whether it's school vouchers, faith-based initiatives or the premise that there's a worldwide clash of civilizations -- and the Lynde and Harry Bradley Foundation is apt to have its fingerprints on it.

Milwukee Journal Sentinel
April 3, 2003
Bradley Fighting Vehicle
*A comprehensive **new report** makes clear the foundation's import in the feeding and nurturing of the Neoconservative Movement that has led the US to war in the Middle East.*

It directly ascribes the war on Iraq to the "playbook" of the neocons, a group of "mostly Republicans," "many of whom have gotten funding from Milwaukee's Bradley Foundation."

A Newly Enriched Foundation Hires Chairman

Things changed dramatically in 1985, when the Allen-Bradley Company was sold to Rockwell International, a leading defense and aerospace conglomerate, for a whopping $1.651 billion. The Foundation benefited heavily from the sale, seeing its assets shoot up overnight from less than $14 million to more than $290 million, catapulting it into the ranks of the country's largest foundations. At that point its name was changed to the Lynde and Harry Bradley Foundation, to publicly separate it from the company. Flush with new money and an understanding that they were now poised to play a more national role, foundation trustees decided it was time to hire a professional to run the organization. They found their man in New York at the *John M. Olin Foundation*.

** Now I flip to page 106 of my 2000 CFR Annual Report which lists foundations that offered generous grants to the CFR and right after The Norwegian Ministry Of Foreign Affairs comes, surprise, surprise The John M. Olin Foundation. I said previously that I'd prove Pipes gets his money directly or indirectly from the CFR and I just did.
Now would you trust him with YOUR country? **

ALM 4 - THE MIDDLE EAST PLANS OF THE TRILATERAL COMMISSION

It's always a welcome moment when I have a chance to meet a member of my update list in person. A sign of a changing world is I usually recognize them, not by name, but by e-mail address. Such was the case last Wednesday when I met Chaim Hayman at a lecture in Jerusalem. We went out with a small group for drinks and then ended up in his nearby apartment where he assured me that he has collected some vital documentation.

How true he was to his word. Among his remarkable finds was one gem that immediately caught my eye. It was a worn, partly dog-chewed internal document prepared for the Trilateral Commission called, The Israeli-Palestinian Issue. Here, at long last, was the Trilateral Commission's real Middle East agenda.

For those unacquainted with this powerful group, it is a very good idea to get to know them. In 1974, the chairman of the Council On Foreign Relations (CFR), David Rockefeller decided to create an international branch of his insidious think tank, encompassing select American members of the CFR along with the chosen elite from NATO countries and Japan. Hence, the tri of Trilateral.

Although the original organization had fewer than 200 members, by 1976, they had taken over the White House. Among the Trilateralists in the new administration were Carter, Vance, Brown, Mondale and the man with the hardest name to spell in diplomatic history, Zbigniew Brzezinski.

Unlike the CFR, the Trilateral Commission is secretive and rarely makes public policy announcements. But when they decide on a policy, the whole world will feel it.

Which makes the document about to be revealed so important. The Israeli-Palestinian Issue was prepared for the Trilateral Commission's meeting in Washington between April 21-23,1990 by one Garret Fitzgerald, a former Irish Prime Minister and then-Deputy European Chairman of the Commission. Why these credentials have anything to do with Middle East expertise is never explained and the 42 page report is superficial and riddled with mistakes.

Here is what really happened during the Winter of 1990 in Israel, followed by Fitzgerald's twisted interpretation of the events.

In the Autumn of 1989 Israel enjoyed a unity government, with Shamir at the head. Peres was determined to overthrow Shamir and his stategy focused on the Internal Affairs Minister he had promoted to power, Arieh Deri of the Shas Party.

Peres had accepted the post as Finance Minister and appointed Yossi Beilin his deputy minister. They recorded every pruta Deri was stealing from the Treasury and by late 1989 Peres sent Beilin to blackmail him. Either he would join the coup against Shamir and lead his party out of the government, or he would go to prison for massive embezzlement. Needless to say, Deri buckled and Beilin started bragging that he had Shas in his "back pocket." (Details of the coup are found in my article in the National Review, March 14, 1994 or in my book Traitors And Carpetbaggers In The Promised Land - Hearthstone Publishing, 1997).

With Shas in on the junta, Peres had enough Knesset members to fell the government in a non-confidence motion. All he needed was an excuse the public would buy. So he went concocting an issue that would appear to justify his felling of the government.

In January of 1990, he leaked Ezer Weizman's secret meetings with the PLO in Geneva, hoping Shamir would take the bait. He did at first, demanding Weizman's resignation from the government.

And the public played along, further demanding that Weizman be put on trial for his illegal rendezvous with the enemy. Into the fray walked Peres, avidly defending Weizman and threatening a non-confidence motion if he was sacked. Shamir saw the trap for what it was and reached a silly compromise: Weizman would be expelled to the outer cabinet and not take part in sensitive security meetings. The public, wanting its government to survive, reluctantly accepted this plan.

So Peres called for help and it arrived in the form of Secretary Of State James Baker. He flew to Cairo and

278

cooked up the infamous six point Baker Peace Plan with President Mubarak, knowing its clauses would be unacceptable to Shamir. One clause more than subtly called for the division of Jerusalem and Shamir rejected the Baker Plan. He fell into the trap.

Peres called for the Israeli government to, "Say Yes To Baker," and announced that he would initiate a non-confidence motion over the issue. To the nation's surprise, the Orthodox Right Wing Shas Party joined with Peres and the government fell. By June, Shas's constituency pressed the party to re-join Shamir and Peres' plot failed. He retaliated by releasing proof of Deri's crimes to the right addresses and the Deri Scandal began in earnest. As we shall see shortly, Yitzhak Rabin was utterly disgusted by Peres' manipulations but first let's look at what Fitzgerald told the Trilateral Commission:

After praising Mubarak's "courageous" peace work with Baker, and noting Shamir's rejection of it, Fitzgerald observes, "the collapse of the Israeli government in mid-March 1990 was a result of a Shamir bluff being called by the Palestinians, the Americans and the Israeli Labour Party. This interpretation sees Shamir as having been forced to make an excuse to get out of accepting the initiation of the dialogue, even if necessary at the expense of the collapse of his government."

Or, "the Jerusalem issue was an excuse to cover a much more general concern on their part at the idea of commencing such a dialogue, which some fear, could undermine the longer-term objectives of the Right with regard to the Occupied territories."

Finally concluding, "The initiation of a peace process became for the first time in Israel's history the major issue between the parties, causing the collapse of the government."

And if you think he got everything wrong so far, look at

this: "Earlier differences between Peres and Rabin, which, at times had appeared to have an explosive potential, disappeared temporarily, with Rabin, despite his aggressive attitude towards the Intifadah, supporting Peres."

Of course, Rabin as Defence Minister took all the steps necessary to keep the Intifada on hot but that's not the point here. Rabin despised Peres' exploitation of Israeli democracy and called the coup against Shamir, "the stinking deal," one of Rabin's most remembered quotes.

Now, let's look at the Trilateral Commission's overall attitude towards the conflict. First of all, Arabs are gentle, peace-loving folks:

"The recent period has seen a very substantial shift in attitudes by the PLO and the Palestinians. This may reflect a recognition that the earlier policy of using violence against Israel was indeed counterproductive to their interests." pp 7
"The position taken up by Arafat and the Palestinian leadership in dropping lethal violence in favour of the Intifadah and of negotiations has involved a serious risk for them." pp 9

"There are many in the Trilateral countries who fear the consequences of such a scenario for peace...although others are less pessimistic because they believe that none of Israel's neighbours wants war." pp 22

With so many non-violent, peace-loving Arabs in the region, the only thing left to reach a peace agreement is the right political party:

"Would there be a better chance that the process might evolve in this way if the delegation represented a Labour-led government? It would appear to be the case." pp 19

But those nasty Rightists and those pesty settlements are

getting in the way of the peace-loving Arabs and Labour Party, the very people who two years later brought us the Trilateral Commision-backed, Oslo Agreement.

"...the main impact of this new immigration has been upon the pattern of settlements in occupied territories in East Jerusalem, but there are fears that this new wave of immigration could also lead to a renewed attempt to accelerate the process of peopling other parts of the West Bank with Jewish settlers..." pp 3

"Most of these settlements are official ones established on land confiscated on the dubious grounds that its present occupants lack formal title to it. But there are also unofficial settlements of a highly provocative character, for example in the center of the Palestinian town of Hebron."

Of course, Fitzgerald fails to recall that the "Palestinians" who didn't exist at the time in anyone's lexicon, occupied Hebron illegally in 1929 by slaughtering its very longtime Jewish residents. Still, the settlers have to go and here is the Trilateral Commission plan:

"It might be possible to secure agreement to the re-location of many settlers scattered at present throughout the West Bank into settlements nearer to the Green Line as part of agreed border rectifications." pp 27

Naturally, this plan is a formula for war, so how can it possibly be implemented? Easy, the armies of the New World Order will take over the region. And that is the point of this whole exercise in the first place:

"Both the United States and Europe would need to be prepared, regardless of past inhibitions, to exert the pressure necessary to break the deadlock." pp 22

"...the concern of the Palestinians about possible Israeli military intervention being met in turn by international guarantees and the presence of an international force policing the area." pp 24

"In these circumstances, the reassurance could be provided only in a massive reduction of arms...Such a process would need to be subject to international controls...In the international situation now emerging it could be possible to visualise an agreement involving all arms-producing States guaranteeing that no replacement arms would be supplied to any party which committed aggression against the other." pp 25-26

"There is an obvious need for an impartial authority to manage the available water in the land of Palestine...This problem would seem more appropriately dealt with by some joint or international water control arrangement." pp 28-29

Now that Israel has been disarmed and dehydrated by the international forces within her "Palestinian" boundaries, what will her future be? Why she will be a cog in a copy of the EU.

"Close economic links between a Palestinian/Jordanian Confederation and Israel, involving a Common Market or a Benelux structure are acceptable to the PLO and Palestinians and to many Israelis..." pp 31

And that is an inside peek at the thinking of the Trilateral Commission. Those flexible Palestinians and Jordanians, all of them, would love to be part of a trading bloc with Israel. They don't mind giving up their sovereignty and if the Israelis do, well, all those international troops enforcing all those international commissions will change their minds in time.

ALM 1 - THE DEUTSCH DEVILS

Rabbi Marvin Antelman was right all along. Way back in 1974, he identified the source of all the evil against Jews and humanity but his message and style were too unaccessible to get through to anyone but the most advanced students of anti-semitism. What he lacked most was simplicity, a common enough failure of thinkers decades in advance of their contemporaries. What he needed was someone to put out a Cliff's Notes simplified explanation of his thesis...and someone, without intention, just did.

The name of the book is, 50 Jewish Messiahs by Jerry Rabow (Gefen Publishing, Jerusalem). It is an informative but shallow overview of just what the title says, but in its shallowness lies vital depth. We begin with Chapter 17, about the "most damaging messiah to the Jewish people," Shabbatai Zvi. First we'll read Rabow and then add commentary opening Rabbi Antelman's work to the wide world. Recall that there are various accepted English spellings for Shabtai Tzvi, and the Sabbataians. The spelling presented depends on the writer:

pp 91 - Shabbatai Zvi was born in Smyrna, Turkey on the ninth of Av, 1626. The ninth day of Av is the day of a triple tragedy for the Jewish nation. According to tradition, the First Temple, the Second Temple and Bar Kokhba's Betar fortress all fell on this day.

pp 93 - He changed the holiday celebrations and violated the dietary prohibitions. All of this followed from his declaration that the usual rules were inapplicable to messianic times.

pp 95 - He declared that the coming of the messianic era meant that the biblical commandments were no longer binding. He proclaimed that God now permitted everything.

** This is Rabbi Antelman's central assertion; that Shabbataism was the polar opposite of Judaism. That Shabbatai Zvi's program was to destroy all the tenets of the Torah and replace them with their opposites. Incredibly, more than half the Jews of the world at the time, believed he would be revealed as their promised messiah: **

pp 101 - Then he finally made the announcement for which the Jewish community had been waiting for 1600 years - he would begin the Redemption on the 15th day of the month of Sivan, June 18, 1666.

** There are many who will recognize the significance of the date. June is the sixth month, 18 divided by three is 6+6+6 and 1666 is clear enough. Either he knew what he was doing or the prophesies of the emergence of an evil false messiah or anti-Christ are right, and Shabbatai Zvi was him. **

pp 110 - Through all of this, Shabbatai continued to issue proclamations of the theological changes wrought by the coming of the messianic age. Shabbatai's new prayer was, "Praised be He who permits the forbidden." Since all things would be permitted in the age of the messiah, Shabbatai declared many of the old restrictions of the Torah no longer applicable. He abolished the laws concerning sexual relationships. He eventually declared that all of the thirty six major biblical sins were now permitted and instructed some of his followers that it was their duty to perform such sins in order to hasten the Redemption.

** Shabbatai's fall from grace among the great masses of Jews came in September 1666, when the Sultan of Turkey threatened him with torture unless he converted to Islam. He relented and most of Jewry abandoned him. But not all. A core of his followers kept their messiah alive and kicking hard. **

pp 112 - In order to bring on the Reformation, Shabbatai had descended into the darkness of the Muslim world to gather the scattered fragments of the light of creation hidden there. There was an outward reality and an inner reality. Nathan transformed Shabbatainism into a theology of paradox. Once the followers accepted the concept of paradox, they would be able to keep on believing in Shabbatai Zvi...An inner circle of his followers accepted the explanations of Nathan and continued to believe in Shabbatai the Messiah.

** The Shabbatai followers continued their hidden life in the Turkish sect of the Donmeh, whose activities continue to this day, as reported extensively this year, even by the staid Jerusalem Post. One of the Donmeh followers was Jacob Frank, who would transform Europe and the world into a Shabbataian hell barely a century later. **

pp 121 - The Donmeh now converted the Shabbataian Purim into an annual orgy, when members exchanged spouses for a ceremony called "extinguishing the lights." The Donmeh justified their Purim orgies, and their regular practise of sharing wives and engaging in other sexual activities, by citing biblical precedents.

pp 123 - Although Jacob Frank (1726-1791) was born fifty years after the death Shabbatai Zvi, he deserves to be regarded as Shabbatai's true successor.

pp 125 - Frank's followers requested ecclesiastic protection on the grounds that their own beliefs were not Jewish but rather, "anti-Talmudist."..The bishop declared that the "anti-Talmudists", Frank's followers, were entitled to practise their religion, and ordered that all copies of the Talmud within his diocese be seized and burned. Now under the protection of the crown, adoring followers gave Frank huge donations to his movement.

pp 127 - He extended the paradoxical teachings of Shabbatai Zvi that the coming of the messianic age had transformed sexual prohibitions of the bible into permissions and even obligations. According to Frank, engaging in sexual orgies now became the means to purify the soul from its sins. Debauchery became therapy...Frank convinced his followers that the only way for their special form of Judaism to survive was for them to outwardly become Christians, just as the Donmeh had descended into the world of Islam...In February, 1759, the Frankists told the Church they were ready to be baptized...The Frankists promised to deliver 5000 new Christians from Poland, Moravia, Hungary and Turkey.

pp 130 - The Frankists also became involved in international political intrigue, and sent secret emissaries to the Russian government and the Eastern Orthodox Church offering to help in the overthrow of Poland and the Catholic Church...By 1786, Frank suffered temporary financial problems, and moved his court to Offenbach, near Frankfurt. There Frank's money problems were somehow solved. The source of Frank's immense wealth is not clear. He may have used his movement's system of secret messengers and clandestine cells to engage in the constant political turmoil involving Austria-Hungary, Turkey and the Balkans.

** And now we reach the final depth of Rabow's understanding and let Rabbi Antelman take over. **

Frankfurt at the time was the headquarters of the Jesuit, Adam Weishaupt, founder of the Illuminati, as well as Rothschild Brothers' financial empire. This is worth repeating:

Frankfurt was the birthplace of both the Illuminati and the Rothschild empire. When Jacob Frank entered the city, the alliance between the two had already begun. Weishaupt provided the conspiratorial resources of the Jesuit Order, while the Rothschilds contributed the money. What was missing was a means to spread the agenda of the Illuminati and that the Frankists added with their network of agents throughout the Christian and Islamic worlds.

Jacob Frank became instantly wealthy because he was given a nice handout by Mayer Amshel Rothschild of Frankfurt. There is no other explanation.

And from this starting point, Rabbi Antelman gave us a blueprint for the war against Judaism and all its good, and indeed against humanity and all its moral treasures. A movement of complete evil now took hold. The Jesuits' goal was the destruction of the Protestant Reformation leading to a return of one pope sitting in judgement on all mankind. The Rothschilds goal was to control the wealth of the planet. And the Frankist vision was the destruction of Jewish ethics to be replaced by a religion based on the exact opposite of God's intentions. When these factions blended, a bloody war against humanity, with the Jews on the front lines, erupted and it is reaching its very pinnacle at this moment.

Rabbi Antelman traces the means of the worldwide reach of this ugliness. By the 1770s, the Illuminati was exposed and banned in Germany and then throughout Europe. Weishaupt made a strategic change that worked miracles for the international spread of his goals. He infiltrated agents into the Freemasonic lodges of England and Scotland, changing their highest tenets to his own, until every lodge in every nation accepted them. Thus, the Illuminati now had two centers of activity, Germany and Britain. It was from Germany to London that the apostate Jews Karl Marx and Frederick Engels were sent to devise the rot of communism. Shortly after that task was done, the Rothschilds sent their agents John Jacob Astor and Jacob Schiff from Germany to America. They financed the robber barons like Rockefeller and Morgan, who in 1922, founded the Council On Foreign Relations, to overthrow the American constitution and switch the nation's diplomacy to Illuminatiism.

THE REAL WAR AGAINST THE JEWS AND HUMANITY

In 1932, how many organizations in Germany represented German Jewry? Over 250. In 1933, how many? One, and one only; Labour Zionism. We will return to the significance shortly.

First, Rabbi Antelman's account continues. To corrupt the Jews, the Frankists adopted, at first, a humane policy of sorts. With Rothschild money and Jesuit power, the so-called Enlightenment was initiated by the German Jewish apostate Moses Mendelsohn. Napoleon was financed to liberate the Jews wherever he conquered and from Germany, the Reform and Conservative movements were financed to further dilute the faith and introduce totally foreign concepts to their congregations. But the pace wasn't fast enough. The ornery Jews just weren't cooperating with evil, so those stubbornly accepting Torah morality would have to be removed permanently and only those practising Shabbatainism would be permitted to survive.

Yes, in the 2000 years of European Jewish history there were pogroms, Crusades and Inquisitions, the latter aided and abetted by the Jesuits. But compared to what happened from the 1880s on, life was a tolerable picnic. The turning point in the final war against the Jews was the founding of Zionism by the Shabbataians. The final aim of the movement was to establish a Shabbataian state in the historical land of the Jews, thus taking over Judaism for good.

To foment the idea, life had to made so intolerable for Europe's Jews, that escape to Palestine would appear to be the best option. The Cossack pogroms were the first shot in this campaign and for them, the Frankists turned to the

Jesuits and their influence over the Catholic Church. The Jesuits had done more to spread communism, beginning with their feudal communes in South America, and now they wanted to punish the anti-papists of Europe by imprisoning them behind communal bars. The deal was simple: The Jesuits provided the Cossacks, the Frankists, the communists. And naturally, the Rothschilds would provide the moolah.

Once the situation turned foreboding, the German-writing intellectuals took over. In Vienna in 1885, the journalist Natan Birnbaum fired the opening salvo which successfully planted the fast-growing seeds of Zionism. He was followed by another Vienna writer, Peretz Smoleskin, who provided more intellectual justification for returning to a safe home in Israel. However, neither man had the charisma of still another Vienna writer, Theodore Herzl. He could rally the masses as neither of them could and he was chosen to be the spokesman and symbol of the movement.

Read any honest biography of Herzl and the same quandary appears. Herzl claimed he wrote the Judenstaat one summer in Paris. But Herzl wasn't in Paris when he said he wrote the most influential book of Zionism. It had to have been written for him. Anyone who reads Herzl's dreadful plays, has to doubt his sudden departure from literary mediocrity.

In 1901, Herzl appeared in Britain where he was not well received. We are told he backed another option, creating a Jewish sanctuary in British - controlled East Africa. If the idea caught on, it would neutralize the Shabbataians' game plan. Herzl died not long after and not one biography of him tells us how. He entered a Paris sanatorium for a not known condition and never emerged. This was highly fortunate for the British Freemasons doing the Shabbataians' bidding, for they replaced Herzl with one of their own, a German-educated Jew named Chaim Weizmann. In time, a cockamamie legend was fabricated involving the Balfour declaration creating a Jewish homeland in Palestine as a reward for Weizmann finding a way to make acetone for explosives from dried up paint. Not one explosion in World War One came from this magic process. But the British took great pains to capture Palestine from the Turks and appoint the leaders of the upcoming Shabbataian state.

Meeting in London during the War, Weizmann and Balfour had to deal with the problem of the people already living in Palestine, most of whom were religious Jews, who were the majority in such major centers as Jerusalem, Sfat and Tiberius. The myth of an ancient Palestinian Arab indigenous population is belied by any number of reports by visitors as talented as Twain and Balzac, who accurately noted the paucity of Arabs in the land during the 19th century. The later economic success of the new enterprise drew hundreds of thousands of Arabs from as far away as Iraq to the region with consequences the Illuminati were possibly well aware of.

To neutralize the religious Jews, many of whom had been living in the land since antiquity, Balfour and Weizmann inducted Rabbi Avraham Kook into the fold and after the war, he was appointed the first Chief Rabbi of the enterprise, while Weizmann was made the first head of the Jewish Agency. Kook proceeded to strip the landed Orthodox Jews of their real estate and political rights, while introducing a new concept into Judaism; the purity of land redemption. His philosophy was based on profound historical truth, nonetheless, his followers don't understand how he and they are playing out the Shabbataian nightmare.

Stage one was complete. Now the real business at hand was revved up. Rabbi Antelman proves that the American President Woodrow Wilson was thoroughly corrupted by the Frankists through their agent Colonel House. It was Wilson who put an end to America's open immigration policy. Until then, despite all their despair, most Eastern European Jews rejected Palestine as an escape route, the majority choosing America as their destination.

From now on very few would enjoy that option. It would have to be Palestine or nowhere.

We now jump to 1933. Less than 1% of the German Jews support Zionism. Many tried to escape from Naziism by boat to Latin and North American ports but the international diplomatic order was to turn them back. Any German Jew who rejected Palestine as his shelter would be shipped back to his death.

By 1934, the majority of German Jews got the message and turned to the only Jewish organization allowed by the Nazis, the Labour Zionists. For confirmation of the conspiracy between them and Hitler's thugs read The Transfer Agreement by Edwin Black, Perfidy by Ben Hecht or The Scared And The Doomed by Jacob Nurenberger. The deal cut worked like this. The German Jews would first be indoctrinated into Bolshevism in Labour Zionism camps and then, with British approval, transferred to Palestine. Most were there by the time the British issued the White Paper banning further Jewish immigration. The Labour Zionists got the Jews they wanted, and let the millions of religious Jews and other non-Frankists perish in Europe without any struggle for their survival.

But not all Jews fell for the plan. A noble alternative Zionism arose led by Zeev Jabotinsky. He led the Jews in demanding free passage to Palestine and a worldwide economic boycott of the Nazi regime. The Labour Zionists did all in their power to short-circuit the opposition. First, they forced all the German Jews in Palestine to use their assets to buy only goods from Nazi Germany. This kept the regime afloat. Then Chaim Weizmann and his Jewish Agency employed their appointed agents in the US to neutralize Jabotinsky and his followers using any means at their disposal. This culminated in Jabotinsky's suspicious death in New York in 1941. Later, Jabotinsky's most literate advocate, Ben Hecht, was run over by a truck on a Manhattan sidewalk. His crime was being the first to widely expose the Jewish Agency-Nazi plot.

Into this plot against the Jews we add the Jesuits, who wished with all their hearts, to wreck the land that produced Luther, but the Vatican's role in the Holocaust is not the focus of this overview. We now return to America where the Jewish leadership used all their contacts and resources to make good and certain that the unwanted non-Shabbataian Jews of Europe never again saw the light of day.

We return to a quote from Jerry Rabow:

pp 132 - Frankist families, both those living as Christians and those living as Jews, tried to marry only among themselves. In the summers, the German groups regularly held secret meetings in the resort of Carlsbad...It is said by the middle of the nineteenth century, the majority of the lawyers in Prague and Warsaw were from Frankist families. United States Supreme Court Justice Felix Frankfurter is reported to have received a copy of Eva Frank's portrait from his mother, a descendent of the Prague Frankist family.

Here is a quote from Frankfurter:

"The real rulers in Washington are invisible and exercise their power from behind the scenes."-- Justice Felix Frankfurter, U.S. Supreme Court.

The difference between Rabow and Rabbi Antelman is the latter proves that literally all of FDR's court Jews were German-descended Sabbataians, determined to purge Jewry of its unnecessary European, non-Sabbataian morality-believing cohorts. Here is a short list of these Jewish community leaders:

Felix Brandeis - Received Secondary School education in Germany. There, Englishman Jacob de Haas introduced him to Zionism.

Henry Morgenthau Jr., Stephen Wise, Bernard Baruch, Judah Magnes, Felix Warburg - All descended from

292

German Jews. Here is a telling quote from the latter Frankist family:

"We shall have World Government, whether or not we like it. The only question is whether World Government will be achieved by conquest or consent." -- Statement made before the United States Senate on Feb. 7, 1950 by James Paul Warburg ("Angel" to and active in the United World Federalists), son of Paul Moritz Warburg, nephew of Felix Warburg and of Jacob Schiff, both of Kuhn, Loeb & Co. which poured millions into the Russian Revolution through James' brother Max, banker to the German government.

When World War II ended, barely 100,000 European Jews survived and when they arrived in Palestine they had to obey Bolshevik edicts or starve to death. However, they weren't enough to stave off the number one threat to the Frankist state, the Arabs. The wrath of the savage tribes threatened the whole enterprise and only the infusion of large numbers of soldiers could stave off their invasion. To that end, European-controlled Arab dictators were persuaded to go against their national interests, stir up bloody anti-semitism and get the Sephardic Jews to Israel. Their first reward was wealth through seizure of Jews' assets.

Before the Sabbataians introduced it, there was no such thing as Jewish self-hatred. Their religion and heritage came as naturally as breathing. This was the state the Eastern Jews were in when they were driven to Israel. There, the Frankists had to apply all the lessons they learned turning German Jews into their image to change the newcomers. Every effort was made to divest these peoples of their faith and the results were often shattering. This is one reason, for instance, why Moroccan Jews who fled to France are so much better off than their families in Israel.

Initially, the American Frankists supported the new nation, believing it would soon spread darkness to the nations. But the Jews didn't cooperate and held on to their decency. That is when the CFR unleashed its evilest Frankists on the Jews once again. The most prominent of this lot is the German-born Henry Kissinger but the list is long and includes the Austrian-educated Madeleine Albright, and German descendents such as Joe Lieberman and Sandy Berger.

Today, the Frankist agenda is being promoted through the thinking of the German-born American philosopher, Leo Strauss. To show you all is not what it seems, here are a few words about him from a Jewish writer for the Executive Intelligence Report, run by the Germacentric, Lyndon LaRouche:

"If Strauss' influence on politics in the capital of the most powerful nation on Earth was awesome in 1996, it is even more so today. The leading "Straussian" in the Bush Administration is Deputy Defense Secretary Paul Wolfowitz, who was trained by Strauss' alter-ego and fellow University of Chicago professor Allan Bloom. Wolfowitz leads the "war party" within the civilian bureaucracy at the Pentagon, and his own protege I. Lewis "Scooter" Libby, is Vice President Dick Cheney's chief of staff and chief national security aide, directing a super-hawkish "shadow national security council" out of the Old Executive Office Building, adjacent to the White House. According to Bloom biographer Saul Bellow, the day that President George H.W. Bush rejected Wolfowitz and Cheney's demand that U.S. troops continue on to Baghdad, during Operation Desert Storm in 1991, Wolfowitz called Bloom on his private phone line to bitterly complain. It seems that "Bush 41" was not enough of a Nietzschean "superman" for Wolfowitz's taste."

Compare that report with this one recently published by the Jerusalem Post.

LONDON- A British coroner has rejected a German police claim that a 22 year old Jewish man from London, Jeremiah

Duggan, committed suicide in March after attending a meeting of the far-right Schiller Institute in the German town of Wiesbaden.

The Schiller Institute draws its inspiration from American conspiracy theorist Lyndon LaRouche, who was among the speakers at the meeting...

He said, "Mum, I am in deep trouble. I am frightened." As he attempted to give his location, the line went dead."

Duggan made the fatal mistake of getting too close to the true connection between LaRouche and the Frankists. Their program calls for the brainwashing of Jews to hate themselves and they don't cotton to rebels. Here is how that is accomplished through the Israeli higher education system, as reported by Caroline Glick this week in the Jerusalem Post:

"Students speak of a regime of fear and intimidation in the classroom. Ofra Gracier, a doctoral student in Tel-Aviv University's humanities faculty explains the process as follows: 'It starts with the course syllabus. In a class on introduction to political theory for instance, you will never see the likes of Leo Strauss or Friedrich Hayek or Milton Friedman. You will only get Marx and Rousseau and people like that. So, if you want to argue with Marx, you are on your own. You don't know anything else.'"

The fatal error of Israeli Jews was rejecting the Frankists and their Labour Party. The Shabbataians would rather see the Arabs overrun Israel than witness the revival of a state run by true Judaism. They have thoroughly financed and infiltrated the high leadership and especially, far left groups, to prepare the ground for defeat. And if utter demoralization doesn't do the trick, read another local report issued this week:

PREPARATIONS TO USE FIREPOWER AGAINST JEWS.

Our contacts have reported that the following has been introduced by the people preparing MEGA YAMIT.
IBA "B" reported, *in three consecutive reports following the Geha Junction islamic mass murder assault that* **GERMAN EXTREME RIGHT WING Jews** *were those that performed the bombing. (Refer to the IBA "B" records) .*

Rabbi Antelman was right. He looked at the enemy and saw the mirror opposite of real Judaism. A war to the finish is on in Israel and it is being spread to the rest of the planet. Our salvation can only arise when the Arabs realize the Jews of Israel are fighting the same battle they are and against the same enemies. If they can't overcome the brainwashing and hatred, they'll go down along with Israel. And then the rest of the planet might just follow.

FRIDAY January 9th 2004

Dear Mr Chamish,

I read with particular interest your analysis of the problems related to the Donmeh and the Shabbataians, in particular your concluding remarks in which you state that: "Our salvation can only arise when the Arabs realize the Jews of Israel are fighting the same battle (that) they are (fighting) and against the same enemies." It will perhaps come as something of a surprise to learn that there are some Muslims who agree with much contained in your assessment.
As a convert to Islam (from a somewhat ecumenical family - predominantly Christian but with two converts to Judaism my sister and cousin) so yes, in the words of David Dimbleby, we now do have a long weekend.
I believe that the only way out of the present state of affairs is to seek out the facts, publish, or be damned.

Your piece filled in a number of important gaps which, unless you have the sort of inside information, that you obviously have, would have taken a lot more time than I currently have available to spend on this very important subject.

*My own observations are included in a book we published back in 1991 entitled **Satanic Voices - Ancient & Modern** this was a reply to Salman Rushdie's **Satanic Verses.***

I am in the process of extracting the relevant passages to send to you, which relate to the Donmeh and the Islamic prophecies which precisely predict the events which led to the disastrous state of affairs you describe so well, and with which we largely agree.

With best regards
Shabbat Shalom
Yours sincerely
David M Pidcock
The Islamic Party of Britain

ALM 2 - KERRY, GAZA AND THE NEW SABBATAIAN HOLOCAUST

In the first week of February 2004, two related incidents occurred in Israel and America. Prime Minister Sharon announced his decision to evacuate the Jewish residents of Gaza and John Kerry won enough primaries to just about settle the issue of who will be the Democratic Party candidate in the upcoming American elections.

Here are a few less than publicized facts about Kerry:

- He is a graduate, like both President Bushes, of the occultic Yale University cabal, the Skull And Bones Society. So whoever Americans voted for, they got the same secret society determining their lives.

- Kerry, like Howard Dean, Wesley Clark and Joe Leiberman are all members of the Council On Foreign Relations (CFR). So whoever Americans chose to be the Democratic candidate, they got the same CFR agenda.

- The well publicized CFR agenda insists on Israel withdrawing from Gaza, Judea and Samaria and half of Jerusalem, making Israel unviable as a state. To that end, like Dean before him, Kerry promised to appoint Jimmy Carter (CFR) or Bill Clinton (CFR) as his administration's Middle East advisor.

- Not that Kerry would receive any new advice from either of them, since his campaign manager is Alan Solomant, an executive of Peace Now - America.

- But as his prominence grew, so did the investigation of his past. And what did we recently discover; why Kerry is Jewish on his father's side. Somehow, he forgot the fact that his grandparents were prominent Jewish business people in Prague and that his father is 100% Jewish. Ask yourself, do you know anyone who doesn't know his father's religious background?

As rare as it must be, that affliction runs rampant in CFR circles. Former CFR Secretary-of-State Madeleine Albright also forget that both her parents were Jews, even though she was raised in the Jewish home of her relatives in London.

If you didn't feel like voting Kerry, therewais Wesley Clark waiting in the wings. Uncannily, he is also a CFR member who only discovered his father was Jewish while he was burning Bosnia to ashes.

Now how come, no matter which Democrat you chose, you got a CFR half-Jew who forgot all about it? The answer is found in the Sabbataian (also Shabbataian and similar spellings) policy of having their Jewish apostate followers converting and hiding their roots and beliefs.

Allow me to quickly summarize Sabbataianism/Frankism:

In my previous article, The Deutsch Devils, I revealed the findings of Rabbi Antelman in his books To Eliminate The Opiate Volumes I and II. His focus is the false messiah Shabtai Zvi, and the continuation of his evil ministry through the Turkish sect called the Donmeh. In the eighteenth century, Jacob Frank brought the Donmeh ideology to Europe and joined a fateful alliance. This was described in the article as:

Frankfurt at the time was the headquarters of the Jesuit, Adam Weishaupt, founder of the Illuminati, as well as Rothschild Brothers' financial empire. This is worth repeating: Frankfurt was the birthplace of both the Illuminati and the Rothschild empire. When Jacob Frank entered the city, the alliance between the two had already begun. Weishaupt provided the conspiratorial resources of the Jesuit Order, while the Rothschilds contributed the money. What was missing was a means to spread the agenda of the Illuminati and that the Frankists added with their network of agents throughout the Christian and Islamic worlds.

Jacob Frank became instantly wealthy because he was given a nice handout by the Rothschilds of Frankfurt. There is no other explanation.

And from this starting point, Rabbi Antelman gave us a blueprint for the war against Judaism and all its good, and indeed against humanity and all its moral treasures. A movement of complete evil now took hold. The Jesuits' goal was the destruction of the Protestant Reformation leading to a return of one pope sitting in judgement on all mankind. The Rothschilds goal was to control the wealth of the planet. And the Frankist vision was the destruction of Jewish ethics to be replaced by a religion based on the exact opposite of God's intentions. When these factions blended, a bloody war against humanity, with the Jews on the front lines, erupted and it is reaching its very pinnacle at this moment.

Rabbi Antelman traces the means of the worldwide reach of this ugliness. By the 1770s, the Illuminati was exposed and banned in Germany and then throughout Europe. Weishaupt made a strategic change that worked miracles for the international spread of his goals. He infiltrated agents into the Freemasonic lodges of England and Scotland, changing their highest tenets to his own, until every lodge in every nation accepted them. Thus, the Illuminati now had two centers of activity, Germany and Britain.

** A Visit To A Publisher

Before diving into the proofs that Israel is being set up for another Sabbataian Holocaust, permit me the liberty of explaining the inspiration for this piece. On February 1/04 I visited Gefen Books in Jerusalem to pick up some copies of my Hebrew book, Who Murdered Yitzhak Rabin and David Morrison's book, Lies - The Rabin Assassination And Israel's Secret Service.

Dr. Morrison's book has made a powerful case for a conspiracy behind the Rabin assassination. One of the favors he did for me was, as a psychiatric doctor, confirming that my analysis of Rabin's medical records was the correct one. Though I had met him just once, he has aided my cause enormously.

That time I met him was in my home when he and Gefen publisher, Ilan Greenfield arrived to hear me out and decide whether to publish a Hebrew edition of my Rabin book, or not. Ilan told me something I didn't know. "If it wasn't for David, I would never have published your book. I left your place and told him you were coocoo. He answered that if I didn't publish your book, he'd never talk to me again. As a psychiatrist he watched you carefully and concluded you were totally sane. He told me, "He thinks differently than us, that's why he can see how the truth works. That's not called crazy, it's called gifted."

I told Ilan that without knowing how much I owed him, I had repaid David many times over by reviewing Lies in my book, The Last Days Of Israel, and by selling lots of copies of the book in Hebrew and English at my lectures.

Ilan's eyes lit up and he said, "Do you know we published two other books by him? Maybe you could promote them as well." He then showed me the books. He chose to display the newest book first. It is called, The Gush, and it is very relevant to today's impending withdrawal from Gush Katif. This book tells the human story of the Jewish residents of Gush Etzion, also secretly on the chopping block no matter what Sharon says.

It was a nice book, I told Ilan, but my readers expect deep information from me. Then he showed me the other Morrison book, Heroes, Antiheroes And The Holocaust. I struck gold.

David Morrison's book on the secrets of the Holocaust stands with Perfidy, The Transfer Agreement and, The Scared And The Doomed as one of the great studies of how Labor Zionism prevented the rescue of European Jewry. Morrison doesn't see this as policy but you will with the knowledge we have gained together.

Morrison doesn't realize that he is reporting a Sabbataian massacre, yet he instinctively writes about the Young Turks. We begin and end our overview with that subject. I will add my comments beginning and ending with two stars **.

**The First Sabbataian Holocaust –
The Dry Run**

pp 48 - The Young Turks who led the 1908 revolution were Turkish nationalists and established secular institutions, overthrowing the religious Moslem order. They viewed Armenians as a direct threat to their revolutionary plans. The evidence is overwhelming that the massacre of the Armenians was a deliberate, planned genocide. The Young Turks allied themselves with Germany and used world War I

301

as a cover for their slaughter of Armenians...As did the Nazis in World War II, the Turks used their intended victims as slave laborers building a trans-Turkish railway for German business interests.

** And who were these Young Turks who organized The Armenian genocide? We turn to Sabbataian Messianism as Proto-Secularism: M. Avrum Ehrlich, for the answer. **

The extent to which Jews were involved in the Young Turk revolution is debated, some arguing that Jews and Donme dominated the Committee of the Union and Progress Party (C.U.P) which gained control of the State. Others argue that this was anti-Semitic rhetoric
and exaggerated and that while the Jews supported the revolution on a grass roots level, they were not highly represented in the upper echelons of the party. Indeed British diplomats did report to the home office that a Jewish-Masonic conspiracy was at work favouring the revolution. The Donme are believed to have been equally involved in the revolution but exact details are less known due to a number of reasons...It was via the Masonic lodges that the Donme, the Jews, Bektashi and secularists who were less accepted in mainstream society were able to meet on an equal footing, many of them becoming major instruments of the revolution...Whether the suspicions that Masonry is responsible for sedition and subversive activities are true or not, in this context they were a convenient home for the revolution, providing lodges and personnel, secrecy and structures for the revolution. The Donme thrived in the Masonic environment, allowing them to be both secretive and influential, maintaining their religious ideas in a non-dogmatic atmosphere. Bridging the gap between the Jews and the Muslims, they seemed to represent the happy medium of the secular Young Turk revolution. Even today Donme are involved in the Masonic Lodof Turkey. Sahir

Talat Akev of the Kapanci-Izmir group of Donme was the Grand Master of the Masons until his death in 1999.

Dr Nazim, Nuzhet Faik, Mustafa Arif, Muslihiddin Adil, Sukru Bleda, Halide Edip Adivar and Ahmet Emin Yalman were all active in the Young Turks and of Donme families. Mehmet Kapanci (1839-1924) who was a mayor of Salonica and a well-known banker funded the C.U.P and was a Donme. Other Jews active in the Young Turks were Nissim Mazliah from Izmir and Vitali Faradji , Moise Cohen (later called Munis Tekinalp) who was an active Jew and once rabbinical student who turned to business and actively asserted a proud Turkish identity along with Zionist sentiments...It is curious that Israel's first and second Prime Ministers, David Ben Gurion and Moshe Sharett and her second president Yitzchak Ben Zvi had lived and studied in Istanbul and embraced the concept "lehitatmen", Hebrew for "to become an Ottoman". Ben Zvi is alleged by some to be descendent of a Sabbataian family. Sharett served in the Ottoman army in WW1. Ben Gurion gave up Russian citizenship for Ottoman citizenship, something many others in Palestine were afraid to do. Israeli Presidents Ben Zvi, Zalman Shazar and to a lesser degree Yitzchak Navon became students of Ottomanism.

Mehmet Cavit Bey (1875-1926) was one of the most significant Donme political figures. He was active in the revolution as a highly articulate editor of a tabloid and professor of finance and was three times Finance Minister of Modern Turkey until his execution for his alleged role in the assassination attempt of Ataturk. It is believed that Cavit Bey was an ardent Zionist and saw the advantages for Turkey in the Jewish settlement of Palestine.

No less today than in the early days of its activities, secular Zionism and the Israeli Left in particular show distinctive utopian aspirations that in many ways resemble forms of religious Jewish messianism, oddly enough bolstered by an almost religious dogmatism. Despite a declared and articulate opposition to conservative orthodoxy and religious messianism, this group seems to have unconsciously adopted many messianic characteristics and uses almost religious symbolism to address its message. In contrast with the early Zionists whose goal was a secular political messianism aimed at establishing a political State and securing sovereign territory by force of arms as an essential premise, the latter manifestation of the Israeli Left has more mystical messianic leanings. On one hand the Israeli Left acknowledges its national aspirations for Jewish sovereignty in the Land of Israel, on the other it supports extreme territorial compromise with Israel's enemies. These two values are often perceived to negate one another. In a situation which is quite possibly un-resolvable in real-politick, it is however, considered entirely possible and likely in the paradigm of peace that the Leftist movement professes. Most interesting is the movement's choice of messianic terminology when describing the peace process with Israel's Arab neighbours, including; "new world order in the Middle East", an uncanny political rendition of the messianic "kingdom of heaven on earth".

. Most interesting is the extreme anti-nomian nature of the Israeli Left Wing. A new dimension to anti-nomianism was created in this mutation of messianism that extended beyond the rejection of Jewish ritual into a form of national anti-nomianism. There existed an overwhelming pressure on believers amongst the Israeli Left not only to neglect Jewish tradition but a fundamental imperative to forfeit Jewish sovereignty particularly over Jewish religious sites (Cave of Joseph, Cave of Machpela, Temple Mount) by which peace was directly achievable. Furthermore, a curious similarity between the Israeli Left and the Sabbataian movement is illustrated in the Left's strong public ties with Arabs and Islam while privately rejecting and even despising their lifestyle, *morality and habits. Stark similarities are evident with the Donmeh who showed great public affection with Islam but amongst themselves entirely rejected and even despised Islam. This of course is not so much because of causal influences that Sabbataianism had on Zionism but rather because the same impulses and mechanisms active in both groups. The belief that assimilation was an important utopian/messianic goal is therefore argued to be a motivation in both Sabbataian and Left Wing Zionist messianism.*

** M.A. Ehrlich's great accomplishments include verifying Rabbi Antelman's grand conspiracy involving the British rites of Freemasonry but exceeds Rabbi Antelman in the strong evidential connections to Labor Zionism and today's Israeli Left. They are being guided to acquiesce in a new Israeli Holocaust, no less than the American leaders of Labor Zionism and the Left did so acquiesce in the 30s and 40s. For a revealing look at modern American Sabbataianism, visit: http://www.donmeh-west.com/# **

The Rothschild Connection

** Kerry and Clark are not the only world leaders who deliberately forgot their Jewish fathers. Numerous sources have claimed that Adolph Hitler's real father was a Rothschild and this assertion is not off the wall. Hitler's mother was working as a maid on a Rothschild estate when her son was conceived either through an affair or rape. No less an authority as the History Channel, in a Jan./04 series on dictators, revealed that Hitler razed the Austrian town he was born in, "to destroy all hints of his Jewish father." Could Hitler have been a Sabbataian?

The initial financiers of Labor Zionism and Theodore Herzl were barons of the Rothschild clan. Their goal was the creation of a state in the image of their Sabbataian beliefs: that is, anti-Torah, anti-Talmudic, anti-religious and anti-Jewish. To the Sabbataians, any Jew who does not accept anti-Judaism is fit for execution. Israel has chosen morality and God, and that means execution is the correct punishment.

Rabbi Antelman is not alone in tracing the Rothschild path to an American financial takeover. Hundreds, if not thousands of researchers have proven that the European Rothschilds sent their German agents of the Schiff, Astor and Warburg families to serve the interests of the cabal formed by the Jesuit illuminati, British Freemasonry and Sabbataianism.

We return to David Morrison's book to have a look at who was conducting the affairs of American Jews during the Holocaust era.***

pp.36-37 - "The leading figures were Judge Mayer Sulzberger, Louis Marshall, Cyrus Adler and Jacob Schiff. Schiff was the towering figure of that group that, to a large degree, represented wealthy American Jews of German background. Louis Marshall was named president of the JDC, and Schiff's son-in-law Felix Warburg, the treasurer. Warburg soon became chairman.

** In the 1940s, the Warburg connection to Hitler was exposed in a startling book by one of their own, Sidney Warburg. He wrote that he was sent to Hitler's court to fnance Hitler's rise with American funds funneled through the Warburg banking operation in Hamburg. For further confirmation, read Anthony Sutton's, Wall Street And Hitler. And who was Felix Warburg allied to but Chaim Weizmann? **

pp 63 - When travelling to America Weizmann and his wife enjoyed the company of Felix Warburg and his wife Frieda.

pp 40 - The power behind the group that made up the JDC and American Jewish Committee was Jacob Schiff. From a wealthy banking family in Germany, he joined Kuhn Loeb in

New York in 1873. In 1875 he won the hand in marriage of the daughter of Solomon Loeb and a full partnership in the firm. His speciality was railroad finance. Working with E.H. Harriman, he acquired the Union Pacific Railroad in 1897.

** Now we dive into the bowels of the plot. Schiff backed the Rockefeller/Morgan/ Carnegie railroad interests, which led ultimately to the foundation of the CFR in 1922 by the same J.D. Rockefeller. E.H. Harriman was the company George Jr.'s grandfather, Prescott Bush, was working for when he funneled millions of dollars to Hitler. This connection has been documented by numerous writers including Sutton and John Loftus. The Rothschild method was to identify crooked robber barons and promise them total wealth and control, if they follow and promote the illuminati/Sabbataian line. The CFR is the diplomatic arm guiding America and the world into a global satanism. And no matter who the American voter chooses, he gets the CFR and more. If Bush wasn't elected last time around, Al Gore would have been president. His daughter is married to the grandson of Jacob Schiff, assuredly meaning he is Sabbataian.

Rabbi Antelman asserts that the Sabbataians sent more than financiers from Germany to infiltrate American Jewry. He insists the Conservative, and moreso, the Reform Movements, are tools used to draw American Jews away from their traditions and into the arms of the Sabbataians. ***

pp 39 - Judah Magnes confessed without provocation that in Berlin he had been converted to Orthodoxy and he knew Theodore Herzl.

pp 41 - All three groups courted Judah Magnes for a leadership role. Schiff was a major supporter of the Reform Temple Emanu-El in New York but he and Felix Warburg also contributed to the Jewish Theological Seminary. Solomon Schechter, who came from England in 1902 to become president of the seminary, lent his support and prestige to the Zionist cause.

** Recall: *"We shall have World Government, whether or not we like it. The only question is whether World Government will be achieved by conquest or consent."*

- Statement made before the United States Senate on Feb. 7, 1950 by James Paul Warburg ("Angel" to and active in the United World Federalists), son of Paul Moritz Warburg, nephew of Felix Warburg and of Jacob Schiff, both of Kuhn, Loeb & Co. which poured millions into the Russian Revolution through James' brother Max, banker to the German government.

Sabbataian Labor Zionism concocted a dreadful tradeoff with the Nazis, which resulted in 50,000 indoctrinated German Jews escaping to Palestine from 1933 to 1939. The 3 million Jews of Poland were too religious to join the enterprise. And those who weren't religious largely supported the moral and proud scions of Zeev Jabotinsky, known at the time as the Revisionist Zionists. **

pp 42 - Louis Dembitz Brandeis, an early Zionist leader, protested to the Schiff-Warburg group over the route that Joint Distribution Committee funds took from the United States to Polish Jewry. Millions of dollars were channeled through the Aid Society of German Jews that included Max Warburg. Brandeis protested to Felix Warburg that the German group supported the ban on immigration of Polish Jews into Germany.

pp 47 - At the outset of WWI, Jacob Schiff felt the tug of his German roots. He aided Germany financially and told a friend: "My sympathies are naturally altogether with Germany, as I would think as little to side against my country as I would against my own parents."...Schiff's brother-in-law,

Max Warburg, was a German delegate to the economic talks at Versailles. He had discussions with John Foster Dulles...Dulles brother Allen served in Turkey as assistant to the US High Commissioner. From that post he aided the attempt to cover up the Turkish massacre of the Armenians during the war. His superior, High Commissioner Mark Bristol averred: "The Armenians are a race like the Jews - they have no national spirit and poor moral character."

** There isn't the space to present the machinations of the leaders of American Jewry, so we will focus on just one, the leader of Reform Judaism and the American Jewish Congress, Stephen Wise. His closest friend and correspondent was Felix Frankfurter. Of him, Jerry Rabow in his book, 50 Jewish Messiahs, writes:

"United States Supreme Court Justice Felix Frankfurter is reported to have received a copy of Eva Frank's portrait from his mother, a descendent of the Prague Frankist family." **

pp. 208 - The five or six Supreme Court justices that attended the performance on behalf of European Jewry were deeply impressed but it never crossed their mind that it was up to them to do something about it. They figured that if Frankfurter hadn't done anything, there was little to do.

   ** Here again is the quote from Frankfurter:

"The real rulers in Washington are invisible and exercise their power from behind the scenes."-- Justice Felix Frankfurter, U.S. Supreme Court.

Of Stephen Wise, Rabbi Antelman provides this description in To Eliminate The Opiate Volume II:

"Consider Stephen Wise, head of the Reform movement in the United States during World War II. As the slaughter was

going on in Europe, Wise was more interested in his own gratification. Wise was both a Communist and a Sabbatian. That he was a Communist is attested to by Maurice Malkin, a member of the Communist Party who returned to Judaism, in his book Return To My Father's House. Wise was a Sabbatian, as was shown in Helen Rawlinson's book Stranger At The Party. In her chronicle of a sexual encounter with the so-called Rabbi Wise, she describes how Wise had sex with her in his office on his conference table, and quoted the verse from Psalms which Sabbatians did when engaged in sexual intercourse." pp 217

Now follow David Morrison's chronicle of Wise deliberately condemning European Jews to death by torture. Lest you believe today's American Jewish leaders aren't capable of organizing a second Holocaust, always recall the very same process, using carbon copy American Jewish leaders, is at work against Israel at this moment. PM Sharon is simply doing what the CFR tells him to. **

pp 107 - Wise wrote to Albert Einstein displacing blame for Roosevelt's silence on the Nazi atrocities on the Warburgs: "I must say to you in strictest confidence that I saw the President yesterday...His first word was, 'Max Warburg wrote to me lately that things were so bad in Germany that nothing could be done.' The President threw up his hands as if to say, 'Well, if Max thinks nothing can be done, then nothing can be done.'"

pp 110 - Steven Wise circulated, in January, 1937, an internal memorandum to the Governing Councils in the World Jewish Congress making it clear, "in the most emphatic terms that it cannot be a party to any scheme of the Polish government which looks to a place for Polish-German emigrants."

pp 113 - At the same time, he circulated this memorandum, he wrote to a New York congressman who intended to introduce legislation to ease restrictions on emigration to America: "I have every reason to believe that any effort that is made at this time to ease the immigration laws will result in a serious wave of anti-semitic feeling in this country."

pp 120 - After Austria fell, Wise met with representatives of the American Jewish Committee and some non-Jewish groups. The meeting came in the wake of an attempt by New York Congressman Samuel Dickstein, to introduce legislation that would allow unused refugee quotas to be allocated to those fleeing Hitler. The gathered agreed unanimously: The organizations represented at the conference will take the position that the proposed legislation is inadvisable."

pp 128 - In the week following Kristallnacht, the British offered to give up most of the 65,000 quota for British citizens to emigrate to the United States to increase places for Jewish refugees. Under Secretary Of State Sumner Welles responded: "I reminded the Ambassador that the President stated there was no intention on the part of his government to increase the quota for German nationals. I added that it was my strong impression that the responsible leaders among American Jews would be the first to urge that no change in the present quota for German Jews be made...The influential Sam Rosenman, one of the "responsible" Jewish leaders sent Roosevelt a memorandum telling him that an "increase of quotas is wholly inadvisable. It will merely produce a 'Jewish problem' in the countries increasing the quota."

pp 129 - The General Jewish Council met the following day and spent hours of debate on an agenda that did not include the Kristallnacht. When the leaders of the American Jewish Congress addressed the issue, they did so by adopting a resolution giving the following advice to their constituents across the country: "Resolved that it is the present policy of the General Jewish Council that there should be no parades, public demonstrations or protests by Jews." Stephen Wise on American Jewish Congress stationary sent out a report to his members labeled: CONFIDENTIAL. NOT FOR PUBLICATION IN ANY FORM WHATSOEVER: "In behalf of the American Jewish Congress I send you this report clarifying our policy in meeting the present crisis in the life of our fellow Jews in Germany. The silence of the American Jewish Congress should not be regarded as a lack of activity on our part. It is the result of well considered policy."

pp 145 - In the wake of Kristallnacht, New York Senator Wagner introduced legislation to allow 20,000 German Jewish children into the United States. Stephen Wise testified before the legislation committee: "If there is any conflict between our duty to those children and our duty to our country, our country comes first; and if children cannot he helped, they cannot be helped."...Reynolds saw no difficulty in accommodating the refugee children in the United States. The legislation, without support from the Jewish leadership, got nowhere.

** If the children were not destined from Germany to Palestine, they were not destined to live. The same thing happened when choosing the Polish Jews fit to live. **

pp 154 - A letter to American Jews on United Jewish Appeal stationery continued to support the 'selected' immigration of Jews to Palestine, despite the fact that 3 million Jews were now trapped in Nazi-occupied Poland: "Selectivity is an inescapable factor in dealing with the problem of immigration to Palestine. By selectivity is meant the choice of young men and women who are trained in either agriculture or industry.

pp 178 - During the summer of 1942, Gerhart Riegner sent a cable to the State Department detailing the Nazi plan for

312

exterminating European Jewry. At the behest of Under Secretary Of State Sumner Welles, Wise kept the report secret.

pp 187- In the February, 1943 issue of Wise's American Jewish Congress publication, Opinion, there is an extensive review of the Hitler era to date with articles contributed by 52 people. No one mentioned the word 'rescue.'

pp 200 - When Anthony Eden was in Washington he met with Wise and told him nothing could be done...Eden's private secretary Oliver Harvey noted in his diary: 'Unfortunately, A.E. loves Arabs and hates Jews.'

pp 212 - There was an appeal from Italy which stated that an appeal from the pope might stop the deportation of Jews from Italy. The Zionist Emergency Committee did nothing about this matter. A meeting wasn't even called.

pp 217 - Stephen Wise declared: "We are Americans first. Nothing else that we are, whether by faith or race, qualifies our Americanism...The way to save Jews is to unite the Jewish people behind the victory program of President Roosevelt."

pp 220 - A White House staffer recorded in his diary that, "The President told us from his bedroom that he would not see the delegation of rabbis."... Judge Rosenman, who was also in the bedroom said the group was not representative of the most thoughtful elements in Jewry. Rosenman's statement to Roosevelt that "leading Jews of his acquaintance" opposed the rabbis' march.

pp 227 - While Wise sent private memos clearly stating they thought the rescue of Jews was possible...in public they supported the Roosevelt administration's steadfast assertion that nothing could be done...

pp 230 - Congressman Gillette recalled a visit to his office by Wise and a few of his colleagues:" None of these gentlemen seemed to be enthusiastic for...the saving of the remnant of the Jewish people."

pp 241 - Wise felt strongly that the Gillette legislation did not provide for the "proper type of commission." With all that was known about the obstruction of the Jewish rescue by the State Department, Wise was lobbying to leave the issue in their hands...Henry Morgenthau's aide Josiah Dubois uncovered the State Department's policy relevant to the issue of Jewish rescue... The stunning title to the Dubois memorandum was: REPORT TO THE SECRETARY ON THE ACQUIESCENCE OF THIS GOVERNMENT IN THE MURDER OF JEWS...Dubois pointed to the restrictions on visas as, "the most glaring example of the use of the machinery of this government to actually prevent the rescue of Jews."

pp 270 - The Roosevelt administration took the usual position that there be no special effort for Jewish refugees. Stephen Wise also saw no human course of action: "The issue is in the hands of God."

** David Morrison's conclusions are too generous, but his scholarship is invaluable. He has added an essential contribution to the indisputable fact that America's Jewish leaders, led by Stephen Wise, purposely murdered by proxy, the Jews of Europe. Now they are working on the Jews of Israel, starting with those of Gaza. **

ALM 3 - RINGWORMS

The battleground is now Gaza. The removal of the Jewish residents there will open a new front against Israel. No longer will Israel be able to contain the war being waged

314

against it from Gaza without suffering heavy casualties. If the world wanted peace, the Gaza Strip would be extended into the nearly empty Sinai Peninsula, which would require Egypt to actually bring hope to the Palestinians for once. There is the space in Sinai to create a large and viable new nation, if anyone really wanted such a thing.

The Gaza pullout will be the next stage in the dismemberment of Israel and its advocates point to the success of the south Lebanon pullout as a precedent. During the recent insane prisoner-bodies exchange, former Health Minister Ephraim Sneh revealed why Israel no longer has any bargaining power with Hizbullah. They now have 12,000 missiles pointed at northern Israel and there is nothing we can do to prevent them from turning the Galilee into ashes. With Gaza firmly in enemy hands, the same will go for southern and central Israel.

Which is just what the Sabbataians and the far leftists they are exploiting want. They would rather see the Arabs over-run the place than witness the revival of religious Judaism in the country they built along Sabbataian principles.

To illustrate the utter evil of the Labor party founders of Israel, we return to the early days of the state and the mass immigration of Sephardim. In my book Save Israel!, I interviewed Rabbi Uzi Meshulum, who led the movement seeking justice for the 4500, mostly Yemenite, infants kidnapped by the authorities between 1948-56. He claimed and I reported that there was a huge experimental program between parties in the US and the new Israeli atomic program headed by Shimon Peres, to see how much radiation human beings could suffer. The Yemenite children were mostly sent to America as guinea pigs for radiation experiments. In return Israel received nuclear secrets and money. Rabbi Meshulum estimated that the figure was $5000 per child.

Needless to say, not many people believed him or me. Now they have to. The good Israeli people are finally exposing this horrible story of the mass radiation of Sephardi children in the 1950s.

A film about the subject premiered at the Tel Aviv Cinemateque on April 17 and victims of the radiation are now suing for compensation. Let us begin with a report from Haaretz which is wrong in one important detail:

"The last article in the book is by Prof. Baruch Modan, who died last year, and social worker Shlomit Perry. The article discusses "The Israeli Government's Policy on Irradiated Ringworm Sufferers," describing a shocking medical-ethics incident: During the 1950s, some 20,000 people, most of them recent immigrants to Israel, were exposed to x-rays without their consent and without any explanation. Years later, it emerged that the radiation had had only a negative effect and had increased the chances of the subjects' contracting cancer. However, after several years, it also emerged that, in addition to the damage the radiation inflicted on thousands of individuals, information on this procedure was concealed for many years from the public by senior physicians and by the Ministry of Health. The information is published in the article but without any significant criticism from the authors, who even show a certain amount of understanding for the policy of concealment."

The wrong detail is the number of victims. The following report from the Jerusalem Post last January is more accurate:

"The Knesset Labor, Social Affairs and Health Committee rejected the Treasury's demand to cancel the rights of ringworm sufferers for retroactive compensation for cancer...More than 100,000 new immigrant children during the early years of the state were exposed to radiation treatment for ringworm...The children were exposed to radiation 35,000 times more than used today...The youngest

affected are 50 years old and many have already died. The National Religious Party MK, Shaul Yahalom, called on all the TV stations to broadcast a film on the ringworm tragedy."

I heard the director of the film interviewed on Israel Channel One TV on Feb. 16, while not catching his name. However, the interviewer's name is David Witztom and he said, "You are making claims for a horrible conspiracy," and indeed he was. The American government paid the equivalent of $50 billion in today's terms for the experiments and the cost could not have exceeded a few million dollars at most. The rest of the $50 billion is unaccounted for. Needless to ask, was the American government so concerned about ringworm in Israeli immigrant children that it paid $50 billion to treat the fungus?

The authorities are using the excuse that in 1948, x-rays were a common treatment for head ringworm and that 35,000 times the exposure was standard practise. This is nonsense. The standard treatment was ultra-violet light on the hair and the danger of x-rays was very well understood after nearly 60 years of use. The film director noted that the x-ray technicians knew the kind of blasts the children were receiving and would not stay in the same room when the dose was administered.

The children were often taken out of classrooms and told they were going on a sightseeing trip. They were taken to the x-ray rooms without parental consent and given the blast of radiation at the top of their heads. Most were sickened, many died. Over 100,000 children represents literally the entire generation of Israeli Sephardi children exposed to fatal levels of radiation. Ringworm was merely the excuse, and a poor one, for a massive death ray program.

Why were the Sephardi children so victimized? For the same reason the Sabbataian Labor Zionists let the Jews of Poland perish in the Holocaust. Because they were righteous and religious. For Sabbatainism to triumph, all Jews had to be cleansed from the world but those who could be trained and indoctrinated in the anti-Judaistic evil of Shabtai Tzvi. To those believing in Shabtai Tzvi, burning the Jews of Europe and radiating those of the East was a fulfillment of their master's grand vision.

Bringing terror to Israel in the name of peace is their latest step in the annihilation of the Jews. If they have their way, all of Israel will be radiated and eradicated in the name of the devil Shabtai Tzvi and his living disciples, dwelling in the "peace" camp.

ALM 4 - FROM HUNGARY TO GAZA

June 18, 2004
SIMON WIESENTHAL KNIGHTED FOR "LIFETIME OF SERVICE TO HUMANITY"

Simon Wiesenthal received an honorary knighthood today in recognition of his "lifetime of service to humanity".
British Foreign Secretary Jack Straw recommended Mr. Wiesenthal for knighthood for his "untiring service to the Jewish communities in the UK and elsewhere by helping to right at least some of the awful wrongs of the Holocaust."

Simon Weisenthal of Vienna received his just reward from the British royal family for covering up the full story of the Holocaust and making sure that only a few show trials of minor bureaucrats were ever conducted, worldwide. Thanks to Weisenthal, the Jews were satisfied that a relentless Nazi hunter was seeking justice for them. In fact, he was making sure justice for the Jews was never served.

Nowhere is the nazis' mass-escape from justice clearer than in Israel. In 60 years, with thousands of nazis who murdered her citizens to choose from, exactly two were tried and one was released on a technicality. The other one, Adolph Eichmann, was hunted down because he knew too much about the Jewish Agency's complicity in the murder of 800,000 Hungarian Jews.

For years, people who know people have claimed that Eichmann was not executed and the ashes thrown into the sea weren't his. I have never repeated the assertion because it couldn't be proven. But after you read what is known, you may agree that anything is possible.

I am too often compared to a widely-published Jewish internet writer named Henry Makow. The parallels are pretty uncanny. At the same time but independently, we both uncovered the hidden order ruling the life of the planet, and we both discovered that the Holocaust and Israel's founding were manipulations by the same forces.

And, as Jews, these discoveries shook us both to our cores.

The difference is that Makow has drawn all the wrong conclusions from our

discoveries. He has joined the ranks of the pro-Arab anti-semites who exploit the information to slander Israel. The difference between him and me is I live in Israel and know what's going on intimately, while he lives in the boondocks of Canada and has to rely on mistaken second-hand research. We will return to the present in time, but let us first recall the sorry chapter of Labor Zionism-Nazi ties predating the Holocaust, as recounted by Makow:

http://www.rumormillnews.com/cgi-bin/forum.cgi?read=51211

In 1935 the steamer "Tel Aviv" made its maiden voyage from Nazi Germany to Haifa with Hebrew letters on its bow and a Nazi flag fluttering from its mast. The Captain of the Zionist-owned ship was a member of the Nazi Party. A passenger described the spectacle as a "metaphysical absurdity."
Actually it made perfect sense.
The ship transported German Jews who had taken advantage of the "Haavara" program, which allowed them to exchange their money for its value in Germany products in

319

Palestine. As a result, the fledgling Jewish colony received about 70,000 highly educated German Jews and 140 million Reichmarks worth of German industrial equipment. This laid the foundation of Israel's economic infrastructure.

The arrangement also boosted the Nazi economy at a time when Jews worldwide were boycotting German goods. (My source here is "The Secret Contacts" by Klaus Polkehn a prominent German journalist. It is included in Olivia O'Grady's The Beasts of the Apocalyse, 2001, 421-447.)

Why retell this story of Zionist-Nazi cooperation?

Because "Jewish" leaders have been exploiting their "lesser brethren" for a long time, and are doing so today. Ordinary Jews pay the price and this price could rise...

The Zionists did not protest Nazi persecution such as the removal of 2000 Jewish scholars and scientists from German universities in 1933. The Nazis rewarded this "restraint" by allowing the Zionists to go about their work unhindered. All other Jewish and anti fascist organizations were disbanded and their members imprisoned.

The Nazis required all Jews to join the Zionist-led "Reich Union" whose goal was emigration. Jews were to be converted to Zionism at any cost. The Zionists were able to publish books and newspapers critical of the Nazis so long as the audience was restricted to Jews.

The cooperation extended to political and economic spheres. Adolph Eichmann set up agricultural training camps in Austria to prepare young Jews for Kibbutz life. He visited Palestine and conferred with Zionist leaders who confessed their true expansionist goals. There was even talk of a strategic alliance between Nazi Germany and Jewish Palestine. His report is in Himmler's Archives. (440-447)

One peculiar fact about Eichmann was confusing to many Israelis. When brought to Israel for trial, he could speak a little Hebrew and in fact, recited some Hebrew blessings. In 1937, he visited Palestine and included in his tour talks with the leaders of the Jewish Agency. Those contacts turned into the most embarrassing episode in Labor Jewish history, though their murder of Yitzhak Rabin is destined to supercede it.

In 1952, a Hungarian-born Israeli journalist, Malchiel Greenwald, accused a high-ranking Labor Party official, Rudolph Kastner, of working hand in hand with Eichmann to murder 800,000 Hungarian Jews, while saving several hundred of his own family and associates.

It was Ben Hecht, in 1962, who exposed the Greenwald trial in his classic book, Perfidy. The following report is mostly based on Perfidy, and though lengthy, summarizes the main issues:

http://www.aldeilis.net/zion/zionhol03.html

Dr. Rudolf Verba, a Doctor of Science now serving at the British Medical Research Council, was one of the few escapees from Auschwitz. In his memoirs published in February, 1961, in the London Daily Herald, he wrote:

I am a Jew. In spite of that - indeed because of that - I accuse certain Jewish leaders of one of the most ghastly deeds of the war.
This small group of quislings knew what was happening to their brethren in Hitler's gas chambers and bought their own lives with the price of silence. Among them was Dr. Kastner, leader of the council which spoke for all Jews in Hungary. While I was prisoner number 44070 at Auschwitz - the number is still on my arm - I compiled careful statistics of the exterminations...I took these terrible statistics with me when I escaped in 1944 and I was able to give Hungarian Zionist leaders three weeks notice that Eichmann planned to send a million of their Jews to his gas chambers...Kastner went to Eichmann and told him, 'I know of your plans; spare some Jews of my choice and I shall keep quiet.'

Eichmann not only agreed, but dressed Kastner up in S.S. uniform and took him to Belsen to trace some of his friends. Nor did the sordid bargaining end there.

Kastner paid Eichmann several thousand dollars. With this little fortune, Eichmann was able to buy his way to freedom when Germany collapsed, to set himself up in the Argentine...(Ben Hecht, Perfidy, pp261-2)

These accusations are confirmed by the 'Eichmann Confessions' published in Life magazine, 28 November and 5 December 1960:

"Dr. Kastner's main concern was to make it possible for a select group of Hungarian Jews to emigrate to Israel...
As a matter of fact, there was a very strong similarity between our attitudes in the S.S. and the viewpoint of these immensely idealistic Zionist leaders....I believe that Kastner would have sacrificed a thousand or a hundred thousand of his blood to achieve his political goal...'You can have the others', he would say, 'but let me have this group here'.'

The Verdict

Let the verdict of Judge Benjamin Halevi (who later became one of the panel of three judges that tried Eichmann) in Israel's District Court of Jerusalem speak for itself, given in criminal case No. 124 of 1953. The Attorney General v. Malchiel Greenwald. This material should be studied carefully.
"The masses of Jews from Hungary's ghettos obediently boarded the deportation trains without knowing their fate. They were full of confidence in the false information that they were being transferred to Kenyermeze.
"The Nazis could not have misled the masses of Jews so conclusively had they not spread their false information through Jewish channels..The Nazi organizers of

extermination and the perpetrators of *extermination permitted Rudolf Kastner and the members of the Jewish Council in Budapest to save themselves, their relatives, and friends...The Nazi chiefs knew that the Zionists were a most vital element in Jewry and the most trusted by the Jews.*

"This meeting of these important German guests in Budapest exposes the 'rescue' work of Becher in its true light. It reveals also the extent of Kastner's involvement in the inner circle of the chief German war criminals...

"Just as the Nazi war criminals knew they needed an alibi and hoped to achieve it by the rescue of a few Jews at the eleventh hour, so Kastner also needed an alibi for himself.

"Collaboration between the Jewish Agency Rescue Committee and the Exterminators of the Jews was solidified in Budapest and Vienna. Kastner's duties were part and parcel of the general duties of the S.S."

At the appeal hearings before the Supreme Court, the Attorney General of Israel, Chaim Cohen, explained clearly why the Government of Israel was defending Kastner so strongly:

"The man Kastner does not stand here as a private individual. He was a recognized representative, official or non-official of the Jewish National Institutes in Palestine and of the Zionist Executive; and I come here in this court to defend the representative of our national institutions." (Hecht, p. 268)

"The truth of this statement cannot be denied. Kastner's collaboration was not that of an individual. It was the collaboration of the Zionist leadership.

"So far, it has only been established that the Government of Israel continued to support a Nazi collaborator after the facts about his collaboration had been conclusively established in an Israeli court" But the story gets worse.

The Supreme Court of Israel unanimously found that Becher was indeed a Nazi war criminal and that Kastner had without justification, and in the name of the Jewish Agency, helped Becher to escape justice. On this point Greenwald was acquitted of libel and Kastner was not 'fully rehabilitated'.

*The Supreme Court also accepted the **facts** established in the lower court - that Kastner **deliberately** concealed the truth about Auschwitz from the majority of Hungarian Jews in exchange for Nazi permission to take a thousand or so to Palestine. Again, Kastner was far from being 'fully rehabilitated'.*

The Majority Judgement

*But now comes the really nasty bit. After unanimously acknowledging these **facts**, the Supreme Court of Israel, by a majority of three to two, found that Kastner's actions were **morally justifiable** and convicted Greenwald of criminal libel for calling this 'collaboration'.*
*Kastner's actions only proved that **he** was a Nazi collaborator. It is the defense of these actions by the Government and Courts of Israel that prove conclusively that **Zionism** approves of Nazi collaboration.*
*The majority of the Supreme Court of Israel did not **rehabilitate** Kastner. They **joined** him.*

The Labor government of Israel had to exonerate Kastner because its very founders were just as guilty of slaying European Jews as he. According to Rabbi Yoel Brand, Eichmann had offered to save all 800,000 Jews in Hungary in return for 700 trucks. Brand contacted the man who would become Israel's second prime minister, Moshe Sharett in Aleppo, where Sharett had him arrested by the British. But the worst of the lot was the chairman of the Jewish Agency, Chaim Weizmann:

324

Chaim Weizmann, the Zionist leader who had arranged the Balfour Declaration and was to become the first president of Israel, made this Zionist policy very explicit:

"The hopes of Europe's six million Jews are centered on emigration. I was asked: 'Can you bring six million Jews to Palestine?' I replied, 'No.' ... From the depths of the tragedy I want to save ... young people [for Palestine]. The old ones will pass. They will bear their fate or they will not. They are dust, economic and moral dust in a cruel world. ... Only the branch of the young shall survive. They have to accept it."

The cover-up of the Hungarian sellout of the Jews by the Labor Zionists meant hushing those who knew too much about it from the inside. Kastner was murdered in a hospital bed by the Israeli internal secret services. I offer new eye-witness testimony to the murder in my book, Save Israel!. Great pains were taken to kidnap Eichmann and get him under control.

And there was another person who knew way too much for his own good. He was Raoul Wallenberg. No one did as much as this Swedish diplomat to save Hungarian Jewry and he was rewarded for learning too much by being "disappeared" by the Russian liberators of Hungary. Only the Jewish Agency would have benefited from his silence.

We return to 1933. There are two branches of Zionism meeting in Prague. News of the transfer agreement with the Nazis by the Labor Zionist leadership has emerged. The moral branch of Zionism, led by the great Zeev Jabotinsky, is threatening to expose the atrocity to world Jewry. But Labor's negotiator with the Nazis over the agreement, Chaim Arlozorov, is murdered on a Tel Aviv beach. A la Rabin, Jabotinsky's followers are falsely accused of the murder and are ejected from the Jewish Agency. The Labor Zionists then proceeded with their cooperation with the Nazis and six million Jews later, got their state.

What makes today's events all the more confusing is that Israel's prime minister knows all about the Holocaust, yet is determined to lead his country into another:

http://www.ahavat-israel.com/ahavat/protest/shoa.asp

About a year before becoming Prime Minister of Israel, Ariel Sharon made an interesting comment. He said that if Zeev Jabotinsky would have been the head of the Jewish Agency instead of David Ben-Gurion, millions of Jews would have been saved from death during the Holocaust. Immediately afterwards, leftist politicians told Sharon he should apologize for having said this. To which Sharon replied, "I was there and I know what happened, if you want we can debate about it in public." No further comments from the left were heard.

And now back to Makow's core error, parroted by vicious anti-semites worldwide. The main thrust is that evil Sharon and wicked Bush have guided America and her allies into quagmires in Iraq and Afghanistan. Not many Hungarian Jews survived the Holocaust, and the ones who did were enormously lucky or had friends in the Jewish Agency. Here is what one such survivor had to say about Sharon:

On November 7th, Jewish multibillionaire financier George Soros, speaking to a Jewish audience in New York said*: "the policies of the Sharon Administration …. are contributing to a resurgence of anti-Semitism in Europe."*

So let's get this straight: As a reward for conspiring with Bush, Israel gets the following rewards; The Roadmap to suicide, the right to tear down dozens of villages, the joy of turning 8000 Gazan Jews into refugees, the thrill of retreating to undefendable borders and, as the icing on the cupcake, our capital city gets to experience the subtle splendor of division.

Now let us make this most obvious point: We are getting just as screwed as the Arabs. The problem is we are prepared to say that, and the Arabs are just too pig-headed and bloodthirsty to make the same admission. We were all divvied up by the British, placed in artificial nations and given leaders we didn't want.

But unlike the Arabs who were moved all around the Middle East at the whim of the imperialists, the Jews were manipulated into their historic and rightful homeland. How we got there is the injustice, that we are is not.

And now the simplest point of all: The Israeli Labor Zionists. often called, generically, the Left, the same monsters who brought us Kastner, Weizmann and the Holocaust, are the same folks who brought us Oslo and the "peace process."

Which brings us to the only conclusion possible. By rejecting the Labor Zionists, true, ethical and good Judaism is triumphing in Israel. Today, the Labor Party boasts only 18 seats of 120 in the Knesset. In the last election, 67% of the country voted Sharon, deluding themselves that he was a rejection of all that Labor Zionism stood for.

Alas, as I knew then, he was not. He was born a Labor Zionist and will lead his nation back to its Sabbataian roots. However, because the elected governing majority is solidly opposed to the current diplomacy, now focused on the Gaza surrender, typical Labor methods must be used to get their way. As I have proven in my two previous articles, that means murdering the Jewish opposition. The hit list has included the most revered rabbis of Yesha. One more brave family member has come forward with his belief that Jews are being murdered by Jews in the name of "peace."

Apropos the Ra'anan murder in 1998: His youngest son, Michael is married to my daughter. After the funeral, I poked around the charred caravan, and around the back. The caravan was situated on a small cliff edge so that for the murderer to have gotten into the window, he had to have either brought a step-ladder or an accomplice to give him a liftup. I go for the latter, since the murderer was able to stab Rav Ra'anan and then set fire to the place. On the assumption that something more than a 2 litre soft-drink bottle would be needed, he would probably have needed someone to hand him the petrol or kerosene through the window. One way or the other, it was a setup job.A few years later, Zahal claimed to have captured "the" perpetrator. And I say, baloney. They caught (or did not) a fake. "Tik sagur". My son-in-law and daughter were so traumatized by the event, that they were not terribly interested in my observations - in my opinion, they are also being have a similar syndrome to my late in-laws who did not want to talk about their experience in concentration camp.

And that is where the Makow world is upside down. The leaders of the Israeli Left, the "peacemakers" are the self-same murderers who let a Holocaust go on to get their way and then covered it up for all time. And now the very same gang is murdering a new generation of Jews, many who wear kippas or others who live on the land of their forefathers. If real peace ever comes to Israel, it will have to be achieved by negotiating directly with them. They're the only moral game in town.

ALM 4 - The Ringworm Children - A Review

On August 14, at 9 PM, Israeli television station, Channel Ten, broke all convention and exposed the ugliest secret of Israel's Labor Zionist founders; the deliberate mass radiation poisoning of nearly all Sephardi youths.

The expose began with the presentation of a documentary film called, The Ringworm Children, and concluded with a panel discussion moderated by TV host

Dan Margalit, surprising because he is infamous for toeing the establishment line.

Film Details:
The Ringworm Children, released by Dimona Productions Ltd. in 2003.

Producer - Dudi Bergman
Directors: David Belhassen & Asher Hemias
Panel Discussion Participants

A Moroccan singer was joined by David Edri, head of the Compensation Committee for Ringworm X-Ray Victims, and Boaz Lev, a spokesman for the Ministry Of Health.

Subject:
In 1951, the director general of the Israeli Health Ministry, Dr. Chaim Sheba flew to America and returned with 7 x-ray machines, supplied to him by the American army.
They were to be used in a mass atomic experiment with an entire generation of Sephardi youths to be used as guinea pigs. Every Sephardi child was to be given 35,000 times the maximum dose of x-rays through his head. For doing so, the American government paid the Israeli government 300 million Israeli liras a year. The entire Health budget was 60 million liras. The money paid by the Americans is equivalent to billions of dollars today. To fool the parents of the victims, the children were taken away on "school trips" and their parents were later told the x-rays were a treatment for the scourge of scalpal ringworm. 6,000 of the children died shortly after their doses were given, while many of the rest developed cancers that killed them over time and are still killing them now. While living, the victims suffered from disorders such as epilepsy, amnesia, Alzheimer's disease, chronic headaches and psychosis.

Yes, that is the subject of the documentary in cold terms. It is another matter to see the victims on the screen.   ie. To watch the Moroccan lady describe what getting 35,000 times the dose of allowable x-rays in her head feels like.

"I screamed make the headache go away. Make the headache go away. Make the headache go away. But it never went away."

To watch the bearded man walk hunched down the street.

"I'm in my fifties and everyone thinks I'm in my seventies. I have to stoop when I walk so I won't fall over. They took my youth away with those x-rays."

To watch the old lady who administered the doses to thousands of children.

"They brought them in lines. First their heads were shaved and smeared in burning gel. Then a ball was put between their legs and the children were ordered not to drop it, so they wouldn't move. The children weren't protected over the rest of their bodies. There were no lead vests for them. I was told I was doing good by helping to remove ringworm. If I knew what dangers the children were facing, I would never have cooperated. Never!"

Because the whole body was exposed to the rays, the genetic makeup of the children was often altered, affecting the next generation. We watch the woman with the distorted face explain, "All three of my children have the same cancers my family suffered. Are you going to tell me that's a coincidence?"

Everyone notices that Israeli Sephardi women in their fifties today, often have sparse patchy hair, which they try to cover with henna. Most of us assumed it was just a characteristic of Sephardi women. We watch the woman on the screen wearing a baseball-style hat. She places a picture of a lovely young teenager with flowing black hair opposite the lens. "That was me before my treatment. Now look at me." She removes her hat. Even the red henna can't cover the horrifying scarred bald spots.

The majority of the victims were Moroccan because they were the most numerous of the Sephardi immigrants. The generation that was poisoned became the country's perpetual poor and criminal class. It didn't make sense. The Moroccans who fled to France became prosperous and highly educated. The common explanation was that France got the rich, thus smart ones. The real explanation is that every French Moroccan child didn't have his brain cells fried with gamma rays.

The film made it perfectly plain that this operation was no accident. The dangers of x-rays had been known for over forty years. We read the official guidelines for x-ray treatment in 1952. The maximum dose to be given a child in Israel was .5 rad. There was no mistake made. The children were deliberately poisoned.

David Deri, makes the point that only Sephardi children received the x-rays.

"I was in class and the men came to take us on a tour. They asked our names. The Ashkenazi children were told to return to their seats. The dark children were put on the bus."

The film presents a historian who first gives a potted history of the eugenics movement. In a later sound bite, he declares that the ringworm operation was a eugenics program aimed at weeding out the perceived weak strains of society. The film now quotes two noted anti-Sephardi racist Jewish leaders, Nahum Goldmann and Levi Eshkol.

Goldmann spent the Holocaust years first in Switzerland, where he made sure few Jewish refugees were given shelter, then flew to New York to become head of the World Jewish Congress headed by Samuel Bronfman. According to Canadian writer Mordecai Richler, Bronfman had cut a deal with Prime Minister Mackenzie King to prevent the immigration of European Jews to Canada.

But Levi Eshkol's role in the Holocaust was far more sinister than merely not saving lives. He was busy taking them instead. From a biography of Levi Eshkol from the Israeli government web site:

"In 1937 Levi Eshkol played a central role in the establishment of the Mekorot Water Company and in this role was instrumental in convincing the German government to allow Jews emigrating to Palestine to take with them some of their assets - mostly in the form of German-made equipment."

While world Jewry was boycotting the Nazi regime in the banned human testing and needed guinea pigs. The Israeli government agreed to supply the humans in exchange for money and nuclear secrets. The initiator of Israel's nuclear program was Defence Ministry director-general Shimon Peres. '30s, the Jewish Agency in Jerusalem was propping up Hitler. A deal, called The Transfer Agreement, was cut whereby the Nazis would chase Germany's Jews to Palestine, and the Labor Zionists would force the immigrants to use their assets to buy only German goods. Once the Jewish Agency got the German Jews it wanted, those they secretly indoctrinated in the anti-Judaism of Shabtai Tzvi and Jacob Frank, they let the Nazis take care of the rest of European Jewry. The Holocaust was a eugenics program and Levi Eshkol played a major role in it.

The Moroccan lady is back on the screen. "It was a Holocaust, a Sephardi Holocaust. And what I want to know is why no one stood up to stop it."

David Deri, on film and then as a panel member, relates the frustration he encountered when trying to find his childhood medical records.

"All I wanted to know was what they did to me. I wanted to know who authorized it. I wanted to trace the chain of command. But the Health Ministry told me my records were missing."

Boaz Lev, the Health Ministry's spokesman chimes in, "Almost all the records were burned in a fire."

So let us help Mr. Deri trace the chain of command. But now I must intrude myself in the review. About six years ago, I investigated the kidnapping of some 4500, mostly Yemenite immigrant infants and children, during the early years of the state. I met the leader of the Yemenite children's movement, Rabbi Uzi Meshulum, imprisoned for trying to get the truth out. He was later returned home in a vegetative state from which he has not emerged. He told me that the kidnapped children were sent to America to die cruelly in nuclear experiments. The American government had

Rabbi David Sevilia of Jerusalem corroborated the crime and later, I even saw photos of the radiation scars on the few surviving children, and the cages the infants were shipped to America in.

Just over five years ago I published my belief on the internet, that Israel's Labor Zionist founders had conducted atomic experiments on Yemenite and other Sephardi children, killing thousands of them. Almost three years ago, I published the same assertion in my last book, Save Israel!. I suffered much scorn for doing so. However, I was right.

We return to the documentary. We are told that a US law in the late '40s put a stop to the human radiation experiments conducted on prisoners, the mentally feeble and the like. The American atomic program needed a new source of human lab rats and the Israeli government supplied it.

Here was the government cabinet at the time of the ringworm atrocities:

Prime Minister - David Ben Gurion
Finance Minister - Eliezer Kaplan
Settlement Minister - Levi Eshkol
Foreign Minister - Moshe Sharrett
Health Minister - Yosef Burg
Labor Minister - Golda Meir
Police Minister - Amos Ben Gurion

The highest ranking non-cabinet post belonged to the Director General Of The Defence Ministry, Shimon Peres.

That a program involving the equivalent of billions of dollars of American government funds should be unknown to the Prime Minister of cash-strapped Israel is ridiculous. Ben Gurion was in on the horrors and undoubtedly chose his son to be Police Minister in case anyone interfered with them.

Now let's have a quick glance at the other plotters, starting with the Finance Minister Eliezer Kaplan. He handled the profits of the operation and was rewarded for eternity with a hospital named after him near Rehovot. But he's not alone in this honor. The racist bigot Chaim Sheba, who ran Ringworm Incorporated, had a whole medical complex named after him. Needless to say, if there is an ounce of decency in the local medical profession, those hospital names will have to change.

Then there is Yosef Burg, who the leaders of the Yemenite Children's movement insist was the most responsible for the kidnappings of their infants. As Health Minister, he certainly played a pivotal role in the Ringworm murders. That would go a great way to explaining the peculiar behavior of his son, the peacemaker, Avraham Burg.

Let us not forget Moshe Sharrett, who had Rabbi Yoel Brand arrested in Aleppo in 1944 for proposing a practical way to save 800,000 Jews trapped in Hungary. Sharrett's most cited quote is, "If Shimon Peres ever enters this government, I will tear my clothes and start to mourn." Several Yemenite Children activists told me Sharrett was referring to the kidnapping of the Yemenite children when he made this statement.

And other amateur historians have told me that Levi Eshkol openly and proudly announced his belief in the tenets of Shabtai Tzvi, but try as I have, I haven't tracked down a citation. However, we do know of Eshkol, that during the period of the radiations, he served first as Settlement Minister, then took over from Kaplan as Finance Minister. From his bio:

"In 1951 Eshkol was appointed Minister of Agriculture and Development, and from 1952 to 1963 - a decade characterized by unprecedented economic growth despite the burden of financing immigrant absorption and the 1956 Sinai Campaign - he served as Minister of Finance. Between 1949 and 1963, Eshkol also served as head of the settlement division of the Jewish Agency. In the first four years of statehood, he was also treasurer of the Jewish Agency, largely responsible for obtaining the funds for the country's development, absorption of the massive waves of immigrants and equipment for the army."

In short, Eshkol was the person most responsible for Israel's immigrants, the ones he sent to radiation torture chambers.

Finally, there is Golda Meir. We don't know her role, but she was in on the secret and rewarded for it. Note that every prime minister thereafter until 1977, when the honorable Menachem Begin was elected, came from this cabal. And note also, that no one from what is called the Right today, was privy to the slaughter of the Sephardi children. Apply that lesson to a contemporary fact: It is the descendants of these butchers who brought us the Oslo "peace" and are determined to wipe out the settlers of Judea, Samaria and Gaza as surely as they had dealt with the inferior dark Jews who came into their clutches fifty years before.

Now try and imagine it is 1952 and you are in a cabinet meeting. You will be debating whether to send the Yemenite babies to America for their final zapping, or whether to have them zapped here. That is what the Luciferian, satanic Sabbataian founders of our nation were prattling on about when they got together to discuss the affairs of state.

After the film ended, TV host Dan Margalit tried to put a better face on what he'd witnessed. Any face had to be better than what he had seen. He explained meekly, "But the state was poor. It was a matter of day to day survival." Then he stopped. He knew there was no excusing the atrocities the Sephardi children endured.

But it was the Moroccan singer who summed up the experience best. "It's going to hurt, but the truth has to be told. If not, the wounds will never heal."

There is one person alive who knows the truth and participated in the atrocities. He is Leader Of The Opposition Shimon Peres, the peacemaker. The only way to get to the truth and start the healing is to investigate him for his role in the kidnapping of 4500 Yemenite infants and the mass poisoning of over 100,000 Sephardi children and youths.

But here is why that won't happen. It is a miracle that The Ringworm Children was broadcast at all. Clearly though, someone fought for it but had to agree to a compromise. The show was aired at the same time as the highest-rated show of the year, the final of Israel's, A Star Is Born. The next day, there was not a word about The Ringworm Children in any paper, but the newly-born star's photo took up half the front pages.

That's how the truth is buried in Israel, and somehow, these tricks work. The same methods were used to cover up the Rabin assassination.

However, a few hundred thousand people saw the film on their screens and they will never forget the truth. If the Rabin assassination doesn't bury Labor Zionism for good, then The Ringworm Children eventually will.

End

EPILOG

THE MURDER OF OFRA HAZA

The missing Yemenite children claimed another victim. Before we begin, please open:

http://chipwich.tripod.com/ofrahaza/videos/Tzedek.html

Journalist (Ofra Haza) decides to investigate the "kidnapped Yemen children" case & even to find her twin brother after he was missing after his birth. She is meeting Gidi Vaxman (Arnon Tzadok), a detective in the homicide department who is in the climax of solving a very complicated murder case. With her determination, she succeeds in breaking his stubbornness to prove to him that he is her lost brother & to lead him to meeting with his biological parents & meeting his past.

Now we begin with some deep political background. Under dire threat, Ariel Sharon has begun the process of the forced removal of 8000 Jews from their homes. The pressure from within the country comes from the top of Labor Zionism. Their goal is to stop the religious revival taking place within Yesha, beginning with Gaza. With the transfer of the Gazan Jews will come a split in the country so profound that over half its citizens will stop accepting the government as their legal authority. This will spell the end of Israel.

The Gazan Jews represent the finest ideals of the Zionism of national liberation. Labor Zionism is a foreign transplant on the body of the Jews and only its removal can spell the salvation of Israel.

In my previous two articles I spelled out the depths of criminality which is Labor Zionism. With ample proof we learned that the Ben Gurion government sanctioned the mass irradiation of Sephardic children and youths in the

337

1950s, while kidnapping some 4500 Yemenite infants for use as guinea pigs in American atomic experiments. For this, Israel was paid today's equivalent of 50 billion dollars.

The expose of the Yemenite kidnappings led readers to insist I explore the murder of the Yemenite-Israeli singer Ofra Haza. I had just begun when, divinely, a member of Haza's family asked to meet with me. What he imparted is going to sound fantastic, but what doesn't anymore? You judge, but I believed him.

Let's start with the motive. Ofra Haza had a cousin kidnapped from a transit camp in the 1950s. In 1985, she released an album of Yemenite Songs which turned her into an international disco star, in fact, the most popular Israeli entertainer ever. She was a hero to the Israeli Yemenite community.

In the early 1990s, Rabbi Uzi Meshulum, leader of the movement on behalf of the missing Yemenite children, ignited a demand for the truth that was spreading throughout the country. His house was surrounded by police and army, shot up, killing an eighteen year old follower, and he was finally imprisoned. He returned home in 1999 lobotomized.

The Yemenite community was enraged but felt powerless. Ofra Haza had power, lots of it within the country and throughout the world. Look at a typical testimony to her influence pulled off the internet:

I have to admit that I was ignorant to the proud history of my own ancestors (OFRA and I are Yemenite). After being exposed to OFRA's music I found myself esearching my ethnic history, asking my mother and grand mother to tell me all they knew of the Yemenite people.

In 1997, Ofra Haza decided to dedicate herself to the missing Yemenite children. She financed and starred in a movie about the issue:

Liat Collins
Jerusalem Post
02-28-1997

"Who kidnapped Ofra Haza?" Under this intriguing title, Ma'ariv writer Michal Kafra interviewed the superstar singer who is starring in an Israeli film examining the disappearances of Yemenite immigrant children in the early years of the state. For Haza it marks a return to the big screen, a return from recording studios in Germany and, above all, a return to her roots.

The film, called Absolute Justice, is directed by Doron Eran and Arnon Zadok, who is also the producer.

Arnon Zadok is no minor director. Yemenite himself, he has directed award winning films like White Night, and Beyond The Walls. In fact, he was the last Israeli director to be nominated for an Oscar. But *Absolute Justice* was shown once at the Tel Aviv Cinemateque and disappeared.

I was heartbroken when she died. I was never sure that a woman this beautiful would be content to be solely a recording artist; I thought that she had been aspiring to a career in film. I believed that her disappearance from the scene was a result of her film career not taking off;
-Tom Schnabel
Producer, <u>KCRW Radio</u>

Any movie starring Ofra Haza would have been a hit in Israel but never more than after her death, they told us, of AIDS. So where did the movie go?

It was also in 1997, while making her movie, that Ofra Haza was pursued by a suitor named Doron Ashkenazi. Not just pursued, hounded. She wanted nothing to do with him but profound family pressure was put on her to give him a chance. After her death, it was revealed that Ashkenazi, supposedly a building contractor, paid off Ofra's cousin to be his matchmaker. When her persuasion led to his marriage to Ofra, the yente was paid off with a $20,000 kitchen.

In the wake of Haza's unexpected death, both Ha'ir and Haaretz published pretty deep exposes of Haza's life with Ashkenazi. With the cooperation of her family and her longtime agent, both articles agreed on most major points. Of Ashkenazi, we learned that:

Though she wanted to live near her family in Yehud, Ashkenazi forced Haza to move to an expensive home in Herzlia. Once separated from her roots, he forbade her from visiting family and friends, and had her fire her longtime manager/producer, Bezalel Aloni. While she was dying, Ashkenazi had her sign the deed to her Yehud home over to him, and on the day of her death, he emptied her bank account. Ofra had informed her family that in her will, she bequeathed her home and worldly domain to them. The family challenged Ashkenazi's claim to her property in court. Note that the lawyer chosen was Rami Tsuberi, author of a stinging book about the kidnapped Yemenite children. This URL is in Hebrew.

http://www.bambili.com/bambili_news/katava_main.asp?news_id=1007&sivug_id=6

Ofra Haza was a traditional Yemenite woman, who was modest by nature and not by any means promiscuous. Yet, Ashkenazi convinced her to abort their baby. URL also in Hebrew:

http://www.bambili.com/bambili_news/katava_main.asp?news_id=990&sivug_id=6

Because of her known modesty, combined with the abortion, the public accused Ashkenazi of passing the AIDS virus on to her. He denied it and promised to take an AIDS test and reveal the results to the public. This was apparently threatening to someone. He never had a chance to take the test...

340

Itim
Jerusalem Post
04-09-2001
Headline: Ofra Haza's widower dies, drugs found
Byline: Itim
Edition; Daily
Section: News
Page: 01

Monday, April 9, 2001 -- The attorney of the family of singer Ofra Haza, who died last February of AIDS, said yesterday the family awaits the results of the autopsy to be performed on her husband, Doron Ashkenazi, who died Saturday night, to determine whether he was an HIV carrier.

Ashkenazi was found unconscious Saturday night in his Herzliya home, evidently by friends, who called Magen David Adom around 9 p.m.

...because he was snuffed out 14 months after Haza. But look who promised to do the HIV test post mortem? Why it's Yehuda Hiss, the coroner who falsified the autopsy of Yitzhak Rabin, and the coroner who was caught counterfeiting a DNA test between a surviving Yemenite child and her biological mother.

In English, how Ashkenazi died:

http://chipwich.tripod.com/ofrahaza/doran.html

By Amit Ben-Aroya
Ha'aretz Correspondent and wires

Doron Ashkenazi - widower of Israel's most successful international singer, Ofra Haza, who died of AIDS in February 2000 - died Saturday night of an overdose of crystallized cocaine, police said.

His autopsy today may shed a light on Haza's death as well.

341

"We are expecting an answer as to whether Doron was HIV positive, and the one who infected Ofra," attorney Arie Sharabi, who represents the Haza family, said yesterday.

Several complaints were filed with the police, accusing Ashkenazi of not informing Haza that he was HIV positive. Ashkenazi, who has an eight-year-old girl and a 15-year-old boy, was never arrested in connection with Haza's death. The Tel Aviv prosecutor is still working on the Haza file. His death is to terminate the investigation, unless the family allows it to be continued, which is very unlikely, Sharabi explained.

On Saturday night, the night of the Seder, Ashkenazi would not celebrate with his family. He said he was still in mourning. A preliminary police investigation indicates he spent the evening with friends, doing "crystal meth" at Ashkenazi's home in Herzliya.

When Ashkenazi suddenly collapsed at 8 P.M., one of the friends called an ambulance, and told Ashkenazi's family. Ashkenazi was rushed to Beilinson Hospital in Petah Tikva, where, after attempts at resuscitation, he was pronounced dead.

Police were only informed at 10:30 PM. Chief Superintendent Avi Sasson, deputy commander of the Gelilot station, which is investigating the case, told Ha'aretz he still did not know why Ashkenazi's car was found parked in south Tel Aviv. Ashkenazi family lawyer Shmuel Zang said Ashkenazi was focused on the legal proceeding that were to begin in a few weeks regarding the validity of Haza's will, a copy of which could not be found.

The medical panel that investigated Haza's death published its findings three months ago. Its report said that, if Haza had admitted herself to hospital earlier, her life might have been saved. But Haza, fearful that her condition would become public knowledge, refused to go to the hospital, even when her situation had become very serious.

Ashkenazi was first exposed to the public eye when, in July 1997, he married Haza, a popular singer. She was

342

discovered at age 12 at the underprivileged Hatikva neighborhood in Tel Aviv, by Bezalel Aloni, who was her personal manager for years - until her marriage to Ashkenazi, when she severed her ties with him. Just weeks before her death, she telephoned Aloni and told him of her condition. "I said a year ago that this man [Ashkenazi] was to blame. He covered himself with a battery of lawyers. His death only serves to emphasize how tragic and futile Ofra's death was. Doron was the first and last man in her life, and that's terrible," Aloni said.

With Ashkenazi out of the way, he would talk no more, nor take an HIV test. Dr. Hiss' post mortem test was never released, so Haaretz was used to put final closure on the issue, publishing a report that Haza had an affair with a bi-sexual German film producer. The disinformation apparently did its job and the Haza death withered away with the elimination of Ashkenazi.

Now, with great trepidation, I introduce Shimon Peres. It was Peres who invited Haza to sing at the signing of the Oslo Accord and at the Nobel Prize ceremony, during which he won a prize for "peace." Recalling that Peres was in charge of the Israeli atomic program during the days when the Yemenite children were kidnapped and turned into guinea pigs for atomic experiments, her appearance beside him was more than a little disconcerting.

When Haza entered the hospital, 13 days before she finally succumbed to her poisoning, Peres called her mother to see how she was doing.

http://www.jpost.com/Editions/2000/02/25/News/News.3176.html

And who gave her eulogy, but Shimon Peres:
http://www3.haaretz.co.il/eng/htmls/kat6_3.htm

343

At the funeral, Peres called Haza "a singer of hope for the nation and the world" and thanked her for "making Israel a nation of song."

What was Peres' great interest in promoting the career of Ofra Haza? I met the Haza family member at a cafe near the Shalom Tower in Tel Aviv. Everything he told me came from within Ofra Haza's closest circles.

FM - She was murdered because of the film. I was there when it was shown at the Cinemateque. It was chopped up. She told us that she named names in the movie. I recall she blamed Yisrael Kessar and Yisrael Yeshiahu for being the capos of the kidnappings. That wasn't in the final edit of the film. The film was never shown again but copies of the original are floating around. They got Arnon to bury it and they got Ofra buried.

BC - How did they do it?

FM - We all believe she was deliberately infected with AIDS. Now there was no reason for her to die of it. She was feeling weak for a year and had seen her doctor to complain. But she wasn't given the HIV cocktail.

BC - Why not?

FM - We found out later that her doctor, Mimi Hatman, was a friend/lover of Doron Ashkenazi's. They were in on the murder together. Do you remember the nonsense the media spread that Ofra kept her AIDS a secret so her fans wouldn't be disappointed? In other words, she preferred to die rather than treat her disease? What a story, but the public bought it. The twist given was that she died of shame.

BC - So Ashkenazi married her to murder her?

FM - Yeah. He was the hitman.

BC - For who, Shabak, Mossad?

FM - No, he was Peres' boy. He was on assignment from him. Peres was about the last survivor of the gang that arranged the kidnappings. He would do anything to keep the lid on the affair. When he found out that Ofra was on the Yemenite children bandwagon, he panicked. She was bigger than he was. She was more popular and, of course, way more trusted. She was the biggest threat the scandal ever faced. She was too naive to realize the danger she placed herself in by making that movie. After they got Ofra out of the way, they decided to finish the job. Ashkenazi was getting unpredictable after everyone thought he gave her AIDS because he had it. He didn't and hated everyone thinking he did. He was going to blow the operation so they had him ODing on a needle. That was perfect because it explained how this heterosexual got the disease in the first place. A couple in their 30s injected him and the woman was murdered too. It's very deadly to get too close to Peres, and Ofra should have known better. She knew him better than anyone ever found out.

BC - Because of Oslo and the Nobel Prize ceremony?

FM - He took her everywhere. If Margaret Thatcher was in town, he'd bring her along to serenade her. I have a picture of that event. His affair with her began way before the 'peace' process. He saw her first role, *HaFrekha, (The Tart),* and he took a shine to her.That's how he got to meet Ofra. Peres is a serial cad, but at least he rewards his conquests with great careers. However, he really took advantage of her.

BC - Are you really saying that Peres had an affair with Ofra Haza?

FM - Oh, for years. There are people in the family who say he raped her, but I call it mind-screwing. She's a young naive singer who comes from the slums. Now she's invited to Stockholm to perform for famous diplomats. How could she refuse him later in the hotel? He was using her to satisfy himself and sell peace. He had it made. And she was getting a big career boost by playing along. But she made a bigger mistake.

BC - Being what?

FM - She wanted to do something for her people. The issue of the Yemenite children took hold. I'm almost positive it had nothing to do with getting even with Peres. I don't think she made the connection to his role. But there is that chance that she wanted revenge for the shame he caused her, at least subconsciously. Whatever the truth, Peres felt betrayed and threatened. So Ofra got the Rabin treatment.

That was **NOT** what I was expecting to hear when I arranged   the   interview.

If any of this tawdry tale is true, and I'm inclined to believe that **ALL** of it may be, then we know just how much wickedness resides in the heart of the leader of the Labor Party, of Labor Zionism, of the peacemaker who brought us Oslo, and who is now leading the battle to annihilate the Jewish presence in Gush Katif.

And that very wickedness just can't be allowed to triumph if we are to remain proud Jews and Zionists. May this New Year finally bring truth to Israel.